Myth, Mind and the Screen
Understanding the heroes of our time

Myth, Mind and the Screen is a systematic attempt to apply Jungian theory to the analysis of films (including *2001: A Space Odyssey, The Silence of the Lambs* and *The Piano*) as well as a variety of cultural icons and products such as Madonna, Michael Jackson and televised sport. Through these and other examples, John Izod shows how Jungian theory can bring new tools to film and media studies and new ways of understanding screen images and narratives. He also demonstrates how Jungian analysis can provide us with fresh insights into the psychological dimensions of contemporary mythology and the subjective experience of audiences. Perhaps most controversially, he argues that in the Western world cinema and television bear much of the responsibility for collective emotional mediation that in previous centuries was borne by organised religion. A valuable resource for students of film and media studies, cultural studies and psychoanalytic studies.

JOHN IZOD is Professor of Screen Analysis in the Department of Film and Media Studies, University of Stirling. He is the author of *Reading the Screen* (1984), *Satellite, Cable and Beyond* (with Alastair Hetherington, 1984), *Hollywood and the Box Office* (1988), *The Films of Nicolas Roeg: Myth and Mind* (1992), and *An Introduction to Television Documentary: Confronting Reality* (with Richard Kilborn, 1997).

Cambridge Studies in Criminology

Editors:
Alfred Blumstein, *Carnegie Mellon University*
David Farrington, *University of Cambridge*

This series publishes high quality research monographs of either theoretical or empirical emphasis in all areas of criminology, including measurement of offending, explanations of offending, police, courts, incapacitation, corrections, sentencing, deterrence, rehabilitation, and other related topics. It is intended to be both interdisciplinary and international in scope.

Also in the series:

Myth, Mind and the Screen

Understanding the heroes of our times

John Izod

Stirling Media Research Institute
University of Stirling

PUBLISHED BY THE PRESS SYNDICATE OF THE UNIVERSITY OF CAMBRIDGE
The Pitt Building, Trumpington Street, Cambridge, United Kingdom

CAMBRIDGE UNIVERSITY PRESS
The Edinburgh Building, Cambridge CB2 2RU, UK
40 West 20th Street, New York, NY 10011-4211, USA
10 Stamford Road, Oakleigh, VIC 3166, Australia
Ruiz de Alarcón 13, 28014 Madrid, Spain
Dock House, The Waterfront, Cape Town 8001, South Africa

http://www.cambridge.org

First published 2001

Printed in the United Kingdom at the University Press, Cambridge

Typeface Plantin 10/12 pt.   *System* LaTeX 2$_\varepsilon$ [TB]

A catalogue record for this book is available from the British Library.

Library of Congress Cataloguing in Publication Data
Izod, John, 1940–
    Myth, mind and the screen : understanding the heroes of our times /
John Izod.
        p.   cm.
    Includes bibliographical references and index.
    ISBN 0 521 79253 3 – ISBN 0 521 79686 5 (pb.)
    1. Motion pictures – Psychological aspects.   2. Television – Psychological
aspects.   I. Title.
    PN1995 .I96   2001
    791.43′01′9 – dc21   2001025629

ISBN 0 521 79253 3 hardback
ISBN 0 521 79686 5 paperback

- For my beloved Sarah and Martin -
May the future shine

The reality of all culture, our own included, consists in realizing these images which lie dormant in the psyche. All art, religion, science, and technology, everything that has ever been done, spoken, or thought, has its origin in this creative center.

(Erich Neumann, *The Origins and History of Consciousness* p. 210)

Contents

Acknowledgements

I wish to thank several of my friends and colleagues, including Raymond Boyle, Pamela Calvert, Jeremy Carrette, Tony Cryer, Don Fredericksen, Harriet Margolis, Peter Meech, Catriona Miller, Kathleen McHugh, Helen Ogilvy, David Punter, Philip Schlesinger, Tim Thornicroft and Kay Weaver, for their warm and constructive advice. Special thanks to Jane Ryan for her enthusiastic support and engagement with the book's ideas.

'Active imagination and the analysis of film', a version of the material in Chapter 1, was published by *The Journal of Analytical Psychology* 45 (April 2000) 267–85. An analysis of *Diva* from which Chapters 2 and 3 later grew was published as 'Beineix's *Diva* and the French cultural unconscious', in Elizabeth Ezra and Sue Harris (eds.), *France in Focus: Film and National Identity* (Oxford: Berg Publishers, 2000) 181–93. An earlier draft of Chapter 4 was originally published as '*The Piano*, the animus, and the colonial experience' in *The Journal of Analytical Psychology* 41, 1 (January 1996) 117–36. 'Androgyny and stardom: cultural meanings of Michael Jackson', now the first part of Chapter 5, first appeared in *The San Francisco Jung Institute Library Journal* 14, 3 (1995) 63–74. The second part of that chapter was published in an earlier version as 'Madonna as Trickster', in Fran Lloyd (ed) *Deconstructing Madonna* (London: Batsford, 1993) 49–59. 'Television sport and the sacrificial hero', Chapter 7 here, first appeared in *The Journal of Sport and Social Issues* 20, 2 (1996) 173–93, and has subsequently been developed. Finally, Chapter 10 formed one section of a double paper, the other half of which was written by Jane Ryan and published as 'Classics Revisited: Accounting for Difference in Two Jungian Readings', *The San Francisco Jung Institute Library Journal* 18, 4 (2000) 7–56. The author is grateful to the editors of these journals for permitting republication.

Passages from *The Collected Works of C. G. Jung* are reprinted by kind permission of Routledge and Princeton University Press.

Introduction

Cinema, television and the related media fascinate their audiences in a variety of ways, but entertainment is what most people want when they pay for leisure products. Well aware of this, the media industries build their profits by seeking to gratify audiences' expectations that what they are buying will give them pleasure. The potent impact of moving pictures on the imagination is plain from audience response. A particularly striking feature film or television drama will be received with the most intense private and public reactions. And ever since they first became sources of popular entertainment, both large and small screens have been channels for deeply felt legends, myths and cults. The most exciting fictional characters catch the public's attention and pass into popular discourse where they may remain familiar figures for years. Then too there is the enduring phenomenon of stardom and the hero-worship associated with it.

Orthodox modes of Media Studies have developed effective means of analysing some aspects of the screen experience, including narratives, characters and settings, not to mention the control of style through sound and imagery. However, most spectators want films to give them a buzz through the arousal of intense emotions. Particularly in the case of movies, with their creation of a world that appears entire unto itself, many viewers want the screen's fantasy to lift them in imagination out of their own daily lives. They hope to enjoy pleasures and experience emotions aroused by events which they themselves are not personally undergoing – even if that means being pained witnesses to the sufferings of characters with whom they empathise.

In general, the producers, distributors and exhibitors of films and television drama work alongside those who market the product to attract audiences by responding to this desire. From the initiation of an idea in the scriptwriter's first treatment, the spectator's likely emotional responses are usually among the prime considerations that shape the way a drama will be made. And indeed, mainstream productions have developed highly sophisticated machineries to support the communication of potent emotions to their audiences. Colour, light, camera angle, lens and movement; the density of voices and effects on the sound track; the nature of accompanying music; the pace, logic and elegance of picture and sound editing – all these factors are habitually deployed to enhance the pleasures the audience takes. To highlight one feature alone, mainstream narratives typically move towards resolutions which the audience is well placed to perceive intuitively. In the attainment, not without difficulty, of those goals, gratifying feelings (invariably deferred through conflict, uncertainty, suspense, horror or pain) are communicated to the spectator.

There is a striking imbalance between the effectiveness of filmmakers in awakening emotion and the lame attempts of academic screen analysts to write compellingly about it. As a profession, we are not good at analysing the pleasures of the text or understanding what those pleasures might mean. This is equally true of most of those who have adapted psychoanalysis to film theory. Given that the primary concern of psychoanalysis is the interior life of the subject, every psychoanalytic theory should be well fitted to account for the inner experiences of moviegoers. However, this is more true of Jungian analytical psychology than of other methods.

The inviting, although inexact, resemblance between the experience of watching a film and dreaming has, since 1916 when Hugo Munsterberg wrote *The Photoplay: a Psychological Study*, enticed a number of theorists to find the screen a ready subject. And in the last quarter of the twentieth century, Sigmund Freud's ideas proved susceptible to sustained attempts to bring them, albeit not without strain, into the orbit of the neo-Marxist theory that dominated media studies in Britain in the 1970s. Once his theories had been established in that field, feminist scholars (once again not without considerable difficulty and the need for some astonishing intellectual acrobatics) absorbed them and the variants proposed by Jacques Lacan into the orthodoxies recognised by some currents of feminist theory.

During the last fifteen or twenty years of the past century, something of a rapprochement occurred between some of the leading post-Jungian and post-Freudian thinkers in what had previously been two warring clans. Andrew Samuels's writings, including *Jung and the Post-Jungians* (1990) and *The Political Psyche* (1993), are alive with his desire to pluck what is useful from all schools of psychoanalysis and create a productive synthesis. From the other tradition, Jonathan Lear's *Open Minded: Working Out the Logic of the Soul* (1998) is a positive reappraisal of Freud's work much of which, like his innovative reading of Sophocles's

Oedipus Tyrannus, sits comfortably with the Jungian uses of myth.[1] However, no comparable rapprochement has taken place between the two traditions in Film, Media and Cultural Studies.

As revamped by screen analysts, Freudian and Lacanian theories proved for several reasons to be at best rather limited, and at worst cack-handed implements. In the first place, in common with most late twentieth-century interpreters of Freudian theory, film theorists insisted on referring every disturbance manifested in adulthood back to the traumatic shocks suffered by the infant as it begins to acquire a separate, gendered identity. At its most naive, this tendency is illustrated by Daniel Dervin's use of the orthodox Freudian assertion that the impact of the primal scene (whether witnessed or fantasised) comes at a time when the child is so emotionally and mentally ill-equipped to deal with it that it gets repressed. Dervin contends that the scene's force is so great that it underlies much cinema – the vast imagery in its darkened chamber recalling the parents so much bigger than the infant in the original nocturnal scene (Dervin 1985: 10–14).

Arguing from the formative power of this trauma, Dervin seeks and finds primal scene signifiers in an improbably wide range of films including those where sex and danger are associated; or where life and death secrets are uncovered; or again where envy, betrayal, desertion and loneliness are experienced; and even where there is a marked interplay between immobility and motion – this last recalling the horrified seizure of the child confronted with the sexual frenzy of its parents (ibid.: 17). The insistence that this hypothetical moment underlies a huge number of films can lead to reductive banality: witness his analysis of the slaughter in the Odessa Steps sequence from *The Battleship Potemkin*.

Chaos is everywhere. And yet the culmination of the total process has purpose, for a message is being received from the archaic unconscious: *Father is murdering mother*, which is translated en route to: *The Czar is destroying Russia*. Infantile distortion is converted into political fact . . . (ibid.: 39)

Robert Eberwein has published a Kleinian account of cinema which focuses on a different aspect of the medium's links with infantile experience in a less cavalier manner.

[1] Lear (1998: 39–55) argues that the tragedy of the tyrant king lay in his ignorance of the unconscious and failure to recognise that, like all humans, he would frequently act in ways he could not understand. On the contrary, like a modern man, Oedipus was confident that any human problem could be solved by the application of practical reason, unaware that the unconscious has its own logic which can influence any individual's future. According to Lear, Freud did not register this the full meaning that was to be found in Sophocles' play. His famous reading to some extent missed the point.

Seated in the darkened theater, observing a film on the cinematic screen, we find ourselves thrust back in time to infancy. At some point in our development, when we drifted off to sleep after feeding, we began to dream. In our mind's eye, we sensed those first oneiric images as being somewhere, projected on a field that provided the screen for the dream . . . This field is a complex psychic structure, a 'dream screen' comprised of two elements: the mother's breast, or a surrogate for it, and our own sense of self, the ego. These elements merge to form a dream screen where dreams appear to the sleeper. (Eberwein 1984: 3–4)

For Eberwein, the child cannot yet imagine any other perspective than its own because, both in space and time, it is locked into the passing moment. 'Film and dreams force us to regress back to a level of child- ish perception inasmuch as we are constantly assaulted with "scenes" that we must appropriate initially as belonging solely to *our* perspective' (ibid.: 47).

Just as Jung always accepted that some dreams were best analysed by reference back to traumas of the infant mind, so, in application, Eberwein's schema (and even occasionally Dervin's) does throw light on some films where the reduction to infancy illuminates, for example, the motivations driving a leading protagonist. But if some movies can productively be read by this means (which we shall term, after Jung's us- age, the reductive method), there are others where the predicaments of adulthood are better understood through the constructive methods that Jung advocates.

The strength of Laura Mulvey's psychoanalytical description of main- stream Hollywood cinema 'Visual Pleasure and Narrative Cinema' (widely recognised at the time of publication) was its polemical iden- tification of the way that cinema functioned to favour the male point of view and gaze at the expense of woman's. For Mulvey, screen texts worked to lock their subjects into viewing positions; and with relatively few exceptions, those positions were constructed as male.

Woman then stands in patriarchal culture as a signifier for the male other, bound by a symbolic order in which man can live out his fantasies and obsessions . . . by imposing them on the silent image of woman still tied to her place as bearer, not maker, of meaning. (Mulvey 1975: 15)

In its claims to have adapted to the screen the concepts of psychoanaly- sis, however, Mulvey's reading was weakened by its conflation with neo- Marxian theory. British film theorists of the 1970s and early 1980s argued that Hollywood films were the product of the dominant ideology that kept the ruling classes in power. One consequence of the ideological freight which mainstream movies were said to bear was that they imposed a 'subject position' – the hypothesis being that films prepare positions for spectators from which to view, and where their role is predetermined, 'subject' to the ideology the film conveys. Spectators in general were construed as passive receivers deceived and locked in by a dominant ideology which, to function effectively, must subject all classes in society to the false belief that it reflects the way things actually are.

The logic of this argument inflicted costly damage on the case that Mulvey was advancing. She had shown to persuasive effect how movies evacuated the anticipated viewing position of women. In the process, however, her materialist philosophy undermined the role of actual women as spectators because she was inhibited by that same philosophy from arguing that they could have an independent existence in front of the screen. In a later essay she herself recognised that 'Lacan brilliantly represents the power relationships of patriarchy, but acknowledges no need for woman to escape. Woman in this scheme becomes merely "not-man" ' (Mulvey 1985: 165). That is uncomfortably close to the position she had inscribed for women in her 1975 paper. What, then, as D. N. Rodowick inquired, is the place for the female subject in this scenario? Only as an object defined in the receiving end of the glance. Female unconsciousness, he added, takes place in Mulvey's analysis 'only as an absence, a negativity defining castration and the not-masculine, or as a yet unrealized possibility' (Rodowick 1991: 12, 16).

Rodowick also argued that the hard-edged opposition between masculine and feminine identification which Mulvey's papers embody (in common with the work of other Freudian and Lacanian film theorists) gave a very different picture from that of the psychoanalysts. Rather, psychoanalysis 'saw a variety of fluctuating configurations in the ratios between masculine and feminine identifications within every individual' (Rodowick: 47). The idea, he writes, that there could be a masculine or a feminine identification, equatable in any direct sense with a man or a woman, does not fit with Freud's theory of sexuality (ibid.). Nor does it fit, we should add, with the thinking of post-Jungians.

A further problem inherent in the work of psychoanalytic film theorists parallels that recognised by Elizabeth Wright in her study of Lacan. She identified the lack of power in his concept of the unconscious, recalling his dictum that 'the unconscious is structured like a language'. It is so, in Lacan's thinking, because the unconscious is no more than those contents in the individual's imagination which escape encoding into the symbolic order – that is, principally, language.

The fact that every word indicates the absence of what it stands for intensifies the frustration of this child of language, the unconscious, since the absence of satisfaction has now to be accepted. Language imposes a chain of words along which the ego must move while the unconscious remains in search of the object it has lost. (Wright 1987: 111)

Thus Lacan appears not to give the unconscious power to correct the order of language that created it (ibid.: 112). It is a feature of Freudian and Lacanian film theory that the unconscious is not conceived as having the power to overthrow or remake elements of the symbolic order and rewrite cinematic and spoken language to meet the insistence of hitherto unvoiced desires. Jungian theory, by contrast, hypothesises the unconscious as containing just such high potential energy.

Don Fredericksen has referred to the Freudian method of screen analysis as depending on a hermeneutic of suspicion (Fredericksen 2000). That suspicion arises, first, from the belief that the unconscious consists exclusively of injurious contents of consciousness repressed in large part during infancy. Secondly, suspicion is augmented by Freud's concept of displacement. This is the idea that nothing coming from the unconscious is what it seems to be because dreams disguise their elements in order to shield the ego from their fearful meanings. We shall see in a moment that the Jungian take on dream images is very different. Thirdly, Freudian and Lacanian film theorists heightened distrust of cinema in their theoretical models when, like Mulvey and Christian Metz, they associated the unconscious roots of mainstream cinema with perversions of the sexual drive. The latter were said to reveal themselves in the fetishism, voyeurism and exhibitionism that these writers believed to underlie cinema's visual regimes (see Wright 1987: 120).

Fredericksen regards the hermeneutic of suspicion as a methodology limited at best in its potential to the interpretation of films whose signifiers are already familiar. It does not serve well screen works that are suffused with the erotic and inviting mysteries of symbolic art – films such as Fellini's, Bergman's, Roeg's and many of those that are analysed in the following pages. These are better read via the Jungian hermeneutic of amplification. Using this method the analyst seeks understanding through a form of extended conversation and argumentation with the screen text. Nor is it incidental that this constructive process (which we shall discuss in detail in chapter 1) makes demands upon the analysts' intuitions such that, while pursuing the work, they find themselves being worked upon (Fredericksen: 2000).

Freudian and Lacanian work has an unwelcome characteristic in that it is conveyed in the rebarbative jargon of high theory. This language, as surely as that of any high church, marks out its users as an elite, separating initiates from laity. Worse, it distances the reader from the feel of the remembered screen text. To work well, Jungian screen analysis must deliver the analyst's evidence and intuitions to the reader in terms aimed at engaging the latter, and therefore should speak as plainly as it can.

For the Jungian, the intensity of the fascination generated among audiences by screen narratives is sufficient grounds for finding the phenomenon interesting. Where large numbers of people find a fiction occupying their emotions, there Jungian analytical psychology leads us to expect we shall discover minds engrossed at levels beneath those of which most of them are conscious. This is no accident: emotion is the key to the deeper levels of the psyche because the expression of deep-seated needs and desires is inextricably bonded to the formation of myths, no matter what medium of communication is employed. Jung recognised in every aspect of his psychology the over-mastering force that emotion can exert on the individual. Indeed, he sometimes reversed the usual formulation, saying rather that a strong emotion possesses the individual than the other way about. Thus *affect* (as emotion is also called) is seen as a primary force exercised by the unconscious over which the individual has little control (Samuels, Shorter and Plaut 1986: 11).

What, then, are the purposes and merits of undertaking a Jungian analysis of contemporary media, and what are its limitations?

Many facets of Jungian theory can readily be adapted to advance the understanding of media texts – not just the characters therein, but also plots, settings and aesthetics. Deploying analytical psychology to interpret a media artifact certainly can reveal information about the psyche of the characters. But it can also do a great deal more.

Jungian analysis makes much of the interrelated (intertextual) nature of all cultural artifacts. It elaborates the reading of characters, plots, settings and images in a given movie or screen drama by extending it through comparison with the language and symbolism of pre-existent texts (both on screen and embodied in other art forms). When working with analysands, Jung termed this practice amplification, and it matches a familiar interpretive procedure in the humanities. It enriches the significance of those texts that can sustain the comparison by setting them against the backdrop of legends and myths both ancient and modern. This is done not as an end in its own right, but because myth has an important function in the Jungian understanding of human psychology. To appreciate this, it is simplest to start with the cultural dimension of analytical psychology.

Jungians consider images that arise in dreams and reveries to be the most direct means available for the unconscious to communicate with the conscious mind. Unlike Freudians, they do not believe that such images cover up secret impulses that are too disruptive to be contemplated. Rather, they hold that such figures compensate for the biases of conscious drives. It is a further distinguishing tenet of Jungian work that some dreams reveal more than the repressed contents of an individual's past life. They do so through their robust links with the dreams that other people have experienced and the myths that other cultures have recorded. For Jungians, myths bear the ineradicable traces of dreams, reveries, desires and fears that have touched many people. They are seen to have a collective dimension (in that they may, for example, express the longings or fears of a community or a nation) as they place in the realm of consciousness previously unconscious impulses. Today's cultural artifacts do so no less than those of our forebears. One function of Jungian textual analysis is to identify and explicate some of the undercurrents of collective feeling that electrify those movies which audiences accept (whether they verbalise the experience in such terms or not) as the shaping myths of our time.

It follows that the emotional impact of media texts on audiences engages the attention of the academic Jungian because the distinctive claims of Jungian screen theory include its capability to model the ways in which the subjective and felt experiences of spectators arise from their encounter with the screen text. Therefore, while a Jungian reading does not attempt to determine subject positioning, it can show how a text seeks to open a viewing position for audiences. More interestingly, it has the potential to speak about the collective psychological disposition of the audiences who invest it with their responses. It can also address the cultural significance of their experience, with the caveat that shifts in the psychology of the audience are the more readily detected in broad currents. This is the case, for example, where the object of study can be linked to a persistently popular phenomenon – a movie to its genre, a televised drama to a series, a leading player to his or her stardom.

Fredericksen has remarked that a Jungian reading, if it is to be distinguishable from any other form of textual analysis, must find its base in the intuitive and emotional response of the interpreter. Where nothing more than a routine equation is offered between, say, a character or event on the screen and a pre-existing archetype, the supposedly Jungian reading dies at birth. This is the case with, among others, the lamentably mechanical books by Clark Branson (1987) and James F. Iaccino (1994 and 1998). As we shall discover in chapter 1, Jungian screen theory institutes a positive role for the subjective experience of the textual analyst. Although the latter is not permitted to depart from an interpretation licensed by the textual evidence, without his or her intuitive understanding of what the screen offers, the Jungian reading has little value. The analyst shares the subjective impact of the text so that the reader tastes its emotional impact vicariously through him or her. In doing so, the Jungian invokes the feel of the remembered text and invites the readers' participation – in a way which Freudian and Lacanian film analyses seldom do.

Inevitably, some of Jung's hypotheses have been overtaken by scientific work undertaken since his lifetime. For instance, knowledge of and speculation about cognitive processes have developed vigorously in ways he could not have anticipated. Jungian theory cannot claim, any more than Freudian or Lacanian psychoanalysis, a holistic scientific base. Nor would this have distressed Jung. He described his model of the psyche as a metaphor intended to aid exploration and insisted that (*pace* Iaccino) it should not be reified and treated as if it were the real thing, cast in iron. Its distinctive qualities as an implement supporting screen studies lie not in its scientificity but in its potential for deepening readings of screen myths and heroes in the context of enhanced appreciation of the psyche.

It is worth noting in this connection that Jungian screen theory does not claim to be the most useful analytical tool for dealing with every screen fiction; rather, as we shall have ample occasion for observing, it serves certain kinds of film – the symbolic, the mythically charged and the visionary – better than others.

Despite its high potential, it is still true, as I wrote several years ago, that theorists of Film and Media Studies have not given the writings of Carl Jung a hundredth part of the attention devoted to Freud. This indifference can be directly attributed to the dominance of materialist theories in academic studies of the screen since the late 1960s. Indeed, neo-Marxists were able to wreck before its inception any attempt to do so by two assertions that were taken to be fatal: first, that the concept of the collective unconscious is at odds with sociological theories that represent human beings as subject to ideological pressures exerted on them through every social and cultural channel, including the language they utter; and, secondly, that Jung's psychology rests on an essentialist philosophical base.

The first challenge alleges that an analysis of media texts according to Jung's theories must be incompatible with models acceptable to social scientists of the ways cultural and social forces impact upon individuals. Whatever the failings of Freudian film theorists in over-determining the position of the viewer, they did perceive links between discourse, culture and society and the formation of the psyche. They recognised the authority of Lacan's Symbolic Order, such as the structures of language and cinema; but they too closely identified the Symbolic Order with the Law of the Father. As Rodowick put it succinctly, feminist Freudian film theorists wrongly took sexual identity as being essentially linked to the possession or lack of cultural and societal power. They mistook,

a biological prop – the penis – as the signifier of patriarchal authority and power, when what is at stake for all social beings is the delegation of that power which under the sign of the phallus takes the form of division and hierarchy. (Rodowick 1991: 32)

With the benefit of hindsight, it is possible to see that this fault sprang from the centrality of ideological concerns in feminist readings of the screen. In effect, their interest in demonstrating the cultural mechanisms of patriarchy led them into psychoanalysis from a starting-point locked in ideology. Nevertheless, given that media products are made, distributed and consumed in a social and cultural context which they themselves reflect and influence, the Freudian film theorists' objection to Jungian work is clearly important. Rather than attempt to discharge it in an introduction, several of the following chapters include, as an integral activity along with Jungian textual analysis, an account of the way in which that analysis is inflected by recent Jungian thought concerning the interaction between psyche and culture. Among the ideas which post-Jungians have been developing during the last quarter of the century, some of the most significant concern the manner and degree to which the psyche of the individual is formed by the interplay between psychological factors and social and cultural pressures. These are complex questions, and the responses of Jung's successors to them are still incomplete. Nevertheless, it is fair to say that sufficient progress has been made to show that Jungian theory is by no means incompatible with due respect for social and cultural processes.

The second objection of materialists to Jungian theory, that it rests on an essentialist philosophical base, is more readily answered. Jung invariably declined, when writing as a psychologist, to speculate on the existence of a divinity. He based his refusal on the grounds that what is beyond our understanding is in all ways out of its reach. As James Hillman wrote on this topic some years later,

Theology takes Gods literally and we do not . . . Religion and psychology have care for the same ultimates, but religion approaches Gods with ritual, prayer, sacrifice, worship, creed. Gods are *believed* in and approached with religious methods. In archetypal psychology Gods are imagined. They are approached through psychological methods of personifying, pathologizing, and psychologizing. They are formulated ambiguously, as metaphors for modes of experience and as numinous borderline persons. (Hillman 1975: 169)

Jung emphatically affirmed the concept of a god as a psychological fact because in countless cases he observed that the psyche presented powerful and apparently autonomous images of deity. These archetypal figures tended to exert a controlling force, often forming both the centre and circumference of the individual's being. He described the *imago Dei* as a dominant and autonomous psychic content which, like other autonomous contents, has the power radically to affect our moods and actions (Jung 1935a: 238). He saw it, therefore, as an archetype identical with the self – an archetypal image which we shall be encountering more than once in the course of this study. Thus, to reiterate, Jungians are concerned not with belief but with the natural place of the divine image in the human psyche. In the context of screen studies, this is not without significance given the role of the media in taking over some of the functions of religion.

The book opens by developing some of the themes that have already been touched on. The first chapter lays out a theoretical methodology for the work that follows. It shows how Jungian procedures of amplification and active imagination can be at the service of textual analysts in bringing into the public arena meanings that they derive from a film. This in turn restores a measure of authority to the subjective experience of not only the textual analyst but of all viewers by showing how the interpretation of what one has seen and heard is always tied to the process of bringing the text into being.

The second chapter introduces Jung's concept of the impersonal or collective unconscious and examines in particular one archetypal image, the anima (the contrasexual female image which often presents as a figure of a man's imagining). It offers an analysis of the roles of the two principal characters in the 1981 film *Diva* and shows how its young hero is anima-struck. The activities of the anima are pursued further through the wider field of genre cinema with specific reference to the Western. The notoriously distorted roles of women in Westerns are interpreted as a warping of the collective anima. This appears to be a perversion of the pastoral ideals in the white American cultural legacy that dates back to the seizure of land by incoming colonists from its original occupants.

The socio-cultural agenda having been opened with discussion of the Western, the third chapter gives a fuller account of Jung's model of activity in the psyche and describes the two-way exchange between the unconscious and the social as mediated by symbols. Post-Jungians have developed Jung's model and taken account of the way that cultural influences shape both the inputs to the unconscious and the manifestations of its impulses. This chapter introduces the concept of the cultural unconscious which arose from such post-Jungian theorising, and illustrates it with further work on *Diva*.

In the fourth chapter, a close reading of Jane Campion's film *The Piano* becomes the pretext for reflections on the other contrasexual archetype, the animus. Jung's ideas about it are revised in the light of work by feminist archetypal theorists, work which demonstrates the necessity of considering archetypal images in the context not only of the unconscious but also of internalised social values. The concept of the cultural unconscious remains in play as the colonial experience of the film's characters is shown to have been the dominant shaping force not only in their social lives but also in moulding their sexual and psychological states of being.

Observed through some of their music videos, two pop icons make the focal points of the fifth chapter. Pop stars have cultural existences which far exceed the screen, but their presence here is justified by a number of factors. First, although video is a distinctive form, the magic of the movies is tasted through those music videos that, like Michael Jackson's and Madonna's, exploit to the maximum the medium's quasi-cinematic appeal, embellishing the glamour of their stardom with sensuously crafted music, action, light and colour. Secondly, the convergence of the media industries welds connections between popular music, TV and video. This is true in terms of their global economy; and in this specific instance, all three media have featured both these stars as icons of their time. Finally, stardom itself opens up the idea of the cultural unconscious through the phenomena of fandom – with reference not only to the feelings and behaviour of fans but also to their cultural formation as self-selecting, though by no means mutually exclusive, groups. The iconography that emblazons Michael Jackson's public presence centres on the image of the androgyne which brings male and female into relation in what can be perceived as either perfect harmony or nightmarish discord. And the iconography sported by Madonna is interpreted in the light of two archetypal figures which on the surface of things seem incompatible: the trickster and a goddess make a combination that is most unusual in the modern era.

The sixth chapter develops the feminist theme (discussed in the previous two chapters) of the need to revise male-dominated archetypal images if they are to accommodate the psychological condition of Western women in the late twentieth century. This chapter examines as splendid exemplar the role of a young woman detective, Clarice Starling in *The Silence of the Lambs,* who has dedicated her life to acting as a hero by emulating her dead father. The interpretation of the film offered here suggests that while she is every bit the hero her father was, she is only truly effective both in her professional role and in fighting her demons (manifested in the terrifying figures of the film's serial killers Hannibal Lecter and Jamie Gumb) when, rather than copying her male colleagues in the FBI, she learns to respect and act in accordance with the promptings of her womanhood.

Chapter 7 continues the scrutiny of heroes in a quite different public arena by examining sports reporting on television. It discovers, ascending from the banal to the sublime, that, beneath the routine celebrations of national sporting heroes, there lies a strong cultural impulse which has kinship with the ancient rituals surrounding the flourishing, slaughter and rebirth of the year gods.

The underlying purposes of a hero's quest include not only the working out of destiny, but also confirmation of his or her identity. For Jungians, the travails of a hero are likely to end in a change in the equilibrium of the self. However, Jungians of differing schools dispute the nature of the self. In chapter 8, Philip Ridley's film *The Passion of Darkly Noon* is interpreted as presenting an analogue for the archetypal school's model of the self as polycentred. According to this school, the self has several archetypal nodes constantly in play with each other.

In Ridley's film an intruder enters a secret forest glade where everything appears to be (like the archetypes in the well-adjusted self) in almost perfect balance between the characters living there; but the newcomer's arrival disturbs the fulcrum and throws all into question. By the end of the film a new balance has been struck; but the only thing sure is that the new status quo will hold only temporarily before one of the archetypal figures gathered into the new grouping shifts in one way or another. Such ceaseless flux can be read as a metaphor for the way the archetypal school of Jungians see the psyche operating.

Jung himself, and his followers in the so-called classical school, model the self as an archetype in which all the contesting forces within the psyche, both conscious and unconscious, are held, albeit provisionally, in tensioned equilibrium. The perfection of this state of being has long been the goal of many faiths, and more lately of classical analytical psychology. Tracing its realisation as a possibility for humanity continues to be, as it has for many centuries, the preoccupation of a robust strand in the fictions of Europe and North America. The ostensible subject of chapter 9 is ghosts; but the enthusiasm with which in the 1990s many ghost stories (both large and small screen) were received suggests that something more than entertainment may have been at stake. Although some of these screen ghosts were nothing other than objects of mild sensation, the more vigorous incarnations (as in *Ghost* and *Truly, Madly, Deeply*) were engaged in animus/anima roles. But in their most potent manifestations (as with *The X-Files* and Dennis Potter's last two plays) they lead the spectator to glimpses of the soul in something resembling the ancient, unified form in which it has appeared for hundreds of years to mystics and the devout.

The final chapter picks up the same theme of the hero's journey in search of perfection of the self; but on this occasion it turns to a majestic imagined future for the onward spiritual journey of the human species.

Stanley Kubrick's *2001: A Space Odyssey* is a great cinematic paean, a symbol of the potential development of the collective self. As such, its journey in space has archetypal elements in common with the citings of Unidentified Flying Objects that Jung described as visions (sometimes shared by large numbers of people) that had the potential to reveal symbols of the self to those that saw them. But Jung's UFOs were coming in to Earth. Kubrick's spaceship is going out. Despite the many banalities in which routine affairs mire Earth's peoples at the end of the twentieth century, the species itself reaches out. In dramatising this great journey, *2001* encourages us to rediscover our sense of religious awe without ignoring or demeaning what at the start of the millennium we know of the universe.

1   Jungian theory, textual analysis and audience play

While all the arts are rich treasure-houses of symbolic material, this is especially true of televisual and cinematic fiction with their ability to employ images, speech, narrative and music. Feature films and television drama are confined only by the limits of form and human imagination when they rework myth and adapt it to the needs of our time. The screen is an aesthetically rich medium, and through its sensuous pleasures spectators hope to be drawn into one or a number of diverse experiences.

How do fictions stir the spectator's psyche? The short answer is through emotion. When they view fiction and drama, most viewers expect to be recompensed for their cash outlay by being entertained. Entertainment encompasses many different kinds of delight from imaginary wish fulfilment to the pleasures of terror experienced in a virtual rather than a real milieu; from the sensuous gratifications of saturated colour and engulfing sound to the power trip of flying with a gravity-defying camera. All these forms of pleasure have in common that they appeal to and stir the emotions. Indeed, from our point of view, the significance of the well-rehearsed storytelling and generic formulae at the heart of mainstream cinema lies in the studios' recognition that the impact of emotion is potent. For the best part of a century Hollywood's executive producers have expected their writers and directors to build into almost every mainstream movie scenes which are designed to rouse strong affects in the minds of audiences. Yet despite its obviousness on both the large and small screen, emotion remains a topic to which theorists writing about film and media studies have given inadequate attention.

What then is the power of the emotions? At base, nothing less than to disturb the equilibrium of the psyche. Such a disturbance can in real life be either beneficial or harmful, according to the individual's circumstances and the nature of the complexes that are energised. As we shall see, they may involve the spectator in a form of narcissistic introspection. However, the effects upon audiences of emotions aroused by drama and fictions (including those played out on screen) are in general benign precisely because they refer to a virtual rather than a real world. Story worlds

15

allow for play with emotions just as much as with characters, situations and ideas vicariously experienced. Spectators make discoveries about a hypothetical, not a real, situation. In doing so they also improve their understanding of human nature in general and of their personal psychology in particular (see Preston 1970: 5–6). The emotions aroused by fictions on screen are real enough, but they and their consequences are by no means inescapable, as they often would be in daily life. Rather, experiencing affects aroused by fictions can resemble being drawn by one's emotions into a rehearsal for a possible, imagined future that just might (but more likely never will) occur in the individual's life in the real world. In most instances (and invariably in the case of the fantasy genres such as science fiction, horror or musicals, for example, where there is little or no direct representation of life in the real world) the imagining stimulated by the fiction is principally invested in psychological role play.

When individuals draw images from the outer world and make them part of an inner world that preoccupies them, they may be responding in a narcissistic way. Heinz Kohut understood narcissism as a condition that naturally persists throughout life – and which can be either healthy or unhealthy. When it is pathological, narcissism shows itself in a psychological predisposition to gather the outer world to the self in order to sustain a pretentious persona that covers up feelings of emptiness. Narcissistic development, by contrast, involves a positive process of self-scrutiny and 'the construction and attainment of ambitions and goals' (Samuels, Shorter and Plaut 1986: 97). In this way healthy narcissism can help a person grow in self-knowledge and contribute to individuation (ibid.: 98; Samuels 1990: 124–5). Screened fiction has this potential to help the individual grow in self-awareness – and in particular to gain fuller experience of his or her own emotional being.

According to Jung, the unconscious in its normal stable state is contained by consciousness. This is the case because the energy of the latter is greater than that of the former. Therefore, when unconscious contents overflow into the conscious, either the level of conscious activity has reduced or the intensity of unconscious activity has increased. Jung demonstrated that there were a considerable number of conditions in which the loss of conscious energy could occur. It happens naturally in sleep when we dream, and also when we daydream or associate freely. Even in the waking state, our emotions, whatever we might prefer to think, are not within our control. Emotions happen to us, and they are capable of overwhelming the individual and allowing drives of which we are wholly or partly unconscious to take over and alter our attitudes (Jung 1939: 278–9; 1956a: 442). They are 'instinctive, involuntary reactions which upset the rational order of consciousness by their elemental outbursts' (ibid.: 1939: 278). Their import for human affairs is great because 'emotion is the chief source of consciousness. There is no change from darkness to light or from inertia to movement without emotion' (ibid., 1954b: 96).

The prospect of losing conscious control frequently arouses fear, particularly if we suspect that control may be seized from us by other people. Here is a source of the cinema's power, one which makes it simultaneously both disturbing and reassuring. In front of the screen, the constant flow of storytelling material occupies sight and sound with lavish colours and sounds. As Konigsberg says, we seek to use the film as a transitional object and 'slip into a state of half-wakefulness, into a reverie that weakens our defenses and sets loose our own fantasies and wishes to interact and fuse with the characters and even the landscape that we see on the screen' (Konigsberg 1996: 885–6). Spectators are likely, therefore, to allow themselves a form of play in which for the moment they adopt, without the risk of becoming locked into it, one of the virtual roles that, as a transitional phenomenon, the film has prepared for them. As fans, they are likely to align themselves with their heroes and heroines and partake imaginatively in patterns of life and adventure with little if any connection to the world they inhabit by day. For all their desire to do this, however, the plenitude of fantastic imagery playing across the screen is likely, for the duration of the film's running time, to inhibit spectators from evolving further their own fantasy material. But after the film has ended, active imagination takes over and develops the recollected cinematic imagery by fusing it more completely with personal fantasy material. In the process both are liable to change.

A lowering of the level of consciousness is experienced in the dark warmth and security of the cinema as it unreels its manifold diversions. Its sumptuous images and sounds, its compelling characters and stories arouse many emotions and stir drives of which the individual may be unconscious. Because of the fictionality of their object, whatever the specific nature of these emotions (fear, anger, desire, wonder, horror), they are usually experienced as virtual rather than actual, and therefore ultimately as pleasurable. When the action on screen greatly excites spectators, it seems probable that their emotions set in train the affective process which alters the configuration in the memory of the images even as they are being screened. So the filter through which the unconscious alters and dissolves images and narrative events in conformity with its own predispositions may be assumed to begin its action at once.[2] We shall describe the way that this automatic process can be brought into the service of criticism when discussing the active imagination.

[2] Tony Cryer is due thanks for help with this point.

To repeat, then, where popular audiences find a fiction engaging their emotions, there Jungian analytical psychology leads us to expect to discover minds engrossed at levels beneath those of which most of them are conscious. Emotion opens the deeper levels of the psyche. The airing of deep-seated collective needs and desires is a driving force in not only the formation but also the reception of myths. Here in the illustrated dark, unconscious and semi-conscious desires form and find their goals. And they do this through the parallel mechanisms of *projection* and *introjection*. Jungian theory shares the Freudian interest in these two mechanisms, both schools of thought finding them meaningful in accounting for the transference of energy between conscious and unconscious. And since affect is the force that drives them, they are activated the more strongly the more fully the movie engages the spectator's emotions.

Whether inside or outside the cinema, psychological *projection* is a potent mechanism. It refers to individuals' propensity to displace difficult emotions or parts of the personality that they refuse to recognise in themselves on to people, objects or other figures encountered in the environment. Through projection, therefore, figures in the individual's surroundings reflect meanings which are profoundly personal back to the subject. For Jung (who differed in this from Freud) this was a normal, even routine aspect of psychological activity. According to him complexes are not limited to being the products of anxiety and mental stress, but are routinely experienced in the course of human existence. Not only that, but if the individual learns to recognise the extent to which images in the environment are projections of his or her own fantasy material, the process known as integration may begin to occur and some understanding of the nature of unconscious impulses may be achieved (Jung 1948c: 264–5; Samuels, Shorter and Plaut 1986: 113–14).

Film and the dreamlike experience that occurs when the barriers between consciousness and the unconscious are lowered would, however, be less potently linked were it not for the phenomenon of *introjection*. It may be described as the opposite to projection, since it involves internalising experience of the world. Introjection also plays a large part in creating empathy because it involves an investment of the object with the libido. Through it the recipient takes into his or her psyche from an exterior source both an image and the energy that it stimulates (Jung 1921: 452; Samuels, Shorter and Plaut 1986: 85). Introjection in the cinema accounts for the kind of process that Murray Smith describes in elaborating the concept commonly called identification: that is the process of recognition and psychological alignment that can occur on the part of fans when they endow characters or film stars with their allegiance (Smith 1995: 73–109).

Experienced in the cinema, psychological projection and introjection seem to resemble the same processes known in daily life, but they occur with high intensity. This is because they are enhanced by the experience of *cinematic* projection, the power of which to complement and intensify *psychological* projection and introjection appears to be considerable.

Although the differences between narrative film and dream are easily established in that fiction is subject to conscious control, the resemblances can be particularly vivid in the moment of a film's delivery and as the walls between conscious and unconscious dissolve to a translucency. A number of factors are in play. The intensity of the cinematic experience arises in large part through the ceaselessness of the illusion playing on the screen, which adds to the dreamlike nature of the fiction, unstoppable as the images that roll past one in sleep. It becomes something that happens to one rather than something one controls. This impression is enhanced by the mixing of the two currents of projection flowing in contrary directions. For the projections of the spectator intersect with those of the equipment that throws the images and sounds on the screen. At the same time, this mechanical projection itself carries the psychological projections of the filmmakers, since their own active imaginings have inevitably found expression through the script, intensified through performance, camera and sound recording, and further distilled in the editing suite (see Beebe 1996: 581). No wonder, under the intense psychological pressure that occurs where their own and the filmmakers' desires coincide, that most spectators suspend disbelief.

Projection and introjection help to explain how and why symbolic representations on the screen interact with the unconscious of large numbers of people. The importance of projection and introjection is that they invest with personally felt significance images and sounds whose original locus is observed reality. They bring about a two-way flow between screen and unconscious. This double process of psychological investment is capable of endowing not only the familiar images of everyday life with potential new meaning, but also of making available to the conscious mind symbols hitherto deep-rooted in the unconscious. The effect on the individual spectator can be almost unbearably intense. In the cinema, as with all forms of artistic representation, the terrors latent in loss of conscious control and the associated fear of going mad are lessened by the knowledge that what one is living through is experienced as if by proxy. Even so, the immediacy of cinematic images and events can have so powerful an impact that the sense of safety is occasionally erased temporarily. (This is, for instance, apparent in the case of those spectators, of whom the present writer is one, who faint at moments of particularly bloody dramatic intensity.) In front of the screen this emotional energy cannot flow outwards into any other world than that provided by the screen narrative, which simply intensifies and returns it to the spectating psyche via his or her introjection of images and plot.

To over-simplify, we may say that in life the processes of projection and introjection cause libido to flow into and out of the individual's psyche in relation to images which, in response to its needs, it selects from among the welter of figures in that person's surroundings. We may contrast this with the current of affect in the cinema, where films proffer the spectators preselected images designed to occupy their attention completely; and with the intention, so far as can be prearranged, of arousing and enticing the libido to flow in directions that the filmmakers foresaw. Here is yet another indication, like the popularity of the major genres, that cinema depends heavily for its success on shared subjective experience.

Although on occasion the unconscious is stimulated to pathological levels and the subject faints, the more usual result is that these images and stories present themselves to the individual as potent symbols. As such, the latter may covertly manoeuvre the individual into beginning to apprehend something of the character of his or her unconscious drives.

As we shall discover in more detail in later chapters, Jung describes symbols as having the power to widen the field of the individual's consciousness (1921: 126). They do this by allowing that to be understood which was previously not known. Through their consciously realised aspects they discipline the unruly instincts; and they anchor unconscious energies in form, giving shape to the archetypal contents which they adapt to the social values and cultural norms of the day. Since they offer for scrutiny representations formed through the compensatory pressure of the unconscious, their ultimate role, if they are well understood, is to surrender their symbolic nature.

Jung refers to the way in which a symbol facilitates the transition from one psychological attitude to another as the transcendent function. It occurs when symbols enhance consciousness by bringing it into fuller relationship with the unconscious (ibid.: 480; Samuels, Shorter and Plaut 1986: 150). This is not a small claim when applied in the domain of textual studies, since the reach of a symbol can extend far beyond the single image alone and may well incorporate an entire narrative. This is the case, for example, in Kubrick's *2001: A Space Odyssey* (analysed in chapter 10), in which the entire journey is a symbol not only of the individual human life-cycle extended beyond death into immortality, but also of an imagined future history of the human soul. Full engagement with a symbolic film or television drama (Jung would have described such a work as 'visionary') has no less potential than to change individuals' consciousness. It can alter the way they feel and think about themselves or the world. We should add that, although this is an experience which many film buffs say they know, it is not necessarily a comfortable process.

In psychotherapy the process to which we are referring, namely the integration of projected contents, is often the objective of the analysis. The process aims to narrow and eventually abolish the gap between unconscious and conscious by integration of the tendencies of the former into the latter. It is a potentially hazardous operation which can lead to problems if the individual identifies with the unconscious contents. In such a case, the patient's ego may either be greatly enlarged (to a state near to megalomania), or may suffer near-annihilation by the new contents. Either way the normal ego-personality is exposed to the risk of being all but extinguished. And although (psychotherapy being an accepted form of treatment) it is obvious that the conscious mind is rarely overwhelmed in this way during the process of integration (far less when being stimulated by the symbols in a screenplay), it does become strongly coloured by unconscious contents (Jung 1946a: 263; 1946b 101–2; 1956a: 442).

Because we are concerned with publicly circulated symbols to which in most instances people have been exposed relatively fleetingly in a public arena (rather than recurrently and over a long period in the obsessive privacy of the skull), they are usually experienced less intensely.[3] However, when a symbol resonates strongly with the energy of an archetype seeking to compensate for a bias in collective consciousness, the reverse may be the case. At such a time, as when in the early 1990s the image of the serial killer exercised a hold over the popular imagination, the textual analyst has occasion to work with images and myths of *numinous* power. How he or she does so can in some small degree affect the integration in the community of the unconscious contents concerned.

Like other psychological processes, integration does not have to attend on the assistance of either a therapist or a textual analyst to occur. It may indeed commence spontaneously if, for instance, a person finds a particular symbol fascinating and devotes close attention to it. In such circumstances it may well have benign effects. As Samuels, Shorter and Plaut remark, integration can lead to a state of mind analogous to enjoying mental health or maturity. It can induce a sense of wholeness and may even be the groundwork that initiates the process of individuation of the self (1986: 83–4).

---

[3] One exception occurs with people whose egos are fragmented or so imperfectly developed that they cannot master those cinematic symbols that trigger their anxieties (see Hewison 2000: 291–3).

But how, since symbols break with established schemata, can we learn to make a constructive reading of Jungian symbols and the contemporary myths to which they contribute? There are two principal mechanisms. The first is provided by a process Jung called *amplification*, an important part of the methodology he deployed in dream analysis. He found it more productive than merely observing a patient's mental associations. He acknowledged that collecting directed associations enabled the patient to make a good beginning in allowing patient and therapist to deal with a complex locked in the personal unconscious. It did so by revealing the hidden links among the components of the complex. However, the limitations of association were that it broke down when the analyst tried to go beyond the personal context of the dream. This always happened at the very point where archetypal images generated by energies derived from the collective unconscious were beginning to appear.

Jung discovered that to engage with such images arising from the collective unconscious, the psychoanalyst must plot the dream's archetypal imagery against parallels drawn from mythology, religion, folklore, works of art or other cultural artifacts in order to clarify the metaphorical content of the dream symbolism. This process allows the patient and the analyst jointly to build a picture of its unknown meanings through the process of synthesising personal associations with these 'historical' parallels (Jung 1943: 81; Fredericksen 1979: 188; Samuels, Shorter and Plaut 1986: 16). The significance of this method for us is that it can be reduplicated in the interpretation of screen images. Indeed, amplification has much in common with, and appears to have borrowed from, the traditional scholarly methods of textual interpretation and comparative linguistics. It depends on finding the apposite 'historical' context for each image.

It is simply [a matter] of seeking the parallels. For instance, in the case of a very rare word which you have never come across before, you try to find parallel text passages, parallel applications perhaps, where that word also occurs, and then you try to put the formula you have established from the knowledge of other texts into the new text. If you make the new text a readable whole, you say, 'Now we can read it'. That is how we learned to read hieroglyphics and cuneiform inscriptions and that is how we can read dreams. (Jung 1935b: 83)

The technique can be adapted to the amplification of the symbolic material in all narratives, including those on the screen. The Jungian textual analyst discovers that ancient myths, religious stories, folklore and artifacts can often illuminate both thematic and psychological meanings that may not otherwise be accessible through them. As we shall see, this is the case with some very different films.

The problem with amplification as a method – whether applied to fiction or dream imagery – is precisely that it stabilises meaning. Objectivity and consciousness dominate it and threaten to domesticate its outcome. Because amplification functions by setting symbolic material into pre-existing and well-known schemata, it renders safe the inherent strangeness of symbols. It is for just this reason that James Hillman has argued against the translation of dream imagery into ideas and concepts. As Thomas Moore says, Hillman sees most modes of interpretation as Herculean but misguided efforts to 'spoil imagination, ultimately to defend against the challenging otherness of the dream or image'. Hillman's preferred method of working with dreams, therefore, requires an appreciation for the integrity of the dream. 'We should not lose the dream in the light of day; rather, we should visit the land of dream and be affected by the peculiarities of that world' (Moore 1990: 6).

The more radical archetypal psychoanalysts led by Hillman prefer that dreams should never be interpreted. Classical Jungians, in contrast, take the view that, since the function of such symbolic matter is to compensate for an imbalance between conscious and unconscious, interpretation has the benefit that it focuses material thrown up by the unconscious. However, if we understand Hillman as wishing to postpone interpreting symbolic material so that it comes to consciousness resonating with the energy that generated it, then we have an idea worth developing in relation to the practice of textual analysis.

For our present purposes it is convenient to divide texts into three classes according to their symbolic register. The first of these has already been mentioned, identified by Jung as *visionary*. Characteristic of such work is that –

it can be a revelation whose heights and depths are beyond our fathoming, or a vision of beauty that we can never put into words . . . [Most works of art] never rend the curtain that veils the cosmos; they do not exceed the bounds of our human capacities . . . But the primordial experiences rend from top to bottom the curtain upon which is painted the picture of an ordered world, and allow a glimpse into the unfathomable abyss of the unborn and of things yet to be. (Jung 1950: 90)

The visionary narrative is one that arises from the collective unconscious almost impersonally (without foregrounding the personal psychologies of the artists who are its vehicles). The work of art of this nature is 'a true symbol – that is, an expression for something real but unknown' (ibid.: 94). Human passion falls within the sphere of conscious experience, while the object of the vision lies beyond it. Through our senses we experience the known, but our intuitions point to things that are unknown and hidden, that by their very nature are secret (ibid.: 94).

If the process of reading is not to kill off their visionary images, narratives of this kind must be responded to with the same delicacy of touch that Hillman advocates psychoanalysts should employ when working on great dreams. The analyst's response has to respect the 'feel' of their magical energy. This makes it necessary to work not only with the conscious tools provided by amplification, but also at an intuitive level. We shall say more about this after mentioning the other two classes of text.

Visionary works having the glorious, demonic or revelatory force that Jung describes are comparatively rare. However, the same tact they require should be used in analysing the second class of narrative. This contains all other screen texts incorporating symbolic material where the entire work is not an extended symbol. Once again, there is an approximate parallel with the work of the therapist. When analysing a patient's dream that may seem less than visionary to the analyst, the latter must nonetheless treat it with all the respect due to the originality it has for the patient.

The final class of movie presents the viewer with no material which seems to him or her to be symbolic (again using the term in Jung's sense). A psychoanalytic approach might be of use in deriving a reading that augmented understanding of the ways that such a text allegorically draws upon established mythological themes. In this case amplification might be an appropriate instrument to enhance knowledge about the way the text functions. However, it is unlikely that such a film would stimulate a Jungian reading of the kind we are about to describe where the analyst's active imagination is fully engaged.

As previously mentioned, amplification is a method that resembles closely standard scholarly practice in the interpretation of perplexing narratives to the extent that the scholar, like the psychoanalyst, seeks out earlier examples of phenomena similar to those which are to be illuminated. Therefore amplification exposes the textual analyst no less than the psychoanalyst to the temptation of finding an easy way to explain symbols by falling back on professional routines and applying them mechanically in order to arrive at an interpretation. However, there is a way of respecting the integrity of the symbol, and this involves analysts of symbolic texts (like the analysts of patients' dreams) in bringing their own subjectivity consciously and methodically into play. When scholars succeed in analysing a film while feeling and relishing the impact of its symbolism's energy upon their own minds, they are more likely to be able to convey to their readers a sense of its numinosity. What is needed is a methodology that allows the textual analyst to switch between objective and subjective stances.

Amplification provides the analyst with a mechanism that supports the objective attitude. The question that arises therefore is what method should be employed that responds to the symbol's transcendent function – the function which resides in its potential for bringing together conscious and unconscious contents. What is needed is provided by adapting the framework of what Jung called the *constructive* treatment of the unconscious. Actually this does not mean abandoning amplification. On the contrary, it continues to have a significant function as a part (but by no means the whole) of the constructive process. Amplification provides a map of the known terrain; application of the constructive method suggests routes through that terrain for each voyager and shows where the map needs to be remade for him or her.

The constructive method entails building up the products of the unconscious by elaborating upon them, and teasing out the concealed purpose of symbols. In this respect Jung's procedure differs radically from what he termed Freud's *reductive* method, because there the analytical process insists, according to Jung, upon 'a reduction to the elementary processes of wishing or striving, which in the last resort are of an infantile or physiological nature'. The reductive method is oriented backwards in time either to reminiscences of actual childhood events or to elementary psychic processes. Another limitation is that it does not allow that the product of the unconscious may be authentic in its own right (Jung 1921: 422, 459). By way of contrast, the constructive method relies upon the hypothesis that the products of the unconscious have value and the potential for meaning in their own right. It is oriented forward towards the future (whether of the individual or the collective) in that the products of the unconscious compensate for the contents of the conscious and counterbalance them. It follows that, when apprehended, they sway consciousness to a greater or lesser degree in their direction. Whereas Freud sought to dissolve symbols in order to uncover the rudimentary elements that he believed they must conceal, Jungians (as Hillman's argument indicates) try to build them up while preparing them for integration. Freudians hold that symbols disguise their true meanings because the latter are repugnant to the conscious mind, which resists by repressing those meanings. Jungians argue that symbols reveal their meanings in as plain and direct a way as possible, given that their function is to communicate that which was previously unknown to the subject.

When Jung employed the constructive method as a psychotherapeutic procedure, the point of departure was the patient's own fantasy material. He developed a technique, which he named *active imagination*, designed to help patients lower the level of their conscious control and let unconscious contents surface. With their fantasies made available by this means, individuals were shown simple methods for elaborating and contemplating them. In practice the training for active imagination was adapted to fit the particular skills and inhibitions of individual patients, but it always started with systematic exercises for eliminating critical attention, thus producing a vacuum in consciousness (Jung 1958: 78). This allows the images to develop according to their own logic and furnishes a means of exposing unconscious contents. As Stevens says,

Active imagination is a matter of allowing the natural mind time and freedom to express itself spontaneously. It is important to make some record of what is produced so as to register it and make it lastingly available to consciousness, otherwise it is soon lost. The medium used is a matter of individual taste. The images may be written down, painted, modelled in clay, danced or acted. The important thing is to allow them to happen.

This is a knack which, given patience, anyone can acquire. Active imagination requires a state of reverie, halfway between sleep and waking. It is like beginning to fall asleep but stopping short before consciousness is lost and remaining in that condition. (Stevens 1991: 202; see also Jung 1955/1956: 495–6)

This procedure starts an operation in which the original symbol is apperceived. That is to say, it compels attention and enforces its apprehension in such a way that it becomes assimilated to a series of associated images that are already constellated in the conscious mind (Jung 1921: 412–13). It makes for a kind of spontaneous amplification of the underlying archetypes that drive the fantasy material (Jung 1954c: 204–5). The individual who contemplates his or her fantasy products in this way commences as a spectator, but later learns to participate in the action as if he or she were one of the figures in the drama that passes before the eyes. The reality of the fantasy is thereby confirmed: it is an integral aspect of the individual's own psyche, and thus of the whole being (Stevens 1991: 202–3).

It may seem odd to recommend that the Jungian screen analyst borrow ideas from a process designed precisely to eliminate critical attention. Indeed it may seem, not least because the materials to be worked on are not of the critic's own origination, that the techniques of active imagination have no relevance whatever to the analysis of screen narrative. However, as John Beebe has recognised, although the images that play on the screen are unalterable, each spectator will perceive them according to his or her predisposition and experience (Beebe 1992). Furthermore, the experience of the movie that seizes the mind continues long after the screen has gone dark. In the spectator's memory the movie's content, form and possible meanings all shift under the pressure of his or her needs and personal history. So the emotional impact on the spectator of symbolic screen images is by no means wholly determined, and what they mean to him or her becomes subjectively inflected. The textual analyst can therefore take advantage of the thrust of the emotional reactions and intuitive responses that he or she may feel to loosen the hold of conscious, directed thinking. The guidance of such personal responses offers a means productively to subvert the kind of programmatic work that professionally recognised and routinised methodologies are always likely to lead to.

As we might expect, Hillman warns of the danger of professionally systematised response, whether to images mediated through a work of art or directly encountered as products of the psyche.

The use of allegory as a defense continues today in the interpretations of dreams and fantasies...Dreams have been yoked to the systems which interpret them...If long things are penises for Freudians, dark things are shadows for Jungians. Images are turned into predefined concepts such as passivity, power, sexuality, anxiety, femininity, much like the conventions of allegorical poetry. Like such poetry, and using similar allegorical techniques, psychology too can become a defense against the psychic power of personified images. (Hillman 1990: 24)

What Hillman advocates is naked, emotionally unguarded self-exposure to the symbol, which should be encountered and watched as if it were alive – almost like a person. We can argue that a comparable kind of expo-sure will be as productive for the textual analyst as it is for the psychoan-alyst and patient. Active imagination has the potential, *mutatis mutandis*, to be fashioned into a key function of a critical methodology which de-liberately incorporates emotional and intuitive responses together with rational analysis and the more formal procedures of amplification.

The following means of proceeding allow the analyst of the text to surrender a measure of control to the symbol. Having viewed the film as often as is found necessary, he or she should then reexperience the symbolic material by watching and listening to it as it runs not on the screen but in the memory. In so doing, the analyst actively imagines it and attends to the resonances it strikes within his or her own psyche. To help with this process, a technique that Hillman advocates can be em-ployed. He suggests slowing down the reading process by withdrawing attention from the narrative sequence ('What happens next? And then? And then?'), and investing it instead in a poetic imagistic reading. He urges this method because he finds that in most narrative sequences what appears at first sight to be their complete meaning emerges right on cue and fully rounded at the end of the story. The reader, driven by the ap-petite to draw everything together, rushes towards that goal, urged on by the story itself with its implied promise that all will be revealed at its climax. (This is indeed the only meaning that interests most spec-tators.) By contrast, in the reading of imagistic poetry, sense emerges throughout, and the poetry usually forces the eye to slow itself, even to move back and forwards within the text, to match the cadence of the images (ibid.: 61). In the case of the screen text, the analyst will find it impossible to slow down the process of perusal while the film is running. But this is the advantage to be gained by attending to the images and sounds in memory and withdrawing conscious attention for a while from the story line. What is most important is that in the encounter with the symbol the analyst should respond to the emotions that the image or sound arouses so as to make its personal value for him- or herself felt. A variety of possible associations may then be experienced. They may be pictorial or aural in nature. They may lead to a revaluation of the recollected narrative, or they may, by intensifying some of the emotions and intuitions to which the observer is exposed, refocus his or her attention on facets of the symbolism that had previously gone unremarked.

Having amplified the text inwardly, the analyst turns outwards again and views the actual text once more. The purpose of this screening is to discover to what degree the actual screenplay licenses these private imaginings. Inevitably, some of the associated images and ideas that active imagination produces from the original material will violate the logic of characters, plot or imagery. Such unfit associative material must be discarded on the grounds that it lacks 'tact' by being out of touch with the original source material. But frequently the associative material produced by active imagination may be used without violating the integrity and internal logic of the screenplay. In such cases it may become the stimulus for new analytical work that opens up a fresh angle of approach to the text and precipitates a critical reframing of the work.

A need for amplification *within* the symbolic text is sometimes uncovered as active imagination proceeds. This can occur when the textual analyst discovers chains or a cluster of images endowed with archetypal energies. And the clue which identifies them as symbolic is once again their unifying emotional power. It follows that the analyst should continue to exercise subjectivity and seek to make connections between those images that demand to be brought into juxtaposition through the emotional force with which they are perceived. When the process of active imagination has been completed, these same figures should also be amplified *externally* in the traditional manner.

To be recognised as such, clusters and chains of images have to share more than simply an emotive charge; scanned together they are likely to provide the schemata that allow the spectator to unlock thematic and even archetypal meanings. For example, the colour red in Nicolas Roeg's *Don't Look Now* (1973) takes its place in a chain which increases until it includes blood/fire/child/dwarf/passion/life/and death, to mention only some of its more obvious associations. It extends from observed images to their metaphoric values. Furthermore, it stands in opposition to another that links blue/water/eyes/glass/blindness/vision with not only life and death but also knowledge/ignorance of the supernatural. Taken together the two chains amount to an unmistakable cluster. Their combination has the effect that the possible interpretations of any one image are both directed and deepened by its association with others in the cluster (Izod 1992: 69–75; see also Palmer and Riley 1995: 14–25).

Having refined the products of active imagination discovered within the text and adapted them to a rationally defensible reading of the text, the analyst looks beyond it to embark upon the process of external amplification which we have already described. This does not necessarily require a scrutiny of folkloric, mythological or religious material as such. Commonly, images, characters and stories are amplified by cross-reference to related symbolic or metaphoric material found within the same or other narrative genres, or indeed in other art forms.

As we have mentioned before, the theory underpinning traditional interpretive critical practice recognises the procedure that we have called 'amplification' as a means by which the reader may establish the meanings of the text. Implicit in this traditional practice of textual analysis is a view of the text as an object which will release the meanings it contains when unlocked with a key that fits. The idea that the active imagination might be engaged in the process of analysis violates this static picture. However, it does complement a view of the text that recognises interpretation as an active process. Sandra Kemp summarises this position when she argues that the object *for* interpretation is an aspect *of* interpretation and cannot exist apart from it.

This [change of perspective] does not just open up art as the plural object of plural readings, nor simply make clear that the object of interpretation cannot have 'origins' outside the interpretative act. More importantly, it redefines the art-object as a temporal matter, a *becoming-object* rather than a *being-object*. Interpretation is always a process of *bringing-into-being*. (1996: 155)

The acknowledgement of the role that the active imagination can play in the critical process marries with this view of interpretation as a bringing into being, and recognises the function of the textual analyst's subjectivity. We have been describing it at its most intense. But active imagination encompasses something far more familiar and less portentous that most of us like to enjoy as often as possible.

To what extent can the spectating subject sitting in front of the screen take part in a constructive psychological process? Krin and

Glen O. Gabbard give us part of an answer. They question why people are attracted to movies like *Alien* (Ridley Scott, 1979) which make use of intense horror; and they note that audiences are often drawn to them even where the credibility of the plot is, to say the least, strained. This leads them to speculate that in such instances people are attracted not so much by narrative as by those scenes that compellingly touch on their most primal terrors. The Gabbards develop this line of thought in the context of a persuasive demonstration that Melanie Klein's theories of infantile desires and anxieties are productive in reading certain kinds of horror and science fiction films. She argued that as infants mature they experience the mother as alternately good and bad, depending on the extent to which she is satisfying their needs.

The Gabbards think that the moment in which the mother is split into a good mother and a bad mother in the infant's mind can be seen as a transformation similar to the one portrayed in horror films which involve the metamorphosis of a good object into an apparently identical bad object. They show how *Alien* draws much of its power from the evocation of infantile desires. It skilfully evokes early but imperfectly repressed anxieties about nurturing figures turning against us; and it does so in a manner which seems to be informed by Klein's account of the way the infant utilises introjection–projection mechanisms to deal with its primitive fears that it will be annihilated. For the child having projected 'bad' or aggressive aspects of the self into objects in the environment (primarily the mother), suffers as a consequence paranoid fears of external attack. In its portrayal of a monster that inhabits the mother ship and can attack equally effectively from without or within its victim, *Alien* evokes anxieties left over from childhood about our own aggressive tendencies that can punish us from within or without. And other horror or sci-fi films represent variants of this pattern. For example, those in which people are matched by terrifying *doppelgängers* (cf. both versions of *Invasion of the Body Snatchers*) replicate the Kleinian situation in which a beloved parent seems to have been taken over by a monster (Gabbard and Gabbard 1987: 226–9).

The Gabbards add to our exploration of audience activity by recalling an assertion of Freud in *Beyond the Pleasure Principle* (1920). He said that people feel a compulsion to repeat traumatic events that they originally experienced passively – and they feel thus compelled in an effort psychologically to master those traumas.

People line up to see movies like *Alien* in order to re-encounter powerful unconscious anxieties while retaining a sense that they have some control of an active nature the second time around. Moreover, the movie provides an aesthetic distance so that the audience knows that the terror on the screen is not actually happening to them, and they can experience relief along with their fright (Gabbard and Gabbard 1987: 226–9).

In the Gabbards' model it is not altogether clear whether people actually begin to take control of their anxiety-producing fantasy material, or merely live through it again knowing they are safe. It is possible, however, to conceive of the experience of cinema as a form of symbol play, a thought which has large consequences for the role of the spectator. To think of symbol play is to set screen narrative in a highly productive context in the Jungian schema, for Jung himself knew well the creative potential of play. He found it allowed him to discover a way forward through periods of loss of direction and mental crisis. Indeed, he learned to use it as a means of finding his own myth, that is, of exploring his unconscious, and beginning to discover the self (Jung 1961: 35–6, 197–9). As we shall see in chapter 7, Jungians believe play is so productive because it allows the rules of the ego to be broken. These are rules which map on to social norms with a quite close fit. Hence, as Samuels has said, in play 'category differences, hierarchy, reality, normality, decency, clarity, and so on, all may be discarded' (Samuels 1990: 130). In social life, on the contrary, they have to be observed if the individual is not to face penalties. Individual, undirected play, then, may be organised according to the rules of the unconscious, and in particular of the self, not those of the ego, consciousness and society.

People also play with symbols. This may be obvious enough when they are in the process of creating them, but they do so even when reading them. A convenient explanatory concept that connects play and the symbol is Winnicott's notion of the *transitional object*. In the first instance, during infancy, it is something tangible which the child holds on to as a defence against separation anxiety. It stands in for the absent mother. So such things as teddybears and comfort blankets are transitional objects; Winnicott refers to them as 'the first not-me possession' (1971: 1, 4–6). Soon the psychological presence of such tangible objects appears to be extended when the young child begins to invent a distinct personality for the teddy. This personality may in part be supplied by the child's unconscious need for a stand-in for an absent parent, but in part arises from the desire for play. The toy develops a distinct personality of its own which often resembles that of a friendly and sometimes wayward child, endowed nonetheless with superior, tutelary powers. At this point the transitional object does more than provide a physical substitute for the missing parent. It has become a quasi-symbolic object in its own right which enables the child to try in play a variety of social roles. The child can do so in the knowledge that it is safe from any social or natural consequences that might follow were its actions real. The breaking of natural laws and social rules (teddies can fly, can be killed off and be reborn a hundred times an hour), the exploration of the actual and realisation of an imaginary universe are all common features of children's play, and they all give the players great delight.

It is apparent then that private play may also be organised on principles that derive an input from the social. No accident, for instance, that the teddy bear, the transitional object par excellence, among the other roles in which it is cast, such as experimental flying machine and accident victim, frequently plays a substitute child. Then its behaviour is described by its owner as either good or bad and the teddy-child praised or castigated according to the degree to which it conforms with norms established for the real child by its parents and school. Thus Wehr's remarks (1987: 22–3) about the mutual interaction of social pressures and drives and images that originate in the unconscious hold equally true for play with both tangible objects and symbols.

As the child matures, he or she increases the range of imaginative games beyond the limits set by transitional objects in discovering that intangible symbols offer comparable opportunities for play. For example, the young person who enjoys reading fiction speaks of the pleasure it gives to enter a different world. Such an imaginary world is a composite built upon elements that the author has contributed through the novel's text but which the reader has to elaborate in order to construct its meaning. For instance, it has long been recognised that readers have to contribute a great deal from their own experience and desires to dress out not only the visual appearance but also the personalities of the main characters of written fiction, clothing them in the lineaments of their own psychic images. At this symbolic level too the pleasures of conspiring in play with a safely absent writer give delight – whether it be caused by the breaking of social or natural laws, or by the creation of an imaginary world.

Although, because of technical differences in the processes of reading print and viewing a film, the interpretive work of the reader differs in detail from that of the viewer, in general terms their active engagement with pre-existent symbols belongs to the same order of play. This process of meaning production and play also enables spectators to take a measure of control over the elements of the fiction they see and hear, and to use them in accordance with 'rules' given by their unconscious.

Eventually the individual may discover that intangible symbols provide ways of getting in touch with psychic reality; and this observation returns us to the kind of concern with symbols upon which a Jungian analysis focuses.

2 Archetypal images: signification and the psyche

Jung developed a relatively simple outline model of the psyche which he thought of as consisting in three concentric spheres. Reading from the outermost inwards, they were the conscious mind, the personal unconscious and the collective or impersonal unconscious. Given the intensity of debate which his thought has aroused over the years, it is important to remember that his model was designed to aid understanding, not to enforce a dogma. Jung himself was well aware that there were no hard boundaries between the various spheres that he had posited. Rather, they were permeable such that energies stirred in any one of the mind's spheres could trouble the quietude of the others. It would not have worried him that some of his successors have, as we shall see, suggested a number of modifications to his original classical model. These include the introduction of a fourth sphere known as the cultural or group unconscious, located between the personal and the collective realms.

Of the two spheres of the unconscious posited by Jung himself, the transpersonal or collective is the one which is remembered as peculiarly his own construct. This is not because the other realm, that of the *personal unconscious*, lacks importance in the life of human beings. Rather it is because the latter resembles the Freudian subconscious in many of its functions. Jung conceived of it as the repository of contents generated through the circumstances of the individual's existence. These contents might be matters repressed from consciousness or alternatively memories that had been forgotten. The personal unconscious is therefore the well from which arise feeling-toned *complexes*. When constellated, the latter have a 'relatively high degree of autonomy', acquiring an energy value that exceeds that of consciousness. Then, as with the emotions, it is not so much a case of our having complexes as that they, being 'strongly accentuated emotionally', have us. 'The unity of consciousness is disrupted and the intentions of the will are impeded or made impossible' because complexes are 'incompatible with the habitual attitude of consciousness' (Jung 1934: 96). In these respects (though not in the limits Freud put upon what might be held in the personal unconscious), Jung broadly agreed with his mentor Freud.

On the other hand, Jung's concept of the *collective unconscious* went beyond Freud's thinking. He posited the idea that, unlike complexes springing from the personal unconscious, the contents of the collective unconscious did not have to arise from the individual's personal experience. Indeed they might never have been in his or her consciousness.

I have chosen the term 'collective' because this part of the unconscious is not individual but universal; in contrast to the personal psyche, it has contents and modes of behaviour that are more or less the same everywhere and in all individuals. (1954a: 3–4)

Whereas the personal unconscious for the most part comprises complexes, the collective unconscious consists of *archetypes*. There is, as Anthony Stevens says, a close functional relationship between complexes and archetypes. 'Complexes are "personifications" of archetypes.' They are the means through which archetypes manifest themselves in the personal unconscious (1991: 28).

Since Jung introduced it, the word 'archetype' has entered popular usage where, at its most common, it means merely a commonly occurring image or idea. For Jung, however, the concept had a more specific meaning. It refers to what he believed was the existence of definite, inherited forms in the psyche that were present always and in all peoples. Archetypes consisted of forms without content: when content did fill them out, they entered consciousness (Jung 1936: 42–3).

There are as many archetypes as there are typical situations in life. Endless repetition has engraved these experiences into our psychic constitution, not in the form of images filled with content, but at first only as *forms without content*, representing merely the possibility of a certain type of perception and action. (ibid.: 48)

The energy attaching to archetypes is such, Jung said, that they form powerful predispositions which can, when activated, govern human behaviour patterns.

In considering how the unconscious interacts with the external world, we have to make a basic distinction between the archetypes themselves and the images generated by them. As we shall demonstrate more fully in chapter 3, the concept of the archetype itself is controversial. This is the case not least because, being forms, the archetypes are by definition theoretical or hypothetical constructs whose presence cannot directly be observed. It is the *archetypal images* that are observable, and in a study of screen narratives and popular icons it is naturally enough with them that we shall be working. In the realm of fiction which will for the most part concern us, we deduce their existence through, first, the recurrence and underlying uniformity of certain images, characters or narrative configurations and, secondly, the energy that attaches to them, revealing itself in the excitement of the audience's emotions. Whatever their outward appearance, these are not ordinary images in terms of their impact. Jung referred to figures that have this kind of power as being pitched from 'the treasure-house of primordial images' into the arena of consciousness. He called them archetypal images because, as contents just surfacing from the unconscious, they dress out the archetypes which he presumed furnished them with their force, and make their hidden actuality knowable (Jung 1954a: 4–5).

The archetypes themselves are said not to change or, if at all, do so at a tempo analogous to that of natural evolution, far too slowly to be detected in the human life-span. But, being sovereign, they endow the images that crystallise around them with their power. Archetypal or primordial images, however, are more exposed to the erosions of time and culture than the forms that they can only fill out provisionally. So although such images feel sovereign to the person experiencing them, they are not immutable and do alter under sustained social, cultural or ideological pressure (Wehr 1987: 93–4). In the classic example illustrating the necessary mutability of archetypal images, Jung argued (using words whose diagnostic acuity has not diminished since he wrote them in 1945) that the weakness of the churches in the twentieth century was brought about by their failure to realise that eternal truth cannot survive locked up in an unchanging symbolism. Rather, it needed a language that alters with the spirit of the times.

The primordial images undergo ceaseless transformation and yet remain ever the same, but only in a new form can they be understood anew. Always they require a new interpretation if, as each formulation becomes obsolete, they are not to lose their spellbinding power . . . (Jung 1946a: 196)

Organised religion in the Western hemisphere failed to adapt its symbolism and narratives to contemporary experience. As a consequence, vast numbers of people in the twentieth century (Jung among them) bypassed the churches' moribund teachings to seek religious experience elsewhere. Many found satisfactions deeper than the simple pleasures of entertainment when they encountered reworkings of ancient mysteries in contemporary stories and myths.

Some people (comparatively few as yet, but a growing number) have discovered in analytical psychology the methods by which to approach a new understanding of both those myths and themselves. When analytical psychology amplifies symbolic narratives (including those that play on our screens), it opens through them a perspective into the unconscious which for some members of the audience feeds some of the appetites for religious knowledge that in former times the churches would have supplied. It is to the advancement of that kind of (self) discovery through an enriched understanding of archetypal imagery on the screen that this book is dedicated.

Archetypal imagery is not confined to static pictures or religious iconography. Any popular icons of the day may carry an archetypal charge. Activities subject to the focused passions of large numbers of people (such as televised international sporting contests) may do so too. In fiction, an entire narrative (in whatever medium) may be archetypal if it springs from a source that feeds (and perhaps springs from) the unconscious needs of substantial audience numbers. The recurrence of a plot type and familiar plot situations may well indicate the activation of archetypes. Indeed, the established genres have well-marked archetypal qualities not only in their plots, but also in their principal characters (for example hero and villain), and their stereotypical images.

Archetypal theory furnishes us with a deeper perspective on genres. It shows that their repetitious and conservative nature does not only derive from spectators' desire for the reassurance gained by reinforcing the familiar. While not denying that the comfort of the well known can be one element of the pleasures audiences take, Jungian theory posits the archetypes as potential sources of great energy in mythic stories. Because archetypal images are collective in nature, and therefore tend to change slowly, the symbols, narratives and fictional protagonists which they invest tend to be conservative in the sense that they embody long-established values. They may also embody desires and fears that, although not yet felt consciously, are stirring numbers of people in various sectors of society. Generic images are the focus of considerable psychic energy for as long as they continue to attract a substantial audience. They connect people to the shared experience of common and potent myths whose source is often deep within the history of each culture; and they do so precisely because they serve the need to express collectively felt urges.

No genre has done this more effectively than the Western – whether written or screened. Its archetypal potency is signalled by its circularity in the way it draws from but also feeds back into American history. This despite the fact that, as has often been shown, when it comes to dealing with facts or the great social and economic forces that shaped America, the Western is almost invariably a trivialiser of the nineteenth-century history which is its basic source material. From its immediate sources such as the series of Leatherstocking novels that James Fenimore Cooper commenced with *The Pioneers* in 1823, the genre's main thrust has always been to fictionalise, to break free from history, first into legend, then swiftly, as it gathered cultural gravitas, to enter the imagination of both American and European readers as myth.

The archetypal power of the Western myth that has always attracted readers and audiences to the genre may not have been true to the facts of the past, but it has been influential in forming the construction of contemporary American history. The evidence is everywhere to be seen, both on the ground and in the record books. Western images hang from the hoardings that clutter every United States highway; its ethos is deeply wound into North American culture; and the Western myth has been accepted as validating the 'philosophy' behind all too many episodes of imperial aggrandisement in America's twentieth-century history as the dominant world power.[4]

In a moment we shall consider what the Western means for twentieth-century American culture; but if archetypes are always present giving form to human drives, it follows that today's myths and archetypal images should be merely the latest in a chain of representations that gather around the same kind of psychological orientations, albeit changing somewhat in tune with the times. This proves to be the case, and we can trace the heritage of older cultural forms in the Western. In the nineteenth century one of the master images imported by Europeans was, even before their arrival, an active symbol in their minds. And it resonated with meaning for those who moved to take up new land in the West and gave spiritual credence to that historic migration (see Smith 1970: 123–32). This was the idea that the new territory was the garden of the world which could be made by the labour of an honest people into the new Eden. In large part its power was great because it carried the sacred energy of an ancient, religiously and mythically charged, image cluster. That cluster extended the symbolism of the garden as the blessed place, a Paradise on earth, to include the farm, the smallholding, the wilderness, nature and even the desert. Looking back at it from the perspective of analytical psychology, we can read it as an emerging symbol of an idealised collective self.

The image had been preserved through an entire pastoral and agrarian literary and artistic tradition which can be traced through many sources besides the Bible. Not the least of these are the verses of Horace, which became the object of voracious imitation by countless British gentlefolk in the seventeenth and eighteenth centuries who not only wrote on the

---

[4] The constant circulation of cultural and symbolic currents between the objective and subjective worlds accounts in large measure for the aesthetic register of the genre. The conflict of realism versus fantasy that characterises so many films in this genre is the expression of the melodramatic register through which it engages with popular subjective fantasies.

theme, but – if they were exceptionally well-to-do – actually aspired to play-act the life of the well-bred farmer.

The pastoral-agrarian myth recurred in different form, as Henry Nash Smith demonstrates, in the North-West states. There, during the 1870s, and under heavy pressure from politicians eager to settle the West, as well as the desires of ordinary people for the good new life, the idea of the garden/farm as a place made good by labour and the plough evolved into a dangerous and equally mythic variant on the theme. This was the belief that God would return the love humanity had shown for the new land and ensure that rain would follow the plough into lands which had hitherto been too arid for cultivation. Unhappily this project was even less realistic than the ideal of the noble frequenter of the King's Court in London to find the honest life by farming – at least he could hire skilled employees to cultivate the land on his behalf. But in America the garden myth encouraged people to migrate on to lands so far West that (because the European farming techniques they brought with them were wholly unadapted for these conditions) they had no hope of thriving. After a few freak years of unusually generous rainfall, disaster struck in the winter of 1885–6. Many of the newcomers had to sell their land to big corporations in order to pay their debts – and sooner or later most had to leave their smallholdings. But the agrarian/pastoral myth had demonstrated once again its extraordinary grip on the human imagination, establishing itself as one of the founding myths that gave many people in the emergent nation their sense of new, shared identity (Smith 1970: 179–88; Slotkin 1973: 3–24).

Although the myth did not work on the ground, it has done so almost ever since as a mental set. The Western in fiction embodies a clear instance of myth finding expression through a populist art form. On the screen it plays as action film peopled by larger-than-life characters who are depicted as the bearers of distinctive moral qualities. These characteristics are so strongly marked that the principal figures (cowboy, gunman, sheriff, American Indian and schoolmarm, for instance) continue to personify certain fundamental archetypal characteristics in the popular imagination even though the screen texts that now carry the Western myth have evolved to a greater degree of sophistication than the bare stereotypes on which those personalities are based. The Western still stands in the popular imagination for a set of weighty oppositions: the good versus the bad; light versus dark; rural versus urban; the wild versus the civilised; and – in the most curious fashion of all – male versus female. We shall examine this classical set of values before looking briefly at one example that shows how archetypal images can dissolve and reconstitute themselves.

White men in the Western are invariably represented in terms that reflect upon their power, and their women are frequently shown as impotent when they step outside the domestic circle. Symptomatically, the male hero is often on horseback, the woman in the kitchen. The combination of a man and his pony conveys an idea of speed and strength which allow the hero to exercise his will and move direct to his goal. It is worth remembering that the horse was the most powerful form of transport and source of energy controlled by humanity until the harnessing of steam. It is typically endowed through that association with magical powers analogous to those possessed by Pegasus, the winged horse which brought thunderbolts to Zeus. And at his most moral, the cowboy loosely resembles Pegasus' master Bellerophon who rode him to swoop on the chimera, a monster that was ravaging his country (Grimal 1986: 73, 332–3). In similar fashion, the classic cowboy rids the land of evil, deploying his god-like powers. As a creature of wild nature tamed with difficulty, the moral quality of the horse (however resistant or tricky to ride) is invariably positive. By contrast the iron horse (because it is a product of the industrialisation which by penetrating the wilderness undermines it) is often portrayed as a threatening force.

It has frequently been remarked that the man–horse couple is quasi-sexual in nature – a displacement of normal relations between man and woman. The pony, though physically the stronger of the partners, has to do what the man commands. In this its role resembles that of women in the genre. Thus the horse, often a stunningly beautiful creature, represents one of a number of images in the Western which symbolise the sublimation of Eros to the exercise of will.

So too the image couple man–gun. The gun can hardly be read as anything other than an emblem of phallic power – but seldom in this context as a symbol of male sexual conquest, given the sexual diffidence of the men and the distance they keep between themselves and women. Rather, the bullet also gives man god-like power. In the classic Western, the hero shoots better than the villain because he sees more clearly. The bullet goes where his steady gaze directs it. It becomes an emblem of conscious moral control and, once again, the expression of will. The villains, on the other hand, do not see clearly. Therefore their shooting is erratic. Thus the classic Western cowboy hero in all his shining glory becomes an emblem of sunny, godlike (but exclusively male) control – consciousness ablaze.

Yet the very repetitiveness of the adventure (which in the genre's glory days preceded the decline of patriarchy) suggests the extraordinary effort required of the American male psyche to exert the conscious will and drive out evil. The role of ego-triumphant had to be played over and over again by those who loved the genre in order to reassure themselves of what they wanted to believe. And in the process the power of Eros was much diminished in the effort to have the will triumph.

The Western, then, is dominated by the presence of men, and in many movies women are keepers of the hearth, whores, or more or less absent. It is worth asking, however, whether an archetype has always to be represented to be powerful. Women have comparatively little time on screen, but exert a fascinating power, be it domestic, sexual or cultural, over the men – thus the archetypes that energise the image of womanhood, although not dominant visibly, are strong.

Why do men dominate? In terms of our needs in understanding the genre, it is not enough to refer back to a history when men supposedly filled the dominant social roles – even if such a doubtful assertion did encapsulate the truth of the past. A psychological explanation is required of relationships between the sexes in the Western. According to Leslie Fiedler, the Western hero knows that what he does is blessed and that nature/the garden/the wilderness is one with God (Fiedler 1967: 182). Slotkin reminds us that in the mythology of Europe, the West was strongly associated (because the sun set there) with the kingdom of death, the underworld and dreams – and hence with the unconscious (Slotkin 1973: 28). Eros is principally attached to the wilderness and not to woman: on the contrary, the hero strives to escape being trapped through marriage in the cow town with its bonds of civilisation or Christianity (Fiedler 1967: 199). In that cultural ambience (which, by comparison with the paganism of the wild, presages the advent of urban life), the hero fears his libido will be extinguished.

Instead the Western hero's feelings towards nature lead him to expect that he will thrive in his love for nature. The idea of the wilderness becomes feminised and evolves into a metaphor for the unconscious. It is linked with the ancient motif of the hero's return to the arms of the Earth Mother. At first glance, nature as the object of his emotions appears to be a less problematic recipient for his feelings than most of the women who might be available for marriage. However, possession of the Mother is a far from tranquil matter for the Western hero. In part this is because (as we shall see in more detail later in the chapter) the typical hero has to strive against the kind of absorption into the undifferentiated unconscious to which the parental imago is likely to tempt him. But there was also an important new factor specific to the lands recently entered by those who migrated from the East (see Rushing and Frentz 1993: 63–4; Slotkin 1973: 156). This was the awkward fact that there were peoples settled in the West who had been there so long that they seemed to be at one with the land in a way that Americans of European descent could not be. So the white man found a dark-skinned rival who had got there first and whose presence intruded on the newcomer's jealous love for the wilderness.

Since the new arrivals intended to take the land into their own use by seizing it from its original inhabitants, they soon intuitively made the latter the object of their collective shadow projection, as all peoples do with the enemy when they prepare to go to war. What matters to us is that these shadow projections endured long after the end of the Indian wars and were absorbed into the Western genre where they remained a staple feature through much of the twentieth century.

It is remarkable how few novels and films have attempted to adopt the perspective of the American Indian. Almost always the latter are seen as hostile and a threat to the new white civilisation which, notwithstanding he despises it, the Western hero protects. In addition to colouring the American Indian as bestial and as a competitor for land, shadow projection also tainted the white view of their sexuality. As it happens, the Indian male had historically enjoyed a measure of sexual freedom, and the comparison with the repressed sexuality of the new Puritanical Americans was striking, as Slotkin demonstrates. The former was permitted sexual freedom before marriage, and to some extent after it. Although women did not have equal rights to sexual liaisons outside their marriage, they did have some limited power in the relationship, because married couples could dissolve the relationship at will. Love-making was seen as both healthy and pleasurable, and in some circumstances sacred (Slotkin 1973: 47). But even if the sexual culture of American Indians had not been noticeably more free than that of the whites, it is probable that the simple fact of their dark skins would have enticed the latter to project the shadow of their unrealised sexuality on to them. In North America, as in so many territories to which Europeans migrated in large numbers, the dark-skinned original inhabitants were laden, in the minds of the incomers, with the burden of white sexual guilt. They were understood to be licentious and unable to control their sexuality. Hence the men were thought to be rapacious and to prefer white women to their own; and for this reason white women had to be defended against them. Meanwhile the dark woman was seen as sexually available (and therefore desirable) in ways that white women were not. This dichotomy lies at the root of the classical Western's somewhat coy characterisation of the good woman as blonde, chaste and fair, and the bad woman as dark, brunette, over-sexed and at risk of being killed in recompense for her temerity.

Either way, the woman as anima (which should have the power to lead ego-consciousness towards the unconscious) is often rebutted and almost invariably marginalised. And the splitting of the female image runs right through the genre until well into the third quarter of the twentieth century. The male hero cultivates his strength (the power of his will) in order to defend from what are in fact his own split-off desires the chaste, civilised, but rather bloodless woman who represents the only type he can accept as a marriage partner. In marrying her he defends the urbanising culture that he despises but of which she is the steadfast representative. Meanwhile, the pagan wilderness towards which the white hero's infantile desires endlessly tend is tainted for him by the fact that his rival in everything, the dark shadow, is indissolubly bound to it just as to the sexualised woman who is forbidden to the white hero. In short, we find that the latter employs his highly focused conscious will ultimately to resist the seductions (both benign and evil) of the unconscious. So the cultural values typically represented by the Western hero celebrate the triumph of Logos and power over Eros; of the conscious mind over the unconscious; and of the focused will to *become* over the diffuse, emotionally free experiencing of *being*.

During the course of the century in which the Western has had a presence on screen, social and cultural changes (as the passage from Jung quoted above predicted) had an inevitable impact on the archetypal images current in the genre. One example must stand for the kind of changes that occurred. Within the genre, American Indians were never the only source of evil. The white baddies in the classic Western are usually villainous because they embody some excessive appetite inimical to the Puritan vision of the Western idyll – often their sin is the urban vice, greed. They too are shadow figures, a detail signalled by their being unshaven and unkempt. They look the obverse of the hero who, in the classical Western, keeps himself clean-shaven and smart. The sharp divide between the appearance (and also the moral attitudes) of hero and white villain dissolved in the 1950s. And the most celebrated sites of that change are the Anthony Mann Westerns in which James Stewart as the hero becomes unshaven and grubby. Lin McAdam in *Winchester 73* (1950), Howard Kemp in *The Naked Spur* (1952), Jeff Webster in *The Far Country* (1954) and Will Lockhart in *The Man from Laramie* (1955) are all obsessed with revenge, all have absorbed part of the dark side of their nature and all are redeemed in the final crisis by recognising the extent to which they have become blackened by the obsessive need that has driven them to exact retribution for the crimes of the men they pursue. For these and other cowboys who learned a measure of cynical self-knowledge through hard experience, the dark wilderness of the unconscious (which Mann actually projects on to the harsh landscape in his films) was not quite as impenetrable as it had been to their forebears. Intriguingly, in these films women play a more active role in resolving the heroes' moral nightmares.

In looking at the Western, we have seen clear signs of the interaction between archetypal images and the culture of a given place and time. We shall return to this issue in more detail later, and develop a more sophisticated model by which to understand this interaction. First, however, let us look at an example of strikingly clear archetypal imagery taken from a quite different source.

The emergence of archetypal images is by no means restricted exclusively to genre pieces. Jean-Jacques Beineix's *Diva* (1981), as its title gives notice, centres on an archetypal figure, the film's leading woman Cynthia Hawkins (Wilhelmenia Wiggins Fernandez). She is an artist with an extraordinarily fine voice, a hard-working and dedicated professional. She knows that her voice arouses passions in her audiences; but she keeps the feelings that it stirs in her own heart hidden even from herself. When her singing awakens deep emotions in a young admirer, Jules (Frédéric Andrei), Cynthia takes on the mantle of a diva in an older sense, and she soon recognises that he wants from her more than any mortal woman can give. She has become his goddess, his *anima*.

The anima is a contrasexual archetype, its counterpart being the *animus* in women. One of the most frequently encountered figures, the contrasexual archetype occurs in dreams and associations, and is often projected outwards upon living people. It represents those aspects of an individual that have the characteristics of the opposite sex and which he or she is unable to express or even acknowledge in daily life. In a man, the anima typically presents herself in the form of a woman who stirs the emotions intensely. She does so precisely because she seems to promise an answer to his deeply felt need to complete himself – to find his other half. In representing a man's want to him, the archetype may present itself as a dream image of an imaginary woman; but often its power is projected upon an actual woman so that she becomes inextricably wound into the man's fantasy life. The energy of the archetype charges her image with a magical force that makes her seem (either benignly or malevolently) divine.

Jules attends (and secretly tapes) a performance in which Cynthia sings an aria from Alfredo Catalina's *La Wally*. In this, a tragic heroine seeks her death in the purity of mountain snows as the proper restitution for her broken heart. Such episodes of high melodrama are characteristic of the anima (no less than the animus). First, they occupy a rhetorical register which signals their importance to the recipient; and second, their heightened, overwrought quality (which may be, as with Cynthia, coupled with a distinctive radiance) embellishes the numinous energies – that vitality which appears to spring direct from the gods – to which they give form (Beebe 1992). Beineix himself admits to a preference for the heightened aesthetics of opera over flat cinematic realism (Auty 1982: 302), and this style invites the reading offered here.

Cynthia Hawkins is a benign anima to Jules. At 32, a full ten years older than him, she has a better understanding of what is moving him than he does himself. Nevertheless she is intrigued by him. The attraction between them resonates with undertones of incestuous desire. Analysed through Jungian theory, this is of considerable significance.

The son/mother incest theme pertains to the maturation of the adolescent male's psyche. One indication that a young man has completed his mental growth into adulthood is the successful reframing of the mother image. As a boy he is drawn to his first and most potent anima in the image of the mother; but he has to break free from his fixation upon her if he is to achieve maturity. A straightforward example of such a plot is found in Bernardo Bertolucci's *La Luna* (1979). The dream or fantasised configuration of incest with the mother has therefore a double-edged significance. On the positive side, a boy has much to draw from her in the nourishing of his feminine side. But on the negative side, should he not manage to break free, he risks being seduced into a lasting union with her. That can cause stultification of his own psyche, if it becomes subordinated to hers. Successful development, on the contrary, is indicated when the anima transfers away from the mother and takes a new form: in the heterosexual male, it typically settles upon a young woman who now becomes the object of desire.

In the hero myth, the completion of such a transformation may be signalled by the young man returning from the encounter with the mother bearing a trophy. It symbolises his having faced the danger of a prolonged incestuous union, and having won the prize which is his newly made psyche. Jules does indeed hunt for trophies, but, in a variant of the traditional pattern, he steals them before he has earned them, taking both Cynthia's robe and (by recording it) her voice. That these are sacramental thefts is indicated by his draping the robe around her picture on his wall, making it a shrine; also by the recording, which, whenever he replays it, engulfs both the characters and the audience with its voluptuous beauty. Because Jules has seized the trophies prematurely, far from freeing him, they bind him more tightly in Cynthia's thrall.

This becomes clear when Jules hires a prostitute to model the robe for him and finds it has lost its magical appeal when Cynthia is not wearing it. He takes it back to its owner and confronts her shyly. His odd mix of diffidence and boldness attracts Cynthia and they begin an intimate friendship. But Jules comports himself more tentatively than might have been expected, largely through shame over his unconfessed theft of her performance. But eventually this diffidence turns to their mutual advantage.

Jules' guilty feelings make him sensitive to every nuance in Cynthia's speech. So he intuits that there is something excessive in her distress when told by her manager that a good-quality pirate recording of her voice has been made. Refusing to sanction its release, she insists that her singing creates an experience of high art all the more intense because she prohibits recordings. Jules, however, perceives that she is covering an unspoken fear beneath her anger. It helps him recognise his diva as a human being no less vulnerable than anyone else. Risking everything, he plays the recording he has stolen to Cynthia – and offers it as both his confession and his gift to her. Moved, she reveals that she has never heard her own glorious voice in playback, and this is the cause of her fear. As the determining factor in her life, her voice has become an overcharged animus that terrifies her through her certainty that it will eventually betray her when age steals it from her.

Our egos, protected by the structures of time, space, and causality that hold them in place, can delay the gratification our contrasexuality brings . . . But they cannot hold anima and animus at bay forever.

Anima and animus demand entry. Their purpose is to open in us a space for interior conversation, where we can consult ourselves about the things we most deeply desire, and those we most dread. (Ann and Barry Ulanov 1994: 222)

We shall study animus theory in greater detail in chapter 4. Meanwhile, at this its end, *Diva* allows us to reverse perspective and see that from Cynthia's point of view, Jules also fulfills an archetypal role – although he does not complement her anima function by being her animus. Despite the contrary indications – namely that at his most gauche he is a somewhat inept lad with a romantic sensibility – Jules embodies an element of the divine. This is signalled through his job. As a postman he is a type of the messenger god, Hermes or Mercurius, two of whose roles are relevant here. First, he is the trickster: his unstable behaviour unsettles Cynthia, makes it more difficult for her to hold on to her set ideas, causes her pain, but ultimately releases her from her daemon. Second, like Hermes, he is her guide, bringing her the revelation how her voice sounds to others, and with it access to a degree of self-knowledge she formerly lacked.

What Jules first stole from the goddess he has now, asking her forgiveness, restored to the woman. The original theft of the tape and the robe, his attempt to grab a hero's trophies without earning them, was plainly unheroic. By restoring them, Jules shows that he has found another way to attain maturity than that of the embattled hero. Rather, he has come to know and accept the anima. As the film ends, the relationship between the pair is newly in balance. So too is the relation between the human and the divine, which is to say that the balance between the personal and the archetypal spheres has been restored in each of them.

So far so good, but in *Diva* there remain vivid features such as its extraordinary, eye-catching imagery and its bizarre characters (for example, the psychotic criminal Le Cure) who are sufficiently strange that they cannot adequately be deciphered by reference to the generic norms of the gangster movie. All these things hold a store of energy that our account of the one set of archetypal images has not fully discharged. We need to look further into Jungian theory to bring them into the frame.

3 Archetypal images: symbols and the cultural unconscious

Jeremy Carrette has made a meticulous examination of the ways in which Jung and his followers have used the term 'archetype'. He shows how an idea which Jung introduced as a means of bringing order to the description of subjective experience has become reified into supposed objectivity. What was originally a convenient hypothesis with which to explain what Jung called the bewildering conglomeration of psychic realities shifted its meaning constantly. It did so in the first instance under the pressure of his own constantly evolving thoughts and the discursive imprecision with which he used the term. After his death, unfortunate developments occurred in that what he intended as a provisional working implement to aid understanding of the unconscious became in the usage of many Jungians something close to a religious dogma itself (Carrette 1994: 168–71, 185–6). The thrust of Carrette's argument is that it is more productive to work with the images themselves than with a theoretical construct that has been reified on dogmatic grounds.

Notwithstanding the fact that if the term is to have any value, archetypal images must have a universalising potential, they must also be shaped and coloured by the culture of their time if they are to communicate through its language and signifying systems. Therefore, while the archetypes themselves may be presumed to remain constant, archetypal images alter in the sense that they take new shapes across the generations and between cultures, and we have already seen some partial evidence of this in the case of the Western. Observation of the mutability of archetypal images is one of the factors that encouraged some of Jung's followers to modify his original model.

An instance where social conditions and ideological values are readily identified as exerting pressure on an archetypal image can be found in one of the classic dreams. This is the one in which the dreamer either misses a train or catches it at the very last moment as it leaves the platform. Plainly this specific dream would not have been possible before the building of the first railway systems; but it is ideologically as well as technologically marked in that it would not convey the same force were the dreamer not living in a society that depends on the punctual response to minutely regulated time. A dream of missing a horse-drawn vehicle would not convey the equivalent stress because the latter is not capable of running to the accurate schedules that supposedly govern mechanised transportation systems.

Thus in this case societal exigency has contributed to the metamorphosis of an archetypal image. However, it is worth noting that the archetype that we can hypothesise as underwriting this figure has not been altered. Notwithstanding its ideological charge, the dream of the train can also be read as a metaphor for an ancient fear – that one is losing contact with the sources of energy in the libido. Libidinous energy cannot be stopped as it arises from the unconscious; it gives vigour and direction to life, but only if (so to speak) the individual climbs aboard. So, expressed another way, the image of the train can be read as a *psychopomp*, a figure whose function is to lead the dreamer to knowledge of different levels of the mind. As such it performs work comparable to that of the white horse and other conductors of the dead, such as the Sibyl who guided Aeneas in the underworld.

One of the most influential of post-Jungian thinkers is Demaris S. Wehr. For her part, she does not abandon the concept of the archetype itself: it remains in her account the hypothetical source of psychic energy. But she does direct the thrust of her scrutiny in a way which Carrette would approve, namely towards observable imagery. She argues that archetypal images are subject to contingent societal influences, and that this can be demonstrated. When a person is persistently exposed by culture and society to coherent symbol-sets to the extent that she or he internalises them, not only do those symbols have 'political' consequences in shaping behavioural patterns and value systems, they also weave the fabric that dresses out pre-existing archetypes and produce archetypal images.

Symbols and images operate pre-verbally and pre-rationally and find their way into the thought-systems by which we live … Because of their pre-verbal, pre-rational, and often unrecognized character, they have great force. (Wehr 1987: 22)

Wehr calls upon Emma Jung's work with negative and positive images of the self-hater (one form of the inflated animus) to demonstrate how women, in internalising men's images of them, have succumbed to the pressure of patriarchal society's persistently promoted pre-verbal symbols (Wehr 1987: 123–4, citing Emma Jung 1957: 20).

It is far deeper than rationality and thought can reach, and therefore, rational thought, or even mere insight, is not powerful enough to silence it. In women, by the time oppression has been internalized, it has the character of fervent conviction. (Wehr 1987: 22)

We shall return to the question of women's internalisation of culturally insistent self-images in the next chapter. Meanwhile, we may note that not only women, but also homosexuals and blacks, can be shown to have internalised the oppressive symbols of white patriarchal society in this way.[5] Thus, Wehr argues, society and the individual psyche are in dialectical relationship with one another.

That means that, as Jungians hold, psychological forces (pre-rational images, mythic themes, fears, needs) do indeed shape society. At the same time, social structures already in existence at the time of each individual's coming into the world exert great influence in shaping the individual personality. (1987: 18)

In the foregoing we have been using the terms 'archetypal image' and symbol without marking the distinction between them. It is now time to do so. At first sight, symbols seem very like archetypal images. They connect the archetypal, the cultural and the personal and are charged with an intense energy whose source is not within the domain of consciousness. However, they do not invariably share the universal quality of the archetypal image. To understand this, we need to know the specialised sense in which Jung used the term 'symbol'. His argument was founded on the observation that not all images communicate with the same force; and he distinguished between images according to the intensity with which they convey an unconscious energy charge. He gave the name *sign* to any image which 'always has a fixed meaning because it is a conventional abbreviation for, or a commonly accepted indication of, something known' (1956a: 124). Such a figure carries a low archetypal charge because both its constituent elements and its meanings are found in the domain of consciousness.

By contrast, the figure Jung termed the *symbol* presents unconscious contents in a form which the conscious mind cannot immediately grasp, though it may eventually be able to apprehend them, if not without difficulty.

The true symbol . . . should be understood as an expression of an intuitive idea that cannot yet be formulated in any other or better way. (1931a: 70)

Jung argued that the symbol is fashioned in the womb of creative fantasy, the unconscious. It remains there as long as the energic value of the conscious contents exceeds that of the unconscious symbol. Energy must be supplied to bring it to the surface, and when such a reversal of values occurs, the symbol rises to the surface and gives fuller expression to the

---

[5] Hopcke (1991: 59) argues that the hatred and fear of which homosexuals are often the target are likely to be more to blame when mental illness occurs among gay people than anything inherent in homosexuality itself.

archetypes from which it finds its source. While emotional distress and the constellation of complexes can reverse the balance of energies in abnormal circumstances, under normal conditions it is the libido that brings the symbol to the surface (1921: 113–15).

The symbol is, for Jung, 'the best possible expression for an unconscious content whose nature can only be guessed, because it is still unknown' (1954a: 6n.). It also has a function in initiating change in the psyche: because it compensates for the inevitable biases of the conscious mind, it points 'to the onward course of life, beckoning the libido towards a still distant goal' (1921: 125). It presents in darkly metaphorical form material hitherto hidden in the unconscious, so that the conscious mind can strive to grasp it and enhance knowledge of the self.

However, we should add that because individuals undergo different experiences in their lives, a figure that is a symbol to some may be no more than a sign to others. The image that has an energy so strong that it exerts an archetypal influence on some people may nevertheless be so familiar a part of the mental landscape of others that its magical force has been discharged for them.

The symbol, like the archetypal image, frequently links the personal with the social and cultural because (unless confined to the secret dreams of an individual) it usually enters the public domain via one medium or another. And this brings us to the idea of the *cultural or group unconscious*. A number of Jungians have posited this concept as a means of refining Jung's model of the spheres of the unconscious. Its significance is that it extends post-Jungian theories of the psyche and builds a new sphere into the unconscious based on the recognition just mentioned, that social and cultural pressures conjoin their considerable influence with many other factors in forming all but the deepest psychic images. As Richard M. Gray observes, 'the closer to consciousness the archetypal influence is led, the more easily its external form is determined by environmental factors' (1996: 72).

Rushing and Frentz describe the cultural unconscious as the site of a collision of psychic energies from two separate origins – archetypal images having their source in the collective unconscious, and repressed contradictions from oppressive social formations (1991: 391). Their hypothesis is well supported by the kind of thinking that Robin Wood exemplifies when he argues that the symbols and stories which constitute the horror genre deal with the return of the culturally repressed: 'One might say that the true subject of the horror genre is the struggle for recognition of all that our civilisation represses or oppresses, its re-emergence dramatised, as in our nightmares, as an object of horror . . . and the happy ending (when it exists) typically signifying the restoration of oppression'

(1986: 75). Wood's position in turn harmonises with Wehr's thinking. As we have seen, she concentrated on the way women internalise the very patriarchal images that have oppressed them. In this shared experience they partake of an already acculturated unconscious.

However, the formulation is too restrictive when it describes repressed contents as the only input from consciousness to the cultural unconscious. We can agree with these writers that repression is often that which builds up the psychic energies that reveal themselves in texts; but we do not have to accept that all the contents that derive from societally shared conscious experience must have entered the unconscious by being repressed (Rushing and Frentz 1991: 391). Andrew Samuels raises the question whether the concept of the group or cultural unconscious implies that it is a repository of cultural experience. Alternatively, he argues, it could be the means, already existing as a potential, by which the human psyche gives birth to cultural difference and then reinforces it. In fact, for analysts of popular culture attempting to account for the production and consumption of symbols, there is much to recommend Samuels' guess that it has both functions (1993: 328). Such a perspective endows the cultural unconscious with a sphere far wider than that described by Rushing and Frentz. The way that film stars are propagated by the studios and received by the public helps to demonstrate our point and shows how culturally available images can be seized upon as markers of difference which arise, seeming to be almost (but not quite) ready-formed, from the cultural repository to which Samuels refers. And we shall see this confirmed in chapter 5.

Up to this point we have in effect been considering the creation of symbols. Reversing the perspective, it becomes apparent that, from the point of view of the individual receiving the symbol (the spectator watching the screen), the specifics of a text's rhetorical address are of great importance. To a significant degree it is the style or manner in which a text addresses spectators which succeeds (or fails) in touching the emotions and the deeper layers of the psyche. When recipients experience a culturally specific symbol that works for them, they feel an excitement which is not aroused by other images, despite the fact that the latter may appeal deeply to other people.

Stardom illustrates this phenomenon well. A star projects an image, a persona, which large numbers of people find deeply attractive. Such people comprise a recognisable social bloc – the fans – the more enthusiastic of whom, like Jules in *Diva*, hunt for trophies and insignia to identify themselves as devoted members of the group. But in the wider community by no means everybody is a fan of the same star. For every passionate follower of, say, Madonna, there will be another person who may take mild pleasure from her songs, a third who is indifferent, and a fourth who actively loathes everything she stands for. The more extreme reactions suggest that her image is intuitively perceived as bearing meaning not only in the lyrics of her songs, but also through every aspect of the style of her performances – that is, through her rhetorical address. The strength of feeling of both her fans and those who hate her arises from the group unconscious in its dual cultural role as first, a repository of differentiated and value-laden experience, and second, the source of drives that oblige the individual to differentiate between the cultural phenomena on which he or she projects libido. We shall study the cultural and archetypal meanings of two stars in chapter 5, but now it is time to return to the film *Diva* which we began to analyse in the previous chapter. We shall look to see how some of the concepts we have been opening up relate to aspects of the text not yet discussed.

The symbolic elements in *Diva* reflect a group unconscious centred on youth culture. The film has an obvious predecessor in Jean-Luc Godard's *A Bout de Souffle* (1959), but the differences, no less than the resemblances, are informative. Both films show the infiltration of French culture by American iconography, and both feature a young American woman encountering France. In addition, both films are not only peopled by young heroes and heroines (with a few exceptions, the middle-aged characters tend to be outcasts, even when they are cops), but they adopt a cinematic register and style which is fresh and invigorating and proclaims the novelty of youth. However, Godard's heroine Patricia (Jean Seberg) is a white tourist who has almost no knowledge of French language or culture (whether high art or popular). She is in Paris to enjoy mildly rebellious kicks, and ekes out her itinerary with casual work selling *The New York Herald Tribune* on the streets. In contrast, Cynthia Hawkins is black, a competent French-speaker, and has come to Paris to perform arias from European operas. Through her, *Diva* emphasises a blending of cultures more complete than the forcible penetration of French ways by American style and values which interested Godard. Indeed, in *Diva* the seamless wedding of French and American culture is only the first symptom of cultural *mélange*. Over all, the film represents Paris as a vivid polyglot scene. Its juxtaposition of radically disparate cultures and styles has the impact of the surreal. The collision of elements runs through its *mise-en-scène*, its characters, the plots that weave them together, its visual and aural styles and finally its symbolism.

The entire city as *mise-en-scène* becomes a metaphor for the cultural unconscious of French youth. Even a selective list of its components makes the point that it is laden with figures that are symbolic in Jungian terms. Jules' apartment is entered via an industrial freight lift which opens on to an area filled with the wrecks of luxury cars. We are dealing, he remarks enthusiastically, in disaster deluxe, a theme developed in his living space which is hung with murals depicting cars as they might occur in a teenager's dream. Bulbous, oversexed American autos cruise palm-lined avenues, others hang like dirigibles in the sky, and all of them seem to thrust into Jules' living space. In some of the cars, ecstatic passengers seem to have found their ultimate delight, but a child is spilling out of another to her death.

The actual vehicles of the film's story world are no less strange. Jules' scooter sports a sound system that fills the streets with overtures to the operas. He rides it everywhere – into his apartment and (in flight from the villains) down beneath the streets and on to the Métro. His rescuer, the 'oneiric' Gorodish (Richard Bohringer) has a car that might have sprung direct from the dreams of a hero. It is a vintage Light 15 Citroën, in mint condition *le transport juste* for the white knight that he is. When the villains blow it up, he calmly unveils an identical white car, and drives off in it: wish-fulfilment of a most magical order. Even the corrupt chief of police gets around in a fantasy vehicle – a large American coupé. In this milieu, when the hired killer Le Curé (who drives a boring Renault) mumbles, 'I don't like cars', it simply confirms his psychotic attitude to life.

The representation of automobiles makes it obvious that Paris is a repository of cultural experience and values. In the 1950s, American cars (along with other American icons, none more than the movies) had been treated as objects of desire in many French books and films. Godard's *A Bout de Souffle* is simply one example among many of the tendency to mythologise the American car and way of life for a heady combination of connotations. They were taken to signify the emergence of a new young generation with a confident taste for speed, personal freedom and inde-pendence. And this was the case even when, as in *A Bout de Souffle*, these same values were undermined by the romantic expectation that their ul-timate outlet was likely to be a James Dean-like immolation of youthful purity in a highway pile-up (Ross 1996: 15–54). Beineix's representation picks up this mythology and changes it. American cars of the 1950s still have a mythic quality about them; but they are associated with death and disaster – both in Jules's apartment and in the fact that the murderous In-spector Saporta drives one. Now the desired dream machine is a pristine 1950s French car which, for the film, combines elegance with the sense of its having sprung from a classic age. The 1980s domestic product, the Renault, is Le Curé's transport – not only boring, but also battered and rendered largely impracticable by the volume of traffic. It adds to the mythology of the white Citroën that it enjoys a freedom of movement im-possible in the Paris of the 1980s. But for mortals who lack the enchanted powers of the white knight, Jules' scooter is an altogether more effective machine for threading (and linking together) the many sectors of Paris that he visits.

The characters themselves add to the sense of the surreal. We have mentioned Gorodish. When we first see him he appears to be a social drop-out dedicating his life to solipsistic pleasures. He passes the first half of the plot (his cool period) in his open-space apartment that is as big as a warehouse. Enveloped by blue objects and light, he divides his time between meditation, completing a vast jigsaw puzzle, and creating the perfect baguette sandwich. When called on to rescue Jules from the gangs that pursue him, he shows the skills of a formidable military strategist, and becomes both the white knight who lays waste to evil, and also the young man's mentor. Alba (Thuy An Luu), his Vietnamese girlfriend, becomes Jules' friend. A common interest in petty larceny brings the latter two together, but they also share the experience of being in love with an older person. Their friendship allows them the chance to chatter uninhibitedly and behave like other teenagers, a freedom which is inhibited in their passionate relationships. Alba's role thus counterpoints that of Cynthia. Although a potential anima figure for Jules, she does not play that part, being instead the canny assistant who augments Gorodish's magical powers in looking after Jules. Gorodish and Alba teach Jules to look beyond himself and can be read as representing Jules' potential. Alba does so through her capacity for joy. Gorodish, as a type of the wise older man, contributes his spirituality and his severe practicality as a role model. And the two together offer Jules their strategic and tactical shrewdness and their wit.

Like many narratives that have as a major strand the uncovering of a crime, *Diva* is also a site where the culturally repressed emerges. There are plenty of characters whose disposition illustrates this point. The personality traits of the malicious Inspector Saporta (Jacques Fabbri) are just the opposite of those inherent in 'saporita' – which means tasty, delicious or witty. With his saturnine disposition and his ruthless destruction of all those who (whatever their service to him in the past) no longer feed his appetite for the corrupt abuse of power, Saporta survives by deception. He is not as visibly demonic a figure as his sidekick, on to whom his evil characteristics are displaced. But the eye-catching killer Le Curé (Dominique Pinon) displays his boss's monstrosity beautifully. Under his bald beetle dome and with his wrap-around sunglasses like a ballgoer's mask, he could have stepped out of Breughel's vision of hell. His words are limited to the curt dismissal of all things: 'J'aime pas ça!' And his speciality is murder by stiletto. The two Thai audio pirates are equivalent types, their coldness and their eyes blanked off by baleful sunglasses shorthand ways of signifying that they too belong to the shadow group.

Another surreal feature is the action, which also consists of clashing elements, there being four dissonant plot threads. Plot A is that of Jules and Cynthia. Plot B concerns the corrupt chief of police, Saporta, the thugs (Le Curé among them) whom he uses to control his ring of Caribbean prostitutes, and the inept cops he bamboozles so they fail to identify their boss as the master criminal they are hunting. Plot C features the sinister pair of Taiwanese bent on getting hold of Jules's recording of Cynthia and selling it on the pirate market. The characters in the latter two plots literally get in the way of each other as each gang of villains pursues Jules for two quite different tapes – the one he knows he has of Cynthia and another he does not know about which incriminates Saporta. But it is Plot D that weaves the others together: Gorodish, replete with wisdom, knowledge and wry humour, gains entry into all their worlds and succeeds stylishly (almost effortlessly, just like a fantasy knight in armour) in eradicating the villains.

The vivid representation of colliding worlds in picture, story and accompanying music, is a further element structuring the spectator's experience. He or she is deliciously battered by the film's exuberant surrealism; its insistent colour-coding through blue and white; its unexpected icons; the overlay of classical music on to pop visuals. All these jarring components cohere in a highly tensioned unity. The factor that tends to pull them apart is obviously enough their extreme diversity. What makes for coherence is principally the characters' own acceptance of the fragmented worlds they pass through. The key figure in this is Jules. All the action centres on him and, despite the boyish excess of his passion for Cynthia, he has a personality as normal as can be imagined in this milieu.

The rhetorical address of the film is startling and charged with energy that the narrative itself does not fully absorb. This is one factor triggering the spectator's appetite to explore its symbolism. Another is the element of fantasy. As Auty says (1982: 302), *Diva* is a traditional morality tale but in modern garb. Its surrealism encourages us to extend the reading of it beyond morality, through myth, and thence to psychology. All told, what we see and hear is a dynamic psychodrama peopled, lit, coloured and resounding with motifs that are energised with a symbolic charge. No one character or motif dominates the others – all are present in roughly equal vigour. The bright and the dark elements are locked together in conflict as countertypes producing what Jung would have termed a *conjunctio oppositorum*. Such a conjunction is a classic representation of the psyche in which conscious and unconscious are in balance. In *Diva* it allows those who respond to the film to see and feel that knowledge of all the passions, both noble and ignoble, is necessary to the well-balanced psyche. The *conjunctio* penetrates even in the magic inner circle which Cynthia and Jules inhabit. Jules is not immune from temptation since he, like several of the villains, indulges in theft (albeit of a special kind). And for her part, Cynthia conceals a terror of her shadow side.

As a vehicle for the cultural unconscious, *Diva* is unusually generous. Through both its characters and its scintillating aesthetics, the film summons the young of heart – the audience with whom it might resonate – as a repository of Parisian cultural experience, both lived and virtual. Audiences are invited to bear witness that full human development demands exposure to many aspects of culture – both light and dark, joyous and potentially murderous. Despite the darker elements it contains, *Diva* is buoyant with an effulgent and emotional optimism which its sound track insists upon. In sum, it is not merely about the cultural unconscious of the young, it invites the audience to assimilate the register and to enter, at least virtually in heart and mind, that social group itself.

4 *The Piano*, the animus and colonial experience

In Jules, the main protagonist of *Diva*, we identified a character whose principal task was to work through and come to terms with an anima complex. We turn now to a film the lead character in which is a woman who faces unresolved problems with an overpowering animus. Like *Diva*, *The Piano* (Jane Campion, 1993) is mainly concerned with both the collective and the cultural unconscious; it barely hints at disturbances in the personal unconscious.

The structure of Campion's film obliges the spectator to recognise that closed interpretations based mainly on analysis of its characters and the narrative are unreliable. The film can be anchored neither to straightforward readings based on its main character's story world, nor to the historical world of mid-Victorian colonialism – which is not to deny that both are presented with clarity. The film's themes are diffuse because its obvious symbolic riches coexist with a lack of hard information about the principal character. Neither the events of the plot nor the heroine's inner narration let us into the secrets of her past.

For this reason, interpretation of *The Piano* has to be augmented by other means, and this chapter rests on the presumption that the film allows us to see not only the exterior, but also the psyche of the main character, revealing in a single sweep how her social milieu touches her interior world. It provides an analysis of the main character in accordance with Jungian principles. But it also seeks explanations for the changes that she brings about in her life outwith the context of simple personal development. To this end it considers the psychological dimension of relationships between the characters in the context of their colonial setting.

Ada (Holly Hunter) has refused to speak since she was 6 years old, but we never find out why. Perhaps she was as stubborn in childhood as in her adulthood and ceased speaking as an act of pride or retribution; perhaps she suffered a trauma at that age. We have no means of knowing. All we are given is her own memory of her father saying that she possesses a dark talent, a strength of will so focused that, were she to decide to stop breathing, she would be dead within the day. We are not told how she came to be a single mother nor who fathered her child. Nor can we make out whether, as her dark apparel (and her daughter's fanciful tales) suggest, she is widowed, or whether the sombre clothes cover an unmarried mother's shame. Finally, we never learn why her father has married her to a man she has not met and dispatched her and the child from his comfortable Glasgow home to the far end of the earth. Although all these circumstances might be explained had there been a long-standing incestuous relationship between father and daughter, we are given no evidence which would enable us to confirm or discredit speculation.

It is not that we don't care. On the contrary, our attention is intensely focused by this resolute figure who, at the end of her long sea journey, seems undaunted at being left alone with her daughter on a wild and empty beach. (She calmly improvises shelter for their first night in New Zealand from her hooped petticoat.) But although our interest in Ada encourages us to search for a more complete understanding of her personality, we can find no anchorage upon which to ground speculation. Again and again we see the evidence of Ada's fierce determination to govern the things that matter to her – principally her daughter and her piano. But the strength of will she directs at the outer world is not matched by (and may even substitute for) an equal power to navigate her inner world. For example, when she speaks of her stubborn nature, she does not report her own thoughts, but recalls her father's words.

These qualities of stubbornness and blind certainty signal a form of semi-emancipation in her personality. Her life has commenced in a familiar Scottish landscape made strange by the virtual absence of a mother. The primal authority of her father is indicated by his autocratic decision to marry her to man she has never seen. Ada submits to his will in this, but might be understood to be continuing her resistance in a form of dumb insolence through her muteness. Certainly this is the personality trait that her husband Stewart (Sam Neill) first encounters in the incongruous figure he finds abandoned on the desolate beach with her piano and all her possessions. For her part, Ada immediately discovers that, although she is now in a wholly unfamiliar landscape, the structures of patriarchy in the expatriate community have been imported wholesale from the homeland. In the face of her absolute refusal to abandon the piano, her new husband declares the instrument too heavy for his men to move, and leaves it on the beach. But where she had no recourse but to submit to her father's will, Ada resists Stewart's by refusing him conjugal rights.

This is a desperate and risky stratagem because in Stewart's mid-Victorian New Zealand, no less than other colonial territories, social norms are set and power is stratified according to competitive economic principles, as Miriam Dixson argues in her discussion of Australian women. White Anglo-Saxon Protestant men are the economic pace-setters, the decision-makers and leaders, and in their cramped style of masculinity they for the most part control sexuality too via a domination–subordination hierarchy in which women are the underdogs (Dixson 1976: 23). Property and propriety go hand in hand. A man in Stewart's position, though deeply repressed in his sexuality, expects to be able to exercise his rights over his wife; and Ada's resistance initiates intense battles over the construction of the family as the basic social unit.

At the same time there is a second power struggle going on in the wider social arena, which centres on the contest for ownership of the land between the white settlers and the Maori who have long lived there. Both these sets of conflicts entwine with Ada's gradually deepening recognition of her own naturalness, set off by the untamed landscape as her exploration of the outer world (her adaptation both to the environment and the isolated colonial community) triggers her exploration and discovery of her inner self. Events in the film's historical world not only stimulate new beginnings in the unconscious mind of its heroine, they also become metaphors for them.

The forest, deep within which lies the dwelling of Ada's new husband Stewart, is therefore a key image in the film. It has many shifting aspects. Campion and her cinematographer Stuart Dryburgh at first represent it as if through the newcomers' eyes as a pathless maze of thickets, trees and mud through whose boundless confusion travellers must force their way as best they can. As the story develops, we explore it with Ada and her daughter Flora, and gradually begin to recognise features of their new surroundings, discovering pathways across the mud that lies deep around the encampment. Then we learn to see the ground further afield in different ways. Ada's husband perceives it as property to be owned, and he sections it with lines of fence poles. For the Maori community, on the other hand, the land is filled with meaning built up through generations of ritual use. They blend into and move through the landscape with an ease that the whites never match. The two cultures come to an impasse when Stewart, obsessed with increasing his holdings of land, offers the people buttons and baubles in exchange for the magically charged places which are their ancestral burial grounds.

Seen through Ada's eyes, the forest gradually changes from being the formidable physical barrier she encountered when first toiling through its snares to reach her new home. She begins to find her way through it with less extreme difficulty, and it eventually becomes instead a mysterious expression of her state of mind. For example, when her piano is installed in her husband's home, she walks uncertainly away from the house while he directs Flora's playing with thumping inaccuracy. The camera tracks with her until it settles on a shot of tree trunks, through which the eye can find no passage. Both the camera and Ada are brought to a standstill, gazing at the trunks that seem to cage them. As we later understand, Ada has reached a crux in her inner life and is in a quandary analogous to Dante's, lost in the middle of the soul's dark forest. As Marie-Louise von Franz notes in her study of fairy tales, a frequent motif is the woman who has to withdraw temporarily into the woods and not go back into life.

From the outside it looks like complete stagnation, but in reality it is a time of initiation and incubation when a deep inner split is cured and inner problems are solved. This motif forms a contrast to the more active quest of the male hero, who has to go into the Beyond and try to slay the monster, or find the treasure, or the bride. (von Franz 1993:106)

Yet another image of the forest emerges as, forced to find her own amusements by her mother's preoccupation with her own affairs, Flora (Anna Paquin) begins to use it as a playground and a way of exploring the world. Her sense of the forest converges with her mother's in being an expression of her inner state of mind; but the things in her mind are rather different and in some ways closer to the Maori view. After spying on her mother making love, Flora leads the indigenous children in a grotesque mimicry of copulation and gets them gleefully to hump trees, much to the amusement of the elders. But in Stewart's eyes, she has defiled herself and the white community. He impresses this on her by making her whitewash all the trunks that the children have played with. It makes the trees look as though they are dying. In this guise they seem to be a metaphor for Stewart's emotional deadness.

To sum up, the woods are the site not merely of values that are in conflict, but of contradictory ways of regulating life. At one extreme lies the Victorian colonial policy of expropriation and property-ownership for which Stewart stands. As the decision-maker and leader of the white community he functions consciously to subordinate both the women and the indigenous people, but it costs him the connection with his own unconscious drives. For the Maori, by contrast, the woods map ritualistically charted ancestral territory organised not by land use but by memories of the dead and projections of the sensed (rather than rationalised) needs of the living. The woods are a topography that helps the people enter the cultural unconscious of their community. For their part, Ada and Flora as white females and incomers cannot initially see the forest from either perspective. They have to work out their own stance or risk subordination into the vacuity to which the other white women in the expatriate Scots community have resigned themselves.

The person who stimulates Ada to adapt is her husband's estate manager, Baines (Harvey Keitel). Pitying her as she yearns for the piano, he buys the instrument from Stewart in exchange for a piece of land. (With marriage, ownership of even Ada's most treasured possession has passed to her husband, a reminder of the extent to which she is still bound by patriarchal law and custom.) Baines has it carried from the beach to his own house and restored to good order. He pretends to Stewart that he wants music lessons, but when she first comes to his house, quickly disabuses Ada of any such idea. He wants to hear her play. Something in her music appears to be stirring his soul. By degrees, Ada enters a relationship with him which is more than that of catalyst and reagent since their influence on each other is equally strong.

Baines represents a distinct sub-type of the settler, the white man who has 'gone native'. As such he arouses the suspicion of his fellow colonists who look askance at mingling between the races. A complex set of cultural responses is in play here that has at its core interracial sexual relations. Throughout the former British colonies (including, as we saw in chapter 2, the states populated by Britons in North America), whites perceived the person who 'went native' as in some way coloured by the darkness of the indigenous people. In most African colonies no less than in America, the supposed sexual insatiability of black men and their rapacious appetite for white women were matters of commonplace white 'knowledge'. White women were sheltered by their menfolk from this danger even while some of the same men fathered children on indigenous women.

A figure like Baines (who has had his face carved and stained with Maori markings and is more comfortable in their company than with his fellow expatriates) would be the object of powerful, contradictory feelings. First he would arouse sexual envy; having left his wife in Scotland he enjoys uninhibited access to the local Maori community which appears to have folded him into its easy-going domestic arrangements. Simultaneously he would suffer social contempt for having supposedly demeaned himself by opting out of white society. And finally he would be the target of moral reprobation for his seeming indifference to Christian values.

Seen from a Jungian perspective, the man who goes native becomes (no less than the indigenous black male) the other, the object of shadow projection by the white community. The latter perceive him as an honorary black man, and discover in him those dangerous desires and fears that they are no longer conscious of possessing themselves, as if they were facets of his personality rather than their own. They distance their dark, unconscious side either because they have forgotten the naked emotions they knew in childhood, or they have had to repress them in order to conform with the requirements of family or society at large. Once again, a comparable pattern of projection occurred involving the white American frontiersman in the dark projections of the people from whom he had sprung. However, in the case of Baines, the projection on to him of the expatriate community's dark traits is ironic. In actuality he is far from being a liberated character, and has a personality quite different from that perceived by Stewart and his family. Although a man of a potential nobility, his qualities will by no means be fully realised until Ada's image reactivates his contrasexual archetype, the anima. And the alteration of Baines's personality also happens *mutatis mutandis* to Ada when her animus transfers to him. We shall follow these transformations later.

Terry Goldie has written a study of the psychological meaning of certain characters in Australian literature. Although both the literature and culture of New Zealand differ from those of its neighbour, the observations he makes seem to apply to *The Piano*. He says that typically the white person gains soul not by becoming aboriginal, but by acquiring aboriginal culture and then resurfacing from it so that the two cultures are blended rather than one overwhelming the other (Goldie 1988: 69–71). Such an entry into and resurfacing from the dark culture is a variant of the familiar transformation journey of the hero into the underworld. The Black is the Other, an object seen from the white point of view, and of interest only to the extent that it offers a social and cultural counterpoint to the white self. The effect is that the indigene is actually represented in order to comment on occidental culture. Interest in the exotic culture is, however, enhanced by the ancient association of the indigene with nature and the natural – that is, with both the unfettered forces of nature (benign or malevolent) and the supposedly uninhibited behaviour of those who are thought to be less encumbered than whites by the moral burdens of civilisation (Goldie 1989: 11–16).

Goldie takes this argument further so that it engages with present-day interests when he argues that some contemporary Australian fiction concerned with a feminist awakening finds an appropriate symbol in a white female protagonist who develops most of the characteristics that the indigenous, dark maiden had displayed in earlier literature. In these cases, 'the pattern of a search for individuation and, to varying degrees, indigenization, is associated with sexual contact with a male indigene'. Goldie agrees with O. Mannoni that in this context romantic literature makes use of racial difference as if it reinforced the appeal of sexual difference: 'The more remote people are, the more they seem to attract our projections – the easier it is for a "crystallization", as Stendhal called it, to take place.' However, the male indigene is 'a transitional figure who is left behind when the white protagonist has achieved certain development.

It is as though the element of "difference" provides a necessary catalyst for the process of individuation but, like other catalysts, it forms no part of the final product' (Goldie 1989: 65, 80; Mannoni 1964: 111). As has been suggested, the case of Ada and Baines forms a variant on this pattern.

The slow stirring in Baines's psyche makes him resemble a reawakening Caliban; it manifests itself through the sex drive in a somewhat awkward physicality rather than in an arousal to spirituality. He strikes a bargain with Ada by which she earns back one of the piano's keys for each visit and in return allows him to caress her as she plays. And although she remains outwardly unresponsive, his caresses become more intimate as the days pass. But after a session in which he persuades her to lie beside him unclothed, he abruptly brings the arrangement to an end. Telling her that the deal is turning her into a whore and making him unhappy, he gives her back her instrument. Once again we have to guess at his motivation, but it seems likely that Ada's playing – virtually the only means by which she communicates with Baines – has soothed his soul. And we can speculate from her then seeking him out and leading him into love that his renunciation of the deal has beguiled her similarly. When they become lovers, Ada, as has been suggested, makes a symbolic connection with her dark side; at the same time, Baines commences his return to the white culture he abandoned in going native. In other words, both make progress towards individuation.

The piano itself is the source of haunting images, none more so than when, abandoned where Ada has disembarked, it seems that its austere symmetry must be overwhelmed by the heavy ocean rollers pounding the long beach. The bizarre conjunction of the wild shore and this potent symbol of Victorian gentility invokes a sense of mystery which is enhanced when we discover that the instrument has suffered little harm from its prolonged exposure. The weird juxtaposition of piano and sea invites the spectator to think of it as a symbol; and it is worth recalling that the sea is also an archetypal image of the maternal unconscious. The conjunction of the two images develops this concept.

It is tempting to think of Ada's music as in some respects substituting for her speaking voice (though Flora helps her communicate with other people through sign language). However, the fact is that until Baines's interest is awakened, she plays primarily for herself, her impassioned performances being the only way she knows to express the romanticism of her soul. We can infer that, just as the piano on the beach does not succumb to the waves, so Ada is able to put herself in contact with the unconscious through her instrument, but its waves have not yet over-whelmed her. Thus her music resounds with nature in a double sense, first reflecting the wilderness of water and wood that surrounds her, and secondly reaching down into some of the unconscious impulses that drive her. It is rightly described by Stewart's Aunt Morag (who hates it) as 'a mood that passes through you...a sound that creeps into you'. As in part a product of the unconscious, it has a predictive aspect. It gives Ada a mysterious foretaste of things that she does not yet fully know; and we can see this in her slowly developing relationship with Baines. Her music is the catalyst for them both in the gradual release of their deep-seated sexual and spiritual repressions: only when there can be no further contact between them through music do they discover their love to each other.

However, Ada's music is also an art, and *The Piano* encourages us to connect the realms of art and life. It does so in a light-hearted way when the expatriate community produce a vaudeville performance of the Blue-beard story for an audience of local whites and indigenous people. When, in a shadow play, Bluebeard prepares to set about his murderous work with an axe, the Maori misunderstand the grand-guignol menace. They rush the stage in order to save the lives of the innocents he threatens, and the drama ends in amusing chaos with the destruction of nothing worse than illusion. This little comedy reminds us that meaning is encoded differently in life and art no matter how closely they resemble each other – and the observation holds good for Ada's subtle playing. No matter how passionate her music, its language is insufficiently specific to communicate to Baines the emotions engendered in her by their new relationship. She has to resort to gesture and action to express her love. Eventually her reentry through love into the world rekindles both the want and the desire for speech to enable her to deal with life in ways the art of the keyboard could not. In this scintillating new arena of her life, music ceases to be adequate to her needs, and even a laborious encumbrance, which explains in part why she jettisons the piano. However, the end of the narrative shows her to have acquired new balance in that she is both learning to speak and playing.

In order for Ada to attain that new balance between her conscious purposes and unconscious drives, however, she has to undergo changes that reach deep into her nature. An explanation of this process can be given with the help of Jungian analytical psychology, which enables us to relate the progress in her own self-discovery to changes in her relationships with the men closest to her. The key to such an explanation lies in animus theory.

The idea of the animus is, as has been mentioned, one aspect of Jung's theory of the contrasexual archetypes. The more complete side of his theory concerned the anima, the contrasexual archetype in a man. Jung argued that the more strongly a man presented himself to his fellows as a manly, even a macho figure, the more likely it was that he would be drawn, either in his dreams or through his projections of psychological energy upon actual women with whom he came into contact, towards an image of woman that would be the complement of his exterior mask. This supple, bewitching, and endlessly transforming image is the anima; it tends, as we saw in *Diva* with Jules and his Cynthia, to play a major role in the lives of men, particularly at times when they themselves are going through periods of psychological change.

Jung's thoughts on the anima were detailed, tested not only through research into myth and literature, but also through his practice with patients and observation of his own dreams and associations. However, his ideas about the animus, the equivalent figure in the psyche of a woman, were altogether more sketchy and necessarily lacked the informative dimension of his own direct experience. Indeed, as several Jungian feminists have shown, his animus theory has proved wholly inadequate to representing women in the many and varied roles they have played in the latter half of the twentieth century. Formed in an era of largely unchallenged patriarchal values, his views plainly ascribe to women a consciousness which, despite his disclaimers, is inferior to that of men in its thinking function. The exercise of reason and differentiation is seen as predominantly a masculine characteristic, while the field in which women are properly comfortable is the realm of personal relations and emotions.

The wide fields of commerce, politics, technology, and science, the whole realm of the applied masculine mind, [a woman] relegates to the penumbra of consciousness; while, on the other hand, she develops a minute consciousness of personal relationships, the infinite nuances of which usually escape the man entirely. (Jung 1935a: 206)

Jung said that anima and animus stood in complementary relationship both to the dominant disposition of consciousness in either sex, and to each other. It followed therefore that each was coloured by what he perceived as the dominant social roles of men and women respectively. However, in developing animus theory, he appears not to have kept firmly in mind the impact upon a woman's unconscious of the specific culture and society in which she lived. With its tendency to draw universal conclusions from the historical circumstances of his own society, Jung's animus theory differs from much of his work which is meticulous in this respect.

As the anima produces *moods*, so the animus produces *opinions*; and as the moods of a man issue from a shadowy background, so the opinions of a woman rest on equally unconscious prior assumptions. Animus opinions very often have the character of solid convictions that are not lightly shaken...But in reality the opinions are not thought out at all; they exist ready made, and they are held so positively and with so much conviction that the woman never has the shadow of a doubt about them. (ibid.: 206–7)

Therefore Jung reckoned that one of the effects of the animus in intellectual women was to encourage disputatiousness and a tendency to harp on irrelevancies so as to make them the main point of an argument. Without knowing it, women suffering from the extraversion of the animus in this way were solely intent upon exasperating the man; a woman possessed by the animus was always in danger of losing her adapted feminine persona, namely her femininity. (ibid.: 208–9)

Read today, this account of the animus demonstrates all too clearly the risks inherent in producing a contrasexual theory for the other sex. In his construction of the animus, Jung portrayed partly his own anima projections and partly his epoch's preconceptions of women's roles. Those preconceptions were actually shared by many women at that time. For although men had a false picture of women's psychology, women as the less powerful sex have for generations tended to internalise men's images of them, and to have made them their own. Of course, now that the present-day occupations and interests of so many women falsify his idea of them, it follows that Jung's concept of the animus must also be revised.

Broadly speaking, feminist writers have confronted Jung's theories via approaches that are bounded by two poles. At one end of the scale lies downright opposition. Jung's ideas are said to be inextricably bound up in patriarchal culture. In their *androcentrism*, or male-centred philosophy, they simultaneously demean women and negate themselves, since a hierarchy of archetypes dominated by a male world view cannot by definition be universal. Feminists who take this position at its extreme tend to deny Jung's work any validity. At the other end of the scale, however, lies the work of a number of writers whose opposition concentrates mainly on those parts of Jung's thought that relate to the lives of women. While they also bring into question those aspects of his archetypal theory upon which his beliefs about women impinge, they usually wish to retain a great deal of the material on myth and mind. It is with this latter group that we shall be concerned.

Demaris S. Wehr took an important new step in developing a feminist Jungian psychology when she argued that society and the individual psyche are in dialectical relationship with one another. As we saw in chapter 3, she believes that psychological forces do indeed shape society. At the same time, social structures also exert great influence in shaping the individual personality (Wehr 1987: 18). The limitation of the classical

Jungian framework was that it showed very little awareness of the social conditions that have created certain character types, and offered no explicit criticism of traditional male and female roles (Wehr 1990: 117).

Although the step Wehr took in arguing for the dialectical relationship of society and psyche was not revolutionary, it did entail a significant change of emphasis from Jung's work. As we have seen, he argued that symbols allow that to be known which was previously not available to consciousness, potentially widening its field. It is possible to identify two stages in Jung's picture of this process of coming to consciousness – though in actuality they form a seamless continuum. In the first preverbal and pre-rational stage, unconscious energies constellate around an archetype. An image surfaces into consciousness when the level is lowered of the mind's preoccupation with other, ongoing conscious activities. As it does so, the ego-conscious, in 'recognising' these partially formed images, dresses them out with the lineaments of its own knowledge and experience. In this latter stage of the movement to consciousness, the pressures of circumstance and ideology fashion to one degree or another the clothing of the archetype, since of course a large part of every individual's experience is socially rooted through participation in language, culture, family and community. Through their consciously realised elements, symbols discipline the unruly instincts, anchoring unconscious energies in form, shaping their contents and adapting them in response to current social and cultural values and styles. Jung says, then, that truly understood, the role of the symbol is to give up its symbolic nature as it enhances consciousness by bringing it into fuller relationship with the unconscious.

As we have seen, Wehr accepts that this describes one of the two ways in which energy flows through symbols; but she argues that a powerful current also thrusts in the reverse direction. Jung does not recognise with the force of Wehr that symbol systems have 'political' ramifications as well as psychological roots. It is an issue that has been clear for some time to the many feminists who have had an interest in Althusserian theory. Indeed as a feminist Wehr does not miss the androcentrism of Jung's own theories: they are themselves political in being centred on the experience of men, and therefore cannot claim to be universal in their original form.

Wehr uses her dialectical model to account for women's 'internalized oppression'. She refers through this phrase to the sense of themselves that all too many women suffer – the belief that they are in some way deficient or inadequate simply because of their gender. She agrees with feminist opinion in attributing this sense of inferiority to women having internalised definitions of them circulated in patriarchal society.

Furthermore, she posits specific psychic consequences that typify the way internalised oppression presents itself to a woman: 'It speaks with a certain voice, and it has a certain effect on her.' And she cites as a typical product of this internalised oppression a symbolic figure called the 'self-hater' who resides in the psyche of Doris Lessing's heroine in *The Four-Gated City*. Its voice becomes a symbol so devastatingly potent as it jeers, mocks and insinuates its hatred in Martha's inner ear that it has the characteristics of negative animus. To survive and mature into her full selfhood, Martha has consciously to confront this inner voice, otherwise she will be at its mercy if she does not take the power to differentiate herself from it. As Wehr says, being able to bring about such a differentiation is one of the main goals of Jungian analysis (1987: 18–19). Lessing, and after her Wehr, have thus identified in the self-hater a powerful archetypal image to which women are vulnerable. It is an image which represents a perversion of negative animus produced by generations of insistent ideological pressure on women. Just such a character exists in the person of Ada in Jane Campion's *The Piano*.

Somewhat unexpectedly, given all we have just said, Jung's original idea that the animus presented a common neurotic complex of women becomes the starting-point for Ann Belford Ulanov's revaluation of the concept. She identifies in Jung's idea a state of mind experienced by those women, whether intellectuals or not, who suffer from certain problems with the animus. The condition can manifest itself as a state of mind in which a woman experiences an inflating compulsion always to be right, feeling that anyone who disagrees with her is wrong or stupid. In *The Piano* there are indications that Ada's temperament is occasionally subject to this kind of inflation when she ignores point blank the wishes of others should they be at odds with her own. Her very muteness itself can be interpreted as her enduring condemnation of the stupidity she finds in the rest of the world.

Discussing it as a matter of particular social interest because the psychological phenomenon remains so common in our own time, Ulanov believes that the same compulsion may also operate in the reverse direction, deflating a woman's ego so that she feels permanently inadequate, as though whatever she does cannot be enough. In this case she does not recognise that her expectations of herself can never be met because after every achievement she obsessively moves her goals again, further out of reach. Whereas Jung seems to claim that the first condition represents a complex experienced by over-intellectual but otherwise well-adjusted women, Ulanov argues that they both emerge when there is insufficient conscious differentiation of the 'I' of the ego from the 'other' of the animus. Where ego and animus are not separated, the latter either inflates the ego, or deflates it when the drive reverses. As a consequence severe emotional problems may be experienced.

In this undigested state, the animus takes the form of emotional expectations of how things ought to be done or understood, expectations which are compulsively expressed and devoid of a sense of timing. (Ulanov 1971: 42–3)

When in this state of mind the animus is projected on a man, problems arise. In the first place the woman may have impossibly high expectations of him as if he really were her unconscious animus image. When inevitably he fails to live up to this image he either becomes weak and not good enough for her, or a menacing enemy (ibid.: 42–5). This, then, is the condition of Ada's psyche represented by Stewart when we read his character as an image that renders one manifestation of her animus.

In this distorted form the archetypal image can spring from either internal or external distress. That is, its source can be either disturbance arising autochthonously in a woman's unconscious, or more commonly it arises from the internalising of social oppression relating to gender roles. By applying Wehr's model to Ada's case, we can identify (seeing Stewart as a manifestation of her animus complex) an oppression which springs in large part from her prescribed gender roles and is redoubled by the colonial power structure that places women at the bottom of the social hierarchy of whites.

However, we can refine matters further. Ulanov demonstrates that things are different where a woman achieves a conscious relationship to the animus. Then she not only relates to the conditioning influence of her father and husband on the personal unconscious; but through the transpersonal archetypal core she also has access to the deepest levels of the psyche.

Just as relating to a man opens a woman to hitherto inaccessible parts of herself, relating to this inner man puts her in touch with as yet unrealised capacities in herself... to focus upon and articulate the deeper aspects of her feminine being, to be assertive and to take definite stands in a feminine way rather than to imitate the masculine way. (Ulanov 1971: 45)

Thus Ulanov constructs a model of the animus which gives it very much the equivalent function of the anima – something that in Jung's writing, despite his claims, it did not have.

Just as the anima's development initiates the development of the masculine personality, the animus in its stages of transformation connects the deeper feminine self to the female ego and initiates the development of the feminine personality. (Ulanov 1971: 241)

When a man learns to relate to his anima, woman to her animus, the contrasexual figures mediate equally for each sex between consciousness and the unconscious.

Neither the anima nor the animus is fully formed at birth. Rather, both develop through a number of phases to full maturity when the individual relates to his or her partner on both the conscious and unconscious levels. Ulanov describes four stages of animus development from infancy to full maturity; and although Ada does not reach the advanced self-knowledge that characterises the final stage, her transition through the other three can be traced.

The infant starts in a state of psychic unity where there is no separation of the ego from the unconscious. In this respect girls and boys are the same, but feminists such as Wehr remind us that because in our society mothers bear most of the burden of looking after children, the early experiences of differentiation by the two sexes are not the same. Jung had thought that the object of the infant's first projections was the parent of the opposite sex (in other words the father, not the mother, would be the first carrier of a projected image for a girl). In contrast, feminist studies suggest that all infants project at first on to the mother, since they are nursed and cared for primarily by women (Jung 1959a: 14; Wehr 1987: 118).

Ulanov argues therefore that for boys self-discovery takes place in opposition to the primary relationship with the mother, which brings about their sense of greater isolation. This in turn leads to a boy's emphasis upon objectivity and ego-consciousness as his awareness develops of his difference from his mother.

He experiences his original identity with his mother as a relation of like to unlike, as a relation to a nonself, to an 'other,' an opposite, symbolized by all the obvious sexual differences. In order to be himself and to have himself to himself he must stand against his early identity with the nonself; he must free his ego and go his own way . . . He identifies his ego with consciousness because his self-discovery coincides with his freeing himself from his mother and from the pre-ego containment in the unconscious that she symbolizes. (Ulanov 1971: 243)

For a girl, however, 'self-discovery is contained in her early relationship with her mother because she feels strongly drawn to her as like to like'. Since there is no pressure on her caused by difference in sexes,

there is less emphasis with a girl than there is with a boy in developing an ego position with which to oppose the unconscious that the mother symbolizes. Instead a girl's ego development takes place not in opposition to but in relation to her unconscious . . . [She] turns toward unconscious processes, not away from them.

The feminine ego is less consciously defined than the male's and often less firm. It stresses objectivity less and is therefore less clear. It is more subjective and as a result less estranged and less isolated from its own roots in the unconscious. (ibid.: 243–4)

For these reasons, women tend to relate by identification while men do so by discriminating (ibid.: 244). The fact that Ada has an unusually strong ego does not negate this pattern. It fits with the (actual or virtual) absence of a mother in her childhood so that she has grown up with a sense of isolation more typical of a boy.

The second stage of feminine development according to Ulanov is triggered by the invasion of the paternal masculine – the animus in its transpersonal or collective form. It is so different from the ego that it makes ego-consciousness aware of its own limits. Springing from the transpersonal unconscious, it is experienced as an overpowering archetypal image charged with magical or numinous energy. Often dressed in the image of an impersonal male divinity (sometimes a ravishing penetrator who breaks into her consciousness), this figure connects a woman to her own instinctual nature, if she can accept it. Then it fundamentally changes her personality and prepares her for profound sexual and intuitive knowledge. If, however, she resists it through fear, as many women do, she may suffer severe difficulties in reconciling herself to her sexuality. A woman fixated in this second stage may act like the Eternal Daughter of a Spiritual Father, and may also retain an excessively strong emotional attachment to her actual father. As a consequence she may find it impossible to get in touch with her own emotionality in the way we mentioned earlier, alternately over- or under-valuing the men with whom she comes into contact (ibid.: 246–52).

The plainest annunciation of an impersonal male divinity in *The Piano* comes in young Flora's fantasies about her absent natural father. Campion heightens the fantasy element by flashing up a cartoon of this imagined romantic figure being consumed by flames. Meanwhile, the child declares to her new aunts that he was an opera singer who courted her mother through song, only to have been struck down by lightning at the height of his vocal passion.

In fact Ada's relation to her animus prior to knowing Baines can also be understood as a variant of Ulanov's second stage; as has been said, it is expressed through her relationships with men. Because her own father commands so much authority in her life, he exerts a godlike power over her. Ada is not connected to her instinctual or emotional nature until she becomes Baines' lover; so it seems that by resisting her father she has blocked herself off from the animus. The implications seem to be that there is unfinished emotional business between them – an unresolved difficulty that might date back to the time when Ada committed herself to muteness. This blockage seems to have left her more or less stuck in relation to her animus, as her relationships with other men imply. It is not hard to imagine that she might have wanted to become pregnant out of an unconscious desire to make up for the absence from the family of her own mother. By stepping into this role, she would symbolically take Flora's father as her own parent – whatever her actual relationship to him. Meanwhile Stewart's relentlessly patriarchal demeanour, together with the fact that Ada's father chose him as his daughter's partner, mark him out as being of the same authoritarian type.

The significance of Baines as a character is different. It fits into what Ulanov discerns as the third stage of feminine development, namely that in which the animus takes on an individual and personal form. A figure familiar from fairy-tales archetypally represents the animus at this stage – the hero who frees the daughter from bondage to her father and then marries her in a relationship in which the inequality between man and woman is less pronounced. For a woman this archetype can be embodied either in a real partner, or may be an 'inner' man. In either case, the feminine ego feels dependent on the masculine and in need of help to break free from the second stage and the encompassing power of the paternal animus. The feminine ego seeks this help in order to establish a more equal relationship with the masculine – as when a woman is helped by her husband to break free from her original family circle and then establishes a new partnership with him. Ulanov says that at this stage a woman is no longer identical with her unconscious feminine interests as she had been in the second stage; rather the animus helps her to find perspective in the materials yielded by her unconscious, and to focus on them directly. 'She remains dependent on her animus function, which acts as an enlivening impulse, stirring up new possibilities of life' (ibid.: 255–6)

This describes Baines's function succinctly. We have already commented on his 'strange' attribute, the consequence of his having gone native. He does indeed help free Ada from bondage not only to her father but also to Stewart, the father surrogate. As a result Ada builds a better balanced relationship with the masculine, witness the fact that she is able to persuade Baines (contrary to his predisposition) to jettison her piano at sea as they sail round the coast to their new home.

All in all, Ulanov's rewriting of Jungian theory achieves nothing less than to give women's animus function the same status as, and a developmental history comparable to, the anima. As it happens we do not observe the fourth stage of animus development in *The Piano* because Ada does not reach it. This final phase parallels the advanced evolution of a man's anima. In it men and women consciously develop and share contrasexual traits in their relationships, so that each can love both the dominant and the subordinate gender characteristics in their partners. The man can admit to his feminine elements, the woman to the masculine in her (ibid.: 257–61). This then represents from the woman's perspective the final stage of animus development with which we began. It enables her to escape from the third stage, fixation in which can mean self-loss because she risks sacrificing the momentum of her own development by never going beyond the patriarchal definition of the feminine role.

Implicit in the drive which urges Ada towards Baines, however, is the desire to escape from the second into the third stage of animus development. The suffering attendant on any such profound change in the personality quickly emerges. When she and Baines become lovers they are spied upon first by Flora and then, eerily, by Stewart who, transfixed by conflicting emotions, cannot break in and confront them, but continues to peer at them through the knotholes of Baines's cabin. However, when she returns home, the will to possess her overwhelms Stewart's voyeuristic impulses, and forbidding her to see Baines again, he seals up the windows and doors and makes her a prisoner in his house. The passion that Baines has aroused in Ada is not easily quietened, and by night (perhaps in her depths stirred by Stewart's display of authority) she comes to him. Whether she is awake or sleepwalking is not clear; what matters is that as she caresses Stewart with the same languorous touch she has used on her piano, she is in the grip of an eroticism that can no longer be denied. As Harvey Greenberg argues, when Stewart rebuffs her, unable to abide his arousal by a woman who (awake or asleep) may be using him as a substitute lover, she feels release. 'It's subtly apparent that while one part of her has been dutifully attempting to shape herself to Stewart's limitations, the larger part has been using her husband as a substitute object' (Greenberg 1994: 48). Her powerful emotions initiate lasting changes in Ada's psyche.

At this point multiple ironies intensify the fairy-tale quality of the piece. Ada takes a key from her piano, inscribes it with a message of love and sends Flora with it to Baines. However, he cannot read, and hitherto, as Lizzie Francke says, the lovers' exchanges have been based on a sensuous play of touch, smell and sound (Francke 1993: 51). As it turns out, Ada's recourse to language harms her when her words are used as the instrument of her betrayal by Flora. The child has become jealous of her mother paying more attention to Baines than to herself. As Greenberg observes, at this moment Stewart represents a lesser evil to her than Baines because, with the failure of his attempt to become Ada's lover, the former no longer seems to Flora to threaten her symbiotic attachment to her mother by interposing himself between herself and her mother as a new father (Greenberg 1994: 48). Baines, however, seems all too likely to do so. Flora therefore secretly defies her mother's wishes and carries the key to Stewart instead.

As dreams often do, at this juncture *The Piano* reworks its basic theme through fresh motifs. Stewart is goaded to a fury by the written evidence of Ada's love for Baines that was not aroused when he spied on their love-making. The deliberate expression of her will violates his authority because language is the medium of the rule-bound world that Stewart expects to govern. To him unspoken emotions are nebulous; but words make things definite and undeniable. He takes an axe and chops off one of Ada's fingers, and makes Flora carry it to Baines.

Although *The Piano* is not a dream, its story does have dramatic situations and motifs in common with the fairy-tale told by the brothers Grimm as 'The Handless Maiden', in which the innocence of the heroine saves her from the Devil when her father makes a bad bargain. Although she survives her test alive, it costs her her hands and she is expelled from her home; as a wanderer, she eventually becomes the wife of a king and the mother of his child, but not without further trials imposed upon her by the Devil's anger. Von Franz has written a Jungian reading of this tale, aspects of which can be adapted to explain the significance of the film's final act. She speaks of the cold father figure (or his surrogate) as suggestive of an aspect of collective consciousness that eventually wears itself out, and through excessive familiarity loses its power to disturb, so that the intensity of its meaning recedes into the background. This will ultimately occur with the Ada's animus in its second stage.

As we have seen, her father and Stewart are the conscious representatives of patriarchal values, and (extending these values into the collectivity of Empire) of colonialist ideology. The woman who attempts to live according to the principles of such an animus figure may well discover the danger of living in a calculated, cold way in which her emotional, feeling side is neglected. If she has no other role model, however, she may actually be reduced to inactivity (that is in metaphoric terms lose the use of her hands) by the fear of ending up like him (von Franz 1993: 88–9). In Ada's case, her cold animus threatens to destroy the one medium in which she is fluent, her musicality contrasting with Stewart's lack of it. Not that he is entirely untouched by the arts; but his dull soul seems to have been stirred (albeit unconsciously) only by Bluebeard's grotesque melodrama which he mimics crudely in attacking Ada with his axe.

Like the king who marries The Handless Maiden and gives her silver hands, Baines fashions a silver fingertip for Ada. Von Franz says that the artificial hands enable the queen to function half way, which is true for Ada too in that, with her metallic fingertip tapping the keys, she is still able to play, but as a less technically perfect pianist than before (ibid.: 94). Although the fairy-tale maiden grows new hands as a reward for piety, Ada can enjoy no such physical renewal. Her injury signifies the suffering of the hero. In this respect the silver finger symbolises both a recompense for injury and her spiritual renewal as consciousness is altered by contact with and recognition of the unconscious (silver being the metal which by traditional association stands for the unconscious) (Jung 1942: 122–3; Chetwynd 1982: 177). It is one of a number of signs of the new ways into which her life is turning, so that her story closes with her old animus, the cold father-figure, no longer a dominant complex in her mind. At the end she belongs to a newer, urban society, yet will remain a stranger to it (her acceptance of the ambivalence caught in her complacent comment that her finger makes her the town freak).

Ada reaches her new state of being after Stewart gives way when he realises that he can neither kill Baines nor shake Ada's will to have him. The lovers depart, accompanied by Flora, and are rowed across the sea to their new home. The piano goes with them, balanced precariously across the boat's transom. Suddenly Ada begins to panic that the instrument's weight will unbalance them, and the reassurances of neither Baines nor the oarsmen can soothe her. Evidently the piano has become a more than physical burden to her, and she commands the bewildered seamen to throw it overboard. Baines swiftly intuits the urgency of her need and jettisons it. But as it sinks, Ada allows catastrophe to seize her as she quietly watches her foot becoming entangled in one of the binding ropes, and is dragged after it into the deeps. While it sucks her down she gazes around calmly for a period, apparently reconciled to the death that she seems to have willed. Then, acting without premonition, she slips her shoe out of the knot that holds it and frees herself: only when facing death, she later reports with astonishment, did her will unexpectedly choose life.

Von Franz refers to the deep relationship which many women have to nature to account for the seven years that the Handless Maiden stayed in the forest. In the Grimms' story the forest is the place where things begin to grow again, and the girl undergoes a healing regression into her innermost nature to find out what it feels like (von Franz: 97–8). As we have seen, Ada's case is not dissimilar. First confused, then unable to find her way, and later (when Stewart tries to force her to love him by attempting rape) literally tangled in its vines, Ada discovers the beginnings of her new life there. But the culmination of her own search into her innermost nature occurs in that half-willed dive into the ocean's deeps. It suggests that she is at risk of becoming a passive suicide until the moment when she chooses life. But as James Hillman has shown, an encounter with the desire for suicide can be a symbolic expression of the need to bring to an end an old way of life (an exhausted state of consciousness) before embarking on a new one. In other words, the death of the old life of the psyche is a prerequisite to resurgence into the new (Hillman 1988: 75–6). Entering the sea, Ada faces not only the idea of death but through it the unconscious, her own personal interest in it (represented by the piano) submerged in the limitless ocean (the collective). Symbolically it reads as if Baines, representing her revitalised animus, were complicit not only in the piano's but also Ada's fall overboard. And by the same token he also represents the source of new life that encourages her to rise back to the surface again.

My argument has concentrated on the process of psychic healing through which Ada goes as she throws off the paternal imago and advances to the third stage of animus development. There remains, however, a sense of loss symbolised by the sunken piano which (although she has a replacement instrument in her new home) haunts her dreams and draws her mind down again and again into the dark depths of the unconscious and the contemplation of her death. Greenberg concludes: "In jettisoning the piano, Ada seems compelled . . . by the need to abjure the dangerous Dionysian thrust of her temperament . . . Her 'will' chooses a tamer Eros over the Thanatos which may well be the ultimate desire prefigured by her muteness" (1994: 50). However, there is another way of reading this: although no course of action can be chosen without excluding the alternatives to it, Ada remains in touch through her dreams both with her unconscious and with the certainty of her eventual death. Arguably this gives her the framework familiar to mystics and the devout alike in which life can be enjoyed the more positively when its end is not merely known as an intelligible fact, but is apprehended by the whole personality.

We may conclude by speaking of two symbols which reinforce this idea. When Ada is last seen with Baines in her new home, she is practising the rediscovered art of speech. We cannot, however, see her face because it is covered by a black veil. Undulating as her breath puffs at it (breath is a traditional figure for the spirit), it reminds us of the constantly fluctuating boundaries between conscious and unconscious across which Ada has peered. Resembling a delicate, living membrane, it also recalls the fragile boundary between life and death and Ada's ambivalent position: although not dead, she is not yet fully reborn into language and life. As an archetypal motif, the veil is (as von Franz says) a symbol appropriate to a person who in seeking truths about herself, has embarked on a religious quest (von Franz 1993: 104).

Ada's new knowledge is personal rather than social or collective: her new life beginning under the veil of mourning for the old does not yet have an obvious political dimension or engage directly with the ideological structures of colonialism, except in so far as she and Baines are refashioning for themselves the power structure of the family. As an inchoate form, her new life is fittingly symbolised by the child, another archetypal image familiar to Jungians which has both a personal and a collective meaning. That figure is represented by Flora.

The first thing to remark about the child archetype is that it has simultaneously a retrospective and a predictive function: where it presents itself in an adult's dreams or associations it can both look back to that person's past or forwards to the future. As a retrospective figure, it represents emotions and unconscious drives that have been excluded or repressed as a necessary precondition to following the route to adulthood, mapped out as it is by the drive to enhance and specialise consciousness which characterises all Western cultures (Jung 1951: 162–3). It is not hard to place Flora in this context. First, she is the invariable channel through whom Ada conveys her angry will to the world; but, equally importantly, by comparison with Ada's repressive self-control, she expresses a wide range of emotions experienced in her own right, taking delight in play, bathing in her mother's affections and later suffering pangs of jealousy so sharp as to drive her to betrayal.

In so far as the archetypal image of the child looks towards the future it does so by representing nascent drives forming in the unconscious which are likely to enter and alter the individual's conscious in the future. Jung remarks –

Our experience of the psychology of the individual . . . shows that the 'child' paves the way for a future change of personality. In the individuation process, it anticipates the figure that comes from the synthesis of conscious and unconscious elements in the personality. It is therefore a symbol which unites the opposites; a mediator, bringer of healing, that is, one who makes whole. (ibid.: 164)

It can therefore signal a change in personality before it occurs, presenting to the conscious mind as it does the early intimations of rebirth. In this respect too, it is easy to read Flora as an archetypal image. To mention one incident, she anticipates her mother's final commitment to her new animus figure when she shelters with Baines from Stewart's wrath.

As the drama unfolds, Flora begins to display, again revealing her archetypal qualities, clear symptoms of interlinked but opposite qualities, both light and dark shining through her personality. There are times when, playing cheerfully around Stewart's house, she wears the wings with which she has been equipped for the village's theatrical evening. Then she seems like a small angel of light. On other occasions black emotions rule her breast, most potently when she betrays her mother's secret to Stewart; then she is a turbulent, presence, murderous by proxy, an angel of death. But since this betrayal triggers Ada's rebirth by cutting her off from Stewart, she simultaneously brings to mind the angel of the resurrection.

The archetypal child represents energies stirring not only in the personal but also in the collective or transpersonal unconscious. It can be seen in Flora's acting out of the tension between opposites, which enables her to achieve a better balance than her mother between independence and solitude on the one hand and dependency on her parents on the other. In this respect Flora's personality hints at the cultural/political future. What is involved here does not directly implicate the evolution of policy, but centres on her development of a new psychological orientation that foreshadows similar changes in the psychology of the community in which she lives.

Even as late as the mid-twentieth century, colonials speaking of 'home' often used to refer to the 'mother country', which suggested that the relationship between an imperial power and its colonies resembled a nurturing matriarchy. However, the metaphor was always badly strained for two main reasons. First, the normal symbiotic relationship between child and mother was ruptured because, although the source of the colonists' culture, the 'mother' was absent and largely indifferent. Second, the imperial power also laid down the law for its colony and applied it in an authoritarian manner, in this regard acting more like an archetypal father than a mother.

These two factors fit Ada's situation precisely and make her a plausible emblem of the white colonial psyche because, until she leaves Stewart, she too is cut off from an indifferent mother, but subject to unbending patriarchal law administered by a succession of father-figures. By the end of *The Piano* however, her daughter's circumstances suggest that the model is altering. First, Flora has both a mother and in Baines a new, caring, father. Second, although not without pain, she is able to express the full range of her emotions; and, even though she lacks the experience to anticipate the effects her actions will have, she intervenes in matters that concern her and alters the course of events irreversibly.

Thus, understood as an archetypal image referring to the collective, Flora hints at the coming of a mind-set of which the colonial whites around her are not yet conscious. Given the nature of her circumstances, the change of collective consciousness that this child anticipates implies a forthcoming alteration in the psychological relation between the colonial 'child' nation and its imperial parent.

5 The pop star as icon

It is not hard to see that the techniques of Jungian textual analysis can be used to interpret the cultural meaning of those music stars who stir the popular imagination. Rock and pop stars have comparable standing as popular icons to their equivalents in film and television. In so far as the production of star personalities is concerned, this occurs because the publicity machines and marketing apparatus behind all the leisure industries construct and promote their stars to audiences through broadly similar mechanisms. What is more, the industry prefers crossovers, with stars working in more than one medium, as a means of broadening the market. So pop stars produce not only CDs, audio tapes and vinyl, but also video tapes for TV broadcast. Web sites are set up in their names; corporate concerns market tie-ins with their images, such as T-shirts advertising concert performances, or personal endorsements of products (Madonna advertising Max Factor make-up in glossy magazines in 1999). And this is to say nothing of their appearances in movies.

Star personalities in every medium possess a form of capital, namely their own image. The right to make use of that image is the saleable commodity that, guided by agents, managers and publicists, they control and exploit. In semiotic terms, what they sell is a sign. As their cross-media activities imply, stars function as signs, no matter in which medium they flourish, that have been more or less deliberately constructed to carry certain meanings. One of their distinguishing traits is that as signs they operate in more registers than the images of other musicians and actors. An actor is a sign whose principal denotative function is to delineate a character in a drama. Movie stars have this function too, but simultaneously they also signify themselves. The audience does not forget the player behind the role as they may do with the actor. Furthermore, the roles of movie stars extend beyond the characters they play in the cinema and encompass their lives off screen (see Dyer 1998: 20). It hardly needs saying that much of the information available to fans (in so far as it comes from sources within the control of the star's publicity machine – press conferences and releases, personal appearances, fan magazines, gossip columns, television and radio interviews) is no less a construction than the on-screen character parts. Like screen actors, pop stars have dual roles, although it may be less obvious in their case because the gap between their performances and lives is usually narrower than in drama.

Taking up the perspective of those who consume the star image, it is clear that fans have a strong desire to discover as much as possible about not only their professional roles but also their private lives. Typically, the more fans find out about the object of their desire, the more they want to know. Like movie stars, pop stars connote some significance more subtle than they denote. Often what the star in any medium connotes is semi-consciously apprehended rather than fully comprehended by fans. The latter may well find it difficult to put a star's meaning or value into analytical words. In part this is usually because those qualities are communicated to them as much by actions, looks (physical appearance, costume, hair-style, make-up, gesture) or sound (the timbre of the voice, characteristic intonation patterns or speech rhythms) as by what is said. But where fans find they cannot analyse exactly what their heroes mean, their very inscrutability adds to the sense of charisma and magic surrounding the personalities of stars. Publicity agents work hard to create such an aura around the figures they offer to the public as stars for the simple reason that fans require to experience this sense of something magical about their heroes if they are to recognise them as stars. It follows in Jungian terms that while a star's image is propagated as a sign, it is received by his or her fans as a symbol. This holds true whether the star's image remains more or less constant throughout his or her career (Tom Jones and Barry Manilow being cases in point) or changes radically from time to time (as have those of Michael Jackson and Madonna). The needs of the audience can be projected as effectively on a pop star as a film star because, for a fan, the admired star carries a distinctive archetypal energy, as the following two case studies make clear.

Androgyny and stardom: cultural meanings of Michael Jackson

Previous chapters have highlighted the contrasexual archetypes – the anima and animus – and have shown instances of their representation on screen. But there exist also powerful myth-bearing figures that mix the two genders. In contemporary popular culture, the androgyne is current as an adolescent figure upon whom are projected the desires of a great many pre-teens and teenagers. The popularity of such figures is sometimes explained through the suggestion that they provide young people with an image that is simultaneously sexy and reassuring. The androgynous star, whether David Bowie, Annie Lennox or Boy George (that is, whatever the gender or private sexual orientation of the individual behind the mask), has an image that displays male and female sexual characteristics with dual emphasis. It is sometimes argued that s/he projects an unthreatening sexuality because of these features. Young girls in particular are said to be able to identify with the androgyne before they attain their own full sexual maturity. The case of Michael Jackson suggests that this explanation may be partially true, but that it leaves a lot unsaid.

The sexually immature androgyne has celebrated forebears. Barbara Greenfield has identified one carrier of the relevant archetypal image in a figure she names (with reference to its classical origins) 'the flower boy'. (We shall encounter other androgynous figures later in the child, the berdache and the syzygy.) Examples of the flower boy in mythology include Adonis, the boy lover of Venus, who was killed when hunting – in other words, when prematurely asserting his independence as a man. Another was Hyacinth: he died in the attempt to compete on equal terms with his mentor (and lover) Apollo, only to be reclaimed by the mothering earth, from which he arose again as a flower. Greenfield says that the appeal of such a boy to girls may be that he is not only young and beautiful, but that he is not yet powerful enough to be threatening. Meanwhile, some older women find that a beautiful boy arouses the desire to mother him. From a Jungian perspective, Greenfield argues that flower boys like these represent a time in life when ego consciousness is a fragile thing. In that phase of life, it remains still at risk of being drawn back into a state of unity with the mother (the unconscious) (Greenfield 1985: 193–4).

Although we shall recognise the signs of the flower boy in Michael Jackson's image, there are other aspects to the pleasure his figure communicates. As Barbara Ehrenreich, Elizabeth Hess and Gloria Jacobs recall, in the early 1960s the Beatles shocked adults and appealed to adolescent girls through the ambiguous sexuality their long hair seemed to connote (Ehrenreich *et al.* 1992: 101–2). For some girls the attraction may indeed have been that the mixed-gender markers sported by the boys made these others seem less sexually threatening than, for instance, the full-blown masculinity of Elvis. But the Beatles were a band, not solo artists. The idea of a pack of flower boys seems absurd, given that young men usually gather in groups to enhance their sense of power. Thus their collective image, like that of Michael Jackson, could be read in a number of ways. For instance, their single most distinctive visual symbol, the famous shoulder-length hair, carried different meanings for different people. For many middle-aged people in Europe and the USA who had grown up with the convention that a short back and sides cut was the only hairstyle that declared a frankly masculine nature, long hair on men made for an all-too-visible and suspicious break with gender uniformity. Time and again young men heard their elders complain that they looked just like girls, an accusation that left open notions of licentiousness too shameful to specify. Further, by invoking such a dark confusion of symbolic categories, long male hair was often read (no doubt by those displacing anxieties aroused by the threat to gender boundaries) as a sign of dirtiness. As Raymond Firth observed, what exacerbated public reaction was the realisation that long male hair was a symbol for deliberate, quasi-political protest against society. Well aware of this, many young men of orthodox and demure heterosexual orientation let their hair grow long as a mark of freedom from the repressed values of their parents' generation (Firth 1973: 276–7).

The Beatles' appearance could be read either as a mark of youthful rebellion or as sexually androgynous, depending on one's perspective. Ehrenreich *et al.* think it likely that the Beatles' sexuality did convey to young women attractive muted suggestions of androgyny because it lifted sex out of the rigid scenario of mid-century American (and we may add British) gender roles. Hitherto, sex, for very young women at least, had been seen as leading directly to marriage and domesticity, but the Beatles treated sex more casually and playfully. They suggested to girls not only that it could be guileless and fun, but also that they could identify with members of the band and seize the power these boys from nowhere had taken, to shape their own lives (Ehrenreich *et al.* 1992: 102–3).

In the 1970s and 1980s, Michael Jackson was in some of these respects one of the Beatles' successors for a new generation of teenagers; but he did not simply replicate the Beatles' appeal. As a solo artist over changing times, he too projected a complex of values. Some embodied the vulnerability of the flower boy; and read in this way today, his girlish voice, long hair, cosmetic surgery and pallid facial make-up supply markers of an insistent feminine softness. Thus, even in his mid-thirties, Jackson was still invoking the archetype of the juvenile androgyne. However, these signs were vividly counterpointed by potent adolescent signifiers of rebellious maleness such as the crotch-grabbing dance routine and the parodies of military costumes. Members of his audience who looked no further could easily read his image (as many did) in one of two complementary ways – either as the unthreatening male, or as the sexual idol who would liberate the young from the bonds of the previous generation's middle-aged and repressive sexuality. The latter image, of the teen hero as a liberator from parental culture, has recurred time and again since its discovery in the mid-1950s as one of the fundamentally marketable stereotypes for an emerging teen culture.

Paradoxically, Michael Jackson's image may actually have offered as much reassurance to young men as young women. The need for it could be due to the impact of feminist values on the culture of young people. Starting in the early 1980s, many young men in school and college in the USA or Britain encountered a new, healthily anti-sexist orthodoxy endorsed not only by their teachers but also by their peers. One product of this orthodoxy, emerging towards the end of the decade, was the idea of the New Man (or Soft Male), a figure who had supposedly discarded (along with many other features of unreconstructed maleness) his old sexual aggressiveness, substituting for it a caring sensitivity. For many young men, however, this new cultural model had too much in common with the faded flower boy to symbolise the urgent drive of the young male sexual hunter. While they might have paid lip service to the pieties of the new sexual decorum, young men transferred their allegiance back to older models of conduct when they were actually out with their friends.

The interesting thing about Michael Jackson's double image as flower boy *and* rebellious youth is that these two can be mapped on to the roles represented by the New Man and the macho male. In other words, Jackson's performances neatly supplied, for the early adolescent young men whose need was to find it, an illusory bridge across the gulf between the two modes of sexual address. Identifying with his image may have helped them persuade themselves that the gentle lover and the macho man are the same thing. In fact, of course, they are far from identical, and this duplicity is merely one instance in which we shall find that concealed splits in the Jackson image mask potentially dangerous conflicts.

For instance, aspects of the Michael Jackson image attract a number of projections that have an unexpectedly dark feeling-tone. A case in point occurs in the videos that repeatedly associate the hero with images of powerful beasts of prey – figures which are well-known metaphors for awakened male sexuality. In *Thriller* a hitherto gentle Michael, who has been sweetly keeping company with his girl, suddenly metamorphoses into a wolf. This image, a shorthand metaphor for rapacious male appetite, springs straight out of the horror genre. Kobena Mercer has argued that the meaning of the metamorphosis is undermined by the incongruity of the college-boy jacket the wolf-man is wearing (Mercer 1991: 311). However, even if seen this way by the spectator, Jackson's association with an aggressive male sexuality still has had to be denied, and opposites are never far to seek in his videos. Mercer believes that, located as they are in the tradition of African-American music, Jackson's androgynous performances challenge dominant stereotypes of macho black masculinity. For this reason he celebrates them as pleasantly subversive (ibid.: 314). But as we have just seen, they could be taken just as subversively as celebrating macho sexuality in an age which had abandoned it, seemingly.

We see further evidence of image/meaning splitting along a different axis in the way in which, in the 1980s, Jackson's appeal appeared actually to have been designed by his image-makers and marketing advisers to straddle the generation gap. Audiences (as they had been twenty-five years earlier with the Beatles) were invited to read his androgynous image in two quite contradictory ways. He was presented to younger viewers as exciting and sexy; yet he appealed to their parents' generation as safe and squeaky clean. Each part of the audience (in part precisely because many of the older group had in their time been fans of bands such as the Beatles and the Rolling Stones) was positioned to ignore this potentially explosive conjunction of opposites. And the rhetorical and commercial success of the strategy of meaning-splitting was signalled when Pepsi-Cola (perhaps not having learned its lesson with an earlier androgynous spokesperson, Joan Crawford) used Jackson to front a major advertising campaign. All in all, as Mercer says, his image attracted and maintained the kind of cultural fascination that made him more like a movie-star than a singer. His face could be thought of as a mask, an aesthetic surface on which society writ large its own preoccupations (ibid.: 313–14).

It has for many decades been typical of Hollywood movies that they are constructed so as to allow different members of their audiences to project entirely contradictory meanings, opinions and beliefs on to their characters and narrative. The ambiguity helps to increase the size of the audience. The music-video industry (in part because of shared owner-ship) simply imitated the practice of the movie business in recognising the commercial benefit of having things both ways. In marketing terms, that is the single most characteristic feature of the music video's postmodernist aesthetics: among students of communication, it is widely recognised that (in the sampling of fragments of imagery, sound and narrative from ear-lier, 'classic' texts) such videos split their signifiers. However, they also bring about a splitting of signifieds. Put less formally, the dazzling abun-dance of references with which the typical postmodernist text sparkles encourages the consumer to find support for whatever values she or he brings to it. Every viewer and listener can be satisfied, so long as they buy the video – or donate the consumer time to watching it.

Because of its diversity of sources, the postmodernist video text ap-pears to be ideologically neutral in its impact, but this claim is plainly disingenuous in relation to its base in and advantage to the image and music industries. Further, such a claim fails to account for what happens when certain images and sounds impact in a way that is experienced as peculiarly potent. And of course it is precisely this emotional potency which causes viewers to inscribe their own desires and fears on to the mask that the star presents to them, driving people, for instance, to make sense for themselves of the multiple meanings that can circulate around a figure such as Michael Jackson.

Considered from a Jungian perspective, the figure of the androgyne – one of the principal symbols with which Jackson is associated – is readily identifiable as an archetypal image precisely because of its fascinating powers. Beyond the ambivalence it arouses in members of our own society, we can easily find evidence that the image of the androgyne has been, in a number of cultures, the vehicle for both positive and negative meanings even more deeply coloured than those we have already touched upon. Positively charged androgynous images include those of the berdache in American Indian culture. These were men living and marrying as women, and honoured by their tribes because of their spiritual leadership. According to Hopcke, they lived out an identification with the androgyne, and were therefore associated with spiritual transformation and meditation (Hopcke 1991: 174–6). Further, a number of figures in religion and myth are associated with deity and endowed with androgynous qualities. The best known of these in the western world is Christ. While all androgynous figures exhibit a common function in that their dual sexuality is an obvious mystery, when positively charged this archetypal image draws the mind on to contemplation of the secret mysteries with which all religions are concerned. Such images do this by deploying the energy which imbues such figures with numinous potency to juxtapose the mind's unconscious disposition to its conscious orientation. The positive androgyne represents the harmonious integration of unconscious drives with consciousness. Conversely, it appears that images of negative androgynes may occur when an imbalance between the unconscious and the conscious needs to be resolved. Then the androgyne can be the vehicle for unconscious energies which are attempting to force themselves into consciousness. We could mention, among the images of accursed androgynes in European mythology, Tiresias, condemned to blindness for his too-complete knowledge of human sexuality, yet given the power to foresee the future by way of compensation. After him come numerous female witches who have distinctively male characteristics accompanied by the power not only to foretell, but also to shape malevolently, what is to come.

It should come as no surprise to find that Jackson's videos incorporate motifs hinting at the monstrous androgyne, including those that tend toward the Frankensteinian. For instance, in the early 1990s the long hair always had a single dishevelled lock falling forward like a crack in the face of a china doll. And one of his trademarks, a single glove, was often fingerless and ragged. It looked like a bandage. As such it brought to mind the cosmetic surgery done to his face and the popular suspicion that his pasty new complexion was the result of unsuccessful repair work. An interesting sign of the way his image continues to be pulled towards the pathological is the fact that doubts have persisted despite Jackson's claim to Oprah Winfrey in 1993 that his pallor had been caused by a medical condition. Here hints of the monstrous in his image come into conjunction with its infantilism, each aspect intensifying the other.

By the early 1990s, Jackson's performances had been presenting audiences with this conjunction for some years: at age 35 he was still evoking the archetype of the (damaged) juvenile androgyne. The signs implicit in the stage and video performances were reinforced by his appearance on a special show hosted by Oprah Winfrey, in which he guided television viewers round his personal Xanadu. (Complete with theatre, carousel and rides, this fabled haven turned out to be nothing less than a child's private theme park. The more bizarre signifiers could be read as implying the psychic damage done to the Peter Pan lost-boy figure by endlessly prolonging childhood.) Mapping Jackson's performances back on to his own life (as the Oprah Winfrey special encouraged us to do), we found that both his girlish mannerisms and the constant gesturing towards his genitals could be read equally well as signs of a deeply unsure masculinity, as of the great potency his hold on the box office suggested.

The enormous scandal that broke in the summer of 1993 played directly on, and greatly amplified, these contrary indications. If confirmation were needed that, along with its other meanings, Jackson's image resonated with something latent in the psyche of considerable numbers of people in North America and beyond, that confirmation came brutally in the instant press response to allegations that he had sexually exploited under-age boys. Although neither charge nor proof of guilt had been brought, massive media coverage was given to the story in both the US and Britain, and it was immediately asserted that his image would be fatally sullied whatever the truth of the matter might turn out to be. Even journalists who reported that Jackson might be the victim of a well-orchestrated extortion attempt confidently predicted that Pepsi would have to cancel the advertising deal and that his career would be in ruins. Jackson did call off his 1993 tour before it had reached its end, and Pepsi-Cola cancelled its deal, claiming that the corporation's obligation had ended because it had undertaken only to sponsor the tour. But in January 1994 Jackson's legal representatives agreed to an out-of-court settlement with the family of a 14-year-old boy who had made the original allegations of misconduct and laid formal charges against him, without an admission of guilt by the singer, who went on to marry Elvis Presley's daughter.

What were the particular cultural and psychological factors with which Jackson's public image and alleged private misdemeanours intersected? How do these help to explain the sudden reversal of the numinous energy that Jackson's presence conveyed and the cynicism with which his continuing popularity is received by the press? To phrase the issue in Jungian terms, what had happened to the sophisticatedly innocent side of the singer's image (an aspect charged with intense archetypal energy for many of his fans)? Had it suffered total eclipse – and if so, why were his many fans still supporting a fallen idol?

At least some parts of an answer are found in the record of a conversation between James Hillman and Michael Ventura. When discussing the sexual abuse of children, they argue that although it has always been inexcusable behaviour, it has actually been going on forever. However, the *obsession* with child abuse is something new, a phenomenon of the 1980s and 1990s, a fact suggesting that a culturally specific syndrome has seized white America and much of Europe. Describing it as an obsession with childhood, Hillman and Ventura trace its source to the prevalent (and erroneous) notion that we are born innocent, which the popularising of psychoanalysis has done much to propagate. The misconception advances on these lines:

1. We are born innocent and happy
2. In adulthood we are neurotic and wretched and have been robbed of our birthright to enduring happiness
3. Since psychoanalytical theory has taught us to look to the first years of our lives to find the source of our current miseries
4. it seems to follow the most casual inquiry that our innocence and happiness must have been stolen from us in childhood.

As a consequence of this new logic of disappointment's development, an obsessive centring on childhood has come to implicate many of the cultural values of North America and Europe as specifically child-abusing. Plain evidence for the power of this conviction is found in the huge numbers of individuals seeking to regain that supposed innocence by purging the hell they believe they must have suffered when they were children, and doing it sometimes on the flimsiest of evidential bases with the help of psychotherapists (Hillman and Ventura 1992: 191–3).

Where a particular figure is loaded with emotional significance for large numbers of people, there an archetypal image is discovered. The abused yet abusing child therefore must be such a figure. In one respect, we can say that its origins reach back deep into folk memories and can be traced there through fairy-tales. But we can also see, as the history of Michael Jackson indicates, that its manifestation in the mid-1990s through his image was a culturally specific episode. It resonated with the unconscious of large numbers of people in Western societies who found themselves becoming absorbed by emotions generated by the allegations about his behaviour.

One of the functions of the child archetype is, obviously enough, to recall the experiences and emotions of childhood. This archetype thus has a compensatory function in a culture bent on early specialisation because, as we saw in chapter 4, it provides access to a more holistic youth that has been lost. It also looks forward to the future and a form of rebirth. As Jung remarked, it is not surprising that so many of the mythological saviours are child gods. Indeed, many of them were androgynous, a factor which reinforced their significance as symbols pointing forward to a goal not yet reached, the *conjunctio oppositorum*, unification of the most striking opposites, the two sharply divided regions of the psyche (Jung 1951: 162–4, 173–4).

But if the child archetype is intended, like an actual child born into a middle-aged family, as an unqualified boon, a sign of hope, why then has its manifestation in Michael Jackson been so ambivalent? Again, to find the answer, we have to look at the career of the star. First, Jackson is someone who has notoriously long since left childhood behind, and has had himself operated upon to erase even the links to that childhood in his physical features, to a degree that Judy Garland and Mickey Rooney never dreamed of. Secondly, and speaking strictly of the archetype as a metaphor, there is an important sense in which many western cultures are massively predisposed towards abuse of the child in the psyche because its symbolic and archetypal qualities are ignored. The very fixation upon childhood described above is actually a symptom of this abuse. The infantile obsession with 'rediscovering' a false innocence occupies the mind with a distorting personal vision which closes off the possibility of seeing the child as the numinous, almost impersonal image that an archetypal representation can be. It is an operation on the child, a perversion of him/her. As Jung taught us, the archetypal child symbolises not only the things that have been lost with the passing of time (not a supposed innocence, but a vivid immediacy of contact with the intuitions and emotions), but also what the future will bring: it is a figure that frequently heralds rebirth both in the individual and the community.

In a number of ways, the infantilism surrounding Jackson has signalled a destructive failure to recognise the archetypal child and, in many ways, a reversal of the values attaching to it. Rather than imply the future this image, like the Reagan era in which it was born, represented an attempt to stop the clock. In a wider sense, it stood for the distortion to the point of absurdity of the desire for unending youth. This desire is so common in western cultures in the second half of the twentieth century in part because advertising has done so much to nurture the appeal of goods and service though association with images of young and beautiful people. The advertiser's calculation is that the desire to possess through their images these succulent but unattainable young bodies will transfer to the purchasable goods with which they are associated. But undoubtedly not all that introjected energy transfers, and the residue leaves many people who are no longer young experiencing the aching need for youth – either by preserving it artificially in themselves or by capturing it through those who are young. Here again is a culturally specific manifestation arising from the group unconscious.

The child god or hero, often abandoned and in danger, is 'smaller than small'. This child hero's awesome power, which makes it 'bigger than big', arises from his vulnerability, the uncertainty of his origins (Jung 1951: 165–7). By the 1980s, however, Jackson was universally recognised as a megastar, a figure surrounded by an army of managers, agents, spokespeople, lawyers, and domestic employees – not to mention his musicians, dancers and fans. He was not a child but an adult masquerading as a sexually precocious child, and his origins were well documented. If, then, it is correct to speculate that in his new Disneyland incarnation he had become the object of widespread infantile projection, those who underwent such a fixation on him would have been blocking, along with their star, their rediscovery of what they had really left behind in childhood. In effect the fixation upon a false image of childhood actually suppressed the true archetype of the child.

A symbol representing something distressing the psyche of those who were preoccupied with his fate, what happened to Michael Jackson's image in 1993–4 demonstrates vividly what occurs when energy constellated by an archetype is repressed.

It is an axiom of psychology that when a part of the psyche is split off from consciousness it is only *apparently* inactivated; in actual fact it brings about a possession of the personality, with the result that the individual's aims are falsified in the interests of the split-off part. If, then, the childhood state of the collective psyche is repressed to the point of total exclusion, the unconscious content overwhelms the conscious aim and inhibits, falsifies, even destroys its realisation. Viable progress only comes from the co-operation of both. (Jung 1951: 164)

Read symbolically, the boy who charged that Jackson had sexually interfered with him was actually effecting the reactivation and return of the child archetype that had been repressed. Jackson began to stand not for the renewal of conscious connection with the unconscious, but for its denial, even its suppression. His image became suddenly the symptom of the deep and widespread reluctance to face the disruptive, often painful energies of a creativity that does not seek to hold the child in place.

Yet, even in Jackson's work, there have been hopeful hints of an eventual recovery of the transpersonal. We must therefore be grateful for the occasional glimpses of the positive and joyous androgyne, the ancient symbol of union. A striking example comes in the video *Black or White*, released just as the scandal was breaking, when the singer's mask metamorphoses into the beautiful faces of a succession of women and men. These young people, who come from many races, are welded by computer-driven dissolves through time into one – a representation both male and female and multiracial. The magic of the new technology makes the blending of all these people into one composite being a fitting image for not only the multicultural societal unity that is the song's theme, but also the free communication of conscious and unconscious that is the present possibility in an age when images can reproduce and metamorphose freely.

A goddess who comes? Madonna as trickster

The image of Madonna, possibly the most famous female media star of her epoch, makes an interesting comparison with that of Michael Jackson. On the surface rather similar in terms of its marked ambivalence, the underlying thrust of the meaning values surrounding her is quite distinct from those generated around Jackson.

When we categorise Madonna's public personality in terms recognised in analytical psychology, we find it belongs to two large classes of archetypal images. Her stage name registers the first of these obviously in that she projects herself as a type of goddess.[6] The second is the *trickster*, a figure which Jung found recurring in numerous places including dreams, myths, religious iconography and rituals, and of which we have seen a restrained example in the case of Jules in *Diva*.

As Jung observed it, the trickster took many different forms. However, almost all of them were male (Jung 1956b: 255–72). Although, as we have mentioned, Jung's imperfect attention to the myths of women has been remedied by a number of his American followers, the archetypal figure of the trickster has not attracted much attention in the arenas of feminism. This may well be because its awkward, irritating characteristics, its unpredictable mannerisms and abrupt reversals of behaviour do not sit comfortably with the self-images of women as they have evolved through the late twentieth century. The trickster is too erratic, too disruptive to be

---

[6] Although Madonna was given this name by her parents, the decision to use it alone without her surname has in effect turned it into a stage name.

a welcome companion on women's route to full self-realisation. No matter how uncomfortable its presence, however, recognition of the trickster can be no less empowering for women than men.

What, then, are the traits of the trickster archetype as Jung discovered it? In common with every other archetypal image that he identified, it embraces the extreme poles of an opposition. To take a rudimentary example, we associate water both with life (because we must drink to survive) and death (it drowns those who fall in it). Such contradictions, in defiance of logic, are an essential feature of the archetypal image. In the case of the trickster archetype, its marked duality consists in its representing simultaneously both the animal and the divine; it is a figure that manages to be both inferior and superior to humanity.

In Europe, the trickster has been seen plainly as a leading player in all those mediaeval customs in which misrule overturns accepted order. He is present too in folklore, carnival, revels and picaresque tales (Jung 1956b: 255–60). Frequently no less grotesque, scurrilous and violent than Punch (one of his numerous manifestations), he may be as unconscious of self as a circus clown, or insinuating as a jester. Significantly, he cannot be tied down: he is a shape shifter, appearing at one moment in one form, only to transmute and make his next entrance in quite another. Such versatility matches his function in running counter to the orientation of the individual's conscious mind. Thus Jung found that in modern life, at the trivial level of personal embarrassment, the trickster disturbs conscious intent with gaffes and *faux pas*. Or, more distressingly, the same archetype may afflict the person who seems suddenly to be at the mercy of a succession of annoying 'accidents' (ibid.: 262).

The trickster is not, however, an exclusively negative figure. Virtually every quality Jung attributes to him maps on to the figure of Mercurius (Mercury), who in turn reproduces the character of the classical Hermes. On the dark side, the latter is a god of thieves and cheats, but at the same time he is also, in his role of messenger, a god of revelation (Jung 1948a: 230–4). That is the very role he played, through Jules, for Cynthia Hawkins in *Diva*. His rooted duality means that he consists of all possible opposites, both material and spiritual. Jung describes him as 'the process by which the lower and material is transformed into the higher and spiritual, and vice versa'. He is potentially both salvific and demonic. Not surprising, then, that the trickster myth can express a longing for the coming of the saviour.

In psychological terms, the trickster's turning away from stupidity towards a measure of good sense indicates that some calamity has either occurred and been overcome, or has been foreseen and integrated at a deep level. In other words the image of the trickster (like every other archetype) contains the seed of a conversion into its opposite (Jung 1956b: 266, 271–2). Jung (naming this principle *enantiodromia*) identified a tendency for every psychological extreme to contain its own opposite and to run towards it.

As a figure of myth (a mythologem) the significance of the trickster is both wider than, but yet linked to, the history of any one individual. For in the history of both the individual and the collective, Jung argues, everything depends on the development of consciousness – and here lies the importance of the trickster figure. Its function is to hold an older, less civilised state of consciousness in conscious view. On the surface of things this is unexpected because, as Jung remarks, we might anticipate that with the progressive development of consciousness the older, cruder version would fall away and disappear. In practice the trickster has been actively sustained and promoted by consciousness as a reference point. The confirmation of this lies in the fact that, far from being subject to repression, this mythologem is frequently a figure of fun which has often given widespread social pleasure.

When recollection of the trickster occurs, it is mainly due to the interest which the conscious mind brings to him, recalling him from the darkness. When that happens, an inevitable concomitant is 'the gradual civilising of a primitive daemonic figure who was originally autonomous and even capable of causing possession' (Jung 1956b: 265, 267; Samuels 1990: 270). Conversely, the absence of the figure in social ritual can be sinister in its implications. When this occurs, a form of repression has taken place, whereupon the contents secreted in the unconscious gradually gain in dynamic energy so that they eventually force an irruption somewhere in the psyche. If they are brought back to the realm of consciousness, they may constellate once again as an image bearing the characteristics of the trickster. If, however, they are unrecognised (that is, refused by consciousness) they may enforce their return as dangerous shadow images which both individuals and the collective project in ignorance of their true meaning on those whom they take to be their enemies. Present-day Europe reveals numerous instances (for example, Northern Ireland and the former Yugoslavia) of entire communities projecting such dark shadows 'over the border' on to their neighbours – who in turn project their own deepest shadows back the other way. It is only a matter of time before inner repression becomes social conflict, perhaps even war. If the anarchic activities of the trickster can (in whatever social arena) inhibit the projection by powerful social groups of such daemonic collective psychological energies onto the victims they intuitively seek out for the split-off shadow, then the value of cultivating this mythologem needs no further demonstration.

Madonna's social arena is not (yet) that of international and intercommunal politics. But for a long time it was that of sexual politics. And for Jungians no less than Freudians this is a particularly interesting field of human activity because it directly links social and cultural practice (and beyond that, certain features of social policy) to the emotional life both of individuals and the collective. As we have remarked previously, Jungian theory holds that changes in human affairs (whether relating to an individual's selfhood or the dominant social ethos) are led through the experience of emotions. Emotions in their turn may be aroused either by personal circumstances or by images and events that occur whether in the objective or the collectively apprehended world. Inevitably we are talking about an image collectively experienced in discussing an immensely popular star who exerts a fascination, as Madonna has done for many years, which all those feel who both love and hate what they take her to stand for. No question then but that her fans apprehend her as an image carrying an archetypal energy, which they recognise through what they perceive as her numinosity or magical charge. She is to them in part a mysterious figure, the full power of which the conscious mind feels readily enough, but has difficulty in understanding. Like other archetypal images, Madonna's image is a centre of energy around which ideas, images, affects and myths cohere. However, she is also, like Michael Jackson, a signifier of the group or cultural unconscious in ways which we explored in chapter 3. That is to say, her image carries an archetypal charge to which her fans and perhaps those who strongly dislike her image respond – but to which others are indifferent. The fans seem to use it as a repository of cultural experience. It is as though her image were the content filling out the empty template of their cultural needs so that she becomes a kind of record of where their intuitions have taken, and are taking them, in the company of a large group of their fellow beings. And simultaneously her image is used as the means of concretising their sense of cultural difference from their peers (see Samuels 1993: 328). Since the same can be said of Jackson's image, it follows that a fan of either star is not necessarily a fan of the (or indeed *any*) other.

Accepting that Madonna's image does function to give body to the cultural unconscious, the shape-shifting characteristic of her work carries with it the risk that her image may jump cultural boundaries that not all her fans are capable of crossing. On the other hand if she does carry them with her, as the immediate success of *Frozen* implies, she may draw them into an unexpected and ultimately civilising interior journey.

Jung demonstrated that every individual experiences the grip of a variety of archetypes in the course of a lifetime. However, as has already been said, he proved most adept at elaborating the archetypes that govern the lives and psyches of men. In redressing the balance, feminist Jungians have in recent years worked at identifying archetypal images that inform the lives of women. In the process, while building on the work of sympathetic archaeo-mythologists such as Marija Gimbutas, they returned to European pre-history and discovered that the dominance of male gods both in the Christian pantheon and in several of the world's most powerful faiths has not been the timeless phenomenon the faiths themselves declare. On the contrary, long before the accession of the male gods the peoples of Old Europe worshipped the Great Goddess, and the male principle had little if any place in their belief system. The gifts of life and death, feast and famine were all in the hands of the Goddess. The symbols of her energy included chevrons, vulvae, snakes, spirals, sprouting seeds and shoots; and images of warfare were strikingly absent from art centred on her (Gimbutas 1989: xvii–xx).

All this changed with the invasion of cattle-herding Indo-European tribes who overran Europe between 3500 and 2500 BC. They imposed their patriarchal culture and bellicose male gods on the conquered people. Yet as Gimbutas and Jean Shinoda Bolen show, the Great Goddess did not disappear without trace. She became the subservient consort of the invaders' gods, and most of the attributes of power that originally belonged to her were given to a male deity. Other attributes were divided among less powerful goddesses. In this way many of her symbols were subsumed into the new patriarchal mythologies. For example, the Birth Giver and the Earth Mother aspects of the Goddess eventually fused with the Virgin Mary. Meanwhile her negative aspects, formerly expressed in her function as the Mother who regenerates life from death, also split off. They became attached to the many women who learned the occult secrets of the Goddess and kept them alive (Gimbutas 1989: 318–19; Bolen 1985: 20–1). Thus the satanic witch hunts organised by the Catholic Church from the fifteenth to the eighteenth centuries (during which more than 8 million women were murdered) can be seen as a consequence of an unbridled collective shadow projection by followers of a faith dominated by a male god. We may guess that, driven by fear of the dethroned Goddess's continuing potency, they projected negative archetypal images upon women whom they believed to be her devotees, then sought to extirpate their demons by killing those whom they had caused to bear them (Jacoby 1992: 201–4). To judge by letters to the press, Madonna has for some years carried the projected shadow of many (both male and female) who loathe her. Her image is for some people malevolent enough that her trickster was tainted with the witch's darkness before she embraced the image herself in 1998.

Long before the Christian era, however, the attributes, symbols and power formerly belonging to the Great Goddess had been divided among a number of powerful Greek goddesses and their Roman successors; and it is these figures who have been recalled to the service of Jungian analysis. Bolen, for instance, has picked out seven classical goddesses who form a pantheon of archetypal images derived from the Great Goddess. On the basis of her observations as a practising analyst, Bolen argues that (whether singly or more typically clustered in groups) they represent the influence exerted by archetypes governing the lives of women.

Even a cursory look at the seven deities reveals that most of them do not at all bear on Madonna's public image. First, she in no way represents Demeter (Ceres to the Romans) who was goddess of motherhood and fertility. Sex in her routines has nothing to do with procreation, and nothing changed in this regard after she herself became a mother.

Second, she is not the child of Demeter, Persephone (the Roman Proserpina) who, in Bolen's opinion, has two dominant aspects. In one she is the Kore, the nameless maiden who does not yet know who she is, the mother's daughter, a child-woman whose sexuality is unawakened. She wears her other aspect as Queen of the Underworld, as the guide for those who visit that place. Where Persephone rules a woman may have reluctant access to her own unconscious, and may have the power to escort other women into the mysteries of their own dark realms. Clearly her first aspect does not match Madonna's public persona. But neither does the second, for although Madonna also mediates between the unconscious and conscious worlds, she is not, like Persephone, a psychological captive, the quality that enables this goddess to help other depressive women (Bolen 1985: 199–203).

Third comes Hera (or Juno), goddess of marriage. She too is not an archetype to fit Madonna, despite the latter's celebrated marital adventures. For Hera embodies an attitude to marriage much in harmony with patriarchal values. This archetype represents a woman's overwhelming desire to be a wife; she does not feel truly alive until she has a husband, and all other activities, such as career or motherhood, come second to the securing and holding of a man (ibid.: 142–3).

The fourth goddess is also completely foreign to Madonna. Hestia (whom the Romans did not represent as a human figure, but as Vesta, a flame) was goddess of the hearth. Bolen describes her as the archetype active in women who find housekeeping a meaningful activity and who through tending to chores discover inner peace and a centring activity equivalent to meditation. Her detachment shields her from the battering of external experience, and her devotion to the inner life gives her the qualities of the wise woman (ibid.: 110–13). She is like an inverted image of the singer.

When we turn to the fifth goddess, Athena (Minerva to the Romans), we meet the first of the archetypal figures who govern Madonna. As goddess of wisdom, Athena was known for her winning skill as a strategist, detached even in the heat of battle and able to plan with clear foresight. Ruled by the head, the woman led by the Athena archetype works to make something of herself: 'The equivalent of a female Horatio Alger is almost always an Athena woman' (ibid.: 78–88). Madonna, who has been described as just such an all-American, rags-to-riches hero, is celebrated for planning her career, polishing her image and relentlessly producing herself as a commodity (see Tetzlaff 1993: 258, 261). It is perhaps her one universally agreed claim to fame.

In addition to these strong resemblances, however, there are equally distinctive mismatches. Bolen observes that the Athena woman shows a tendency to do everything in moderation and to live within the Golden Mean. Indeed she lives in her mind and is often out of touch with her body; typically she is neither sensual nor sexy (Bolen 1985: 92–3).

Resemblances between Madonna and the sixth goddess, Artemis (later Diana) queen of the hunt, are not as strong, but nonetheless exist. Plainly the goddess's virginity and immunity to falling in love have no meaning for the star; but they share the focused intensity and perseverance that Bolen itemises as Artemis' other dominant characteristics. They endow her with the ability to aim and hit the target no matter what the distractions. And there is another important connection with Madonna's public image in that (like today's Artemis women) she treats sex as a recreational sport or a physical experience rather than as an expression of emotional intimacy or commitment (ibid.: 49–50, 60).

In this important detail, then, Madonna's sexual behaviour differs from what might be expected of a woman under the influence of Aphrodite (Venus), the seventh and most potent goddess in Bolen's pantheon, who 'governs women's enjoyment of love and beauty, sexuality and sensuality'. Like Aphrodite, Madonna has potent sex appeal and falls in love easily; she also displays every sign of being overwhelmed by eroticism. But unlike the goddess she does not represent the drive to procreate; nor does she seem to want to become involved to the point of merging with her partner, but rather, Artemis-like, expresses an interest in enjoying the physical experience.

Both Aphrodite and Madonna are tremendous forces for change; and this connects with not only their sexual but also their artistic fertility. Bolen argues that creative work springs from an intense and passionate involvement almost like that with a lover, as the artist interacts with the 'other' to bring something new into being. But while dedication to her work makes Madonna a true Aphrodite woman, there is a significant difference. Women ruled by this goddess tend to live in the immediate present, taking life as if it were no more than a sensory experience and there were no future consequences to their actions (ibid.: 238–41, 255). In this respect, as we have seen, Madonna, a clever strategist, is much closer to Athena.

Thus the two virgin goddesses Athena and Artemis, together with the goddess of love Aphrodite, furnish archetypal images that frame and energise a number of elements of Madonna's public personality. But they do not account for the entire personality for two reasons. First, she is a shape-shifter, only constant like the virgin goddesses in her certainty of aim and command of strategy. Second, her performances, despite her passionate commitment to them noted above, often lack the resonance of lived emotional experience: Madonna seems not to be celebrating love and sexuality in their own right so much as playing with the idea of them, even while she is making them the one constant theme wound through her countless metamorphoses.

Many commentators have noticed these qualities. For example, E. Deirdre Pribram and David Tetzlaff concur in labelling her a chameleon of appearances who refuses all fixed meanings. Behind the postmodern play with masks there is no authentic Madonna, no personal or inspirational centre to the vision (Pribram 1993: 202; Tetzlaff 1993: 255–6). Tetzlaff calls her the Teflon idol.

Nothing sticks to her. The sleaze, the blasphemy, the perversity all slide off. Perhaps the audience recognises that Madonna only inhabits these positions as if she were modelling a collection of fashions . . . unaffected for having worn them for a while. This is represented in the videos themselves, which always end with Madonna seemingly unfazed by the cultures and struggles she has encountered, dancing off screen to the perky disco bounce. (Tetzlaff 1993: 259)

As these remarks hint, Madonna has something in common with the male trickster both in shape-shifting and sexual ambivalence. The shapes and roles she has chosen to perform and then discarded are extraordinarily diverse. We can add to them the roles that her fans and critics have discovered in her acts, through either wish-fulfilment or revulsion playing upon deliberately ambiguous film editing – a further sign of the power of the cultural unconscious to find appropriate contents with which to fill its forms. Earlier personae included the Boy Toy and the Bitch. Later on in the music videos *Justify My Love* and *Express Yourself* her sexual roles were seen as those of a heterosexual partner, lover of a gay man, of an androgynous man/woman, and of a lesbian; she has also dallied with masochism and sadism, and played at group sex. Then, in her stage rendering of 'Like a Virgin' for *In Bed With Madonna (Truth or Dare)*, she simulated masturbation; and seen backstage in the same documentary film, she entertained her dancers by mock-fellating a bottle and hinting that she might be a gay male, claiming that the sight of two men kissing would give her a hard-on.

No question then but she has played to the lesbian and gay audience. Just as some feminists tried to recruit her uninhibited sexuality to support their gender politics, so some lesbians and gays have sought to appropriate her rich sexual ambiguity to back gay activism. On the surface of things they had a good case, since her deployment of artifice, glamour and multiplicity appealed to them as something familiar, because gays too must use such devices to pass in straight society (Henderson 1993: 121). An important aspect of this in her 1980s and early 1990s performances was Madonna's alternation between masquerade (burlesquing feminine norms through excess) and drag (as a performance of gender reversal) (Schwichtenberg 1993: 134–5). In fact Pribram observes how in *Express Yourself* Madonna's clothing (a combination of male business suit and female corset) referred to both genders simultaneously (Pribram 1993: 198).

In practice her long parade of grotesques makes it impossible to enlist Madonna's image in support of any single cause. It is always ambiguous, if for no other reason than that which Tetzlaff notes, the routine commercial recognition that the straight audience is many times larger than the gay one.

It is simply wishful thinking to imagine that anyone who comes up with a good old-fashioned sexist interpretation of these texts is misreading them. Madonna and her creative cohorts are not stupid...After all, the media industry is still controlled by men, and men compose a large part of the mass market. (Tetzlaff 1993: 252)

Despite this adeptness and her multiple transformations, Madonna is in control of her image, not trapped by it. Indeed 'control' and 'power' are terms used repeatedly in connection with her. As Susan Bordo observes, they accumulate to give a sense that the star is self-created (Bordo 1993: 285–6). But this is also a characteristic of archetypes. Not only can they draw the lives of individuals and communities into new channels, but they are autonomous. In other words they charge images with an energy which gives them what appears to be an independent existence of their own. Of no archetype is this more true than the trickster.

Madonna's presentations appeal to (or repel) many different sorts of people in many different ways; but perhaps the one common thread that most of her fans and critics felt tugging at them in her work up to the mid-1990s was that spun from sex and power – the power of seduction, the seduction of power. We said earlier that the trickster simultaneously represents the animal and the divine in humanity. In societies like those of the western world in which sexuality is given high priority and organised religion depreciated, entry into no other sphere of activity than sex is so much desired. No other channel for desire offers so many people the gratifying illusion of power. They seem to sense that through its ecstasies sex might let them breach the limits of the body to touch immortality. Power seems even to many of the powerless to be within reach here – a perspective which informed Madonna's role as the heroine of Alan Parker's *Evita* (1997).

Of course the search for power tends to corrupt no matter where it is found; and for every sexual relationship that empowers its partners, delivering them to ecstasy, there are others dogged by misery. Far from being a romantic, lyric or even comfortable figure, the trickster invariably presents us with an awkward, uncomfortable personality as well as a persuasive, amusing prankster and sexual polymorph. This is all the more significant when we realise that Jung saw the divine as profoundly ambivalent, so that in his psychology the sexual linking of animal and divine, conscious and unconscious can equally well be positive or negative, blessed or cursed.

What then does the wide appeal of Madonna's image signify? We made the point earlier that the fact that a female trickster has emerged in the person of Madonna fits well with the enhanced standing of women – the trickster masked in a star persona confirms that she is not to be taken as pliable. A creature of infinite variety, she bends only to her own whim, not to the fancy of man. Perhaps there is some kind of role model for young women here; however, it is worth suggesting that a model who in the past offered so much parodic sex with so little emotion was not in the longer term a reliable one.

We should therefore go further than this. Jung's writings lament the way in which twentieth-century western humanity continues to bring many of its worst pains upon itself. Complacent in the knowledge of advances in human consciousness which science and technology daily confirm, civilised people undervalue the unconscious. Whether we forget it, repress it or devalue it by ridiculing an interest in the activity of the unconscious as superstition, we cut ourselves off from it at our peril, he argued. The trickster keeps an older state of consciousness in our minds. The rambunctious and downright irritating nature of this mythologem's presence reminds us, however, that among the other characteristics of earlier states of consciousness was an openness to the kinds of intrusion of unconscious impulses that the trickster herself represents.

One strand of imagery that Madonna often favours, and which supplies recurring parodic references to Catholicism, consists of icons such as the crosses and stigmata she receives on her hands in the video *Like A Prayer*, and (more insistently than anything else) her name. She pulls all these images out of their normal context and relocates them centrally in her ceremonies of sex. We can of course say with E. Ann Kaplan that, with the aid of these religious icons, Madonna constructs a thinly disguised autobiographical account of her rebellion against a repressive Catholic upbringing; and we can agree that such an adolescent story may well appeal to some of her fans (Kaplan 1993: 162). But it is questionable whether the subversion of sexual repression accounts for the Madonna phenomenon in its entirety.

From the Jungian point of view, the intrusion of Catholic icons into Madonna's celebrations of sexuality brought into play an all but moribund set of images. They now express a dogma that has lost its spiritual and emotional excitement, and which for most people in Western cultures has no vitality. Reintroducing these icons suits well Madonna's task as trickster because it recalls to mind an older state of consciousness involved in the observance of organised religious practice and the formal approach to the unconscious. So Madonna as trickster draws the old ways back to mind, but in the absence of an effective organised religion, she placed them prior to 1998 in the setting of another fundamental human activity. Her performances proffered sexually electrified images to supply the charge by which those of her fans who (in whatever confusion or uncertainty) sensed the need for self-knowledge, might be stimulated into beginning to feel their way, so to speak, towards that inner goal. It is entirely to the point that, as it confronts our conscious selves with urgent drives and dream images that arise out of the unconscious, sex, like religion, causes us both pleasure and pain, and forces us to experience more fully both the light and the dark, promising both ecstasy and despair.

All this may seem to prepare the way for grandiose claims that Madonna is a priestess. Finally, it does not. The priestess serves organised religion and obeys a pre-existent doctrine which she ministers to the faithful. She must by definition be conscious that she is following the practices of her predecessors in her rituals while mediating between the gods and humans, between the unconscious and the conscious. Madonna may or may not be aware of what she is doing in sponsoring this kind of mediation; but she is by no means observing a doctrine.

As a trickster, however, she has something of the shaman about her. This figure, an unconscious healer, also sometimes plays tricks on people, inflicting discomfort on them (which may well rebound upon him- or herself) in the process of breaking through to and healing the psyche (Jung 1956b: 256). For the shaman is, as Maggy Anthony says, one who works by intuition and seeks a way alone, unaided and one step at a time through the wilderness of the human condition to discover who the gods are and what they say (Anthony 1990: 99). Before 1998 it might have been difficult to claim that Madonna consciously practised such powers or had special insight into the human unconscious. But nonetheless the emotional decentring caused by the force of her performances gave her imagery the catalytic power shared by trickster and shaman. It had the power to stir ancient passions and symbols in the collective unconscious of those people within her audiences in whom the appetite for the inner journey is awakening.

In 1998 with her video *Frozen*, Madonna staged a performance in which she consciously played the role of the shape-shifter, using an imaginative mix of live action, slow motion, visual overlay and computer-generated imagery to give the maximum force to her work. The result is intriguingly complex in that lyrics and imagery pull against each other in the creation of meaning, as this transcript of the opening moments reveals.

Images	*Lyrics*
The Steadicam glides in towards Madonna. Dressed in a flowing black robe, she is found in the empty wastes of a dried-up sea bed. Colour tones are exceptionally muted – blacks, greys and tints of cold blue. Madonna is not standing on, but *above*, the desert floor.	You only see what your eyes want to see. How can I feel what you want it to be? You're frozen When your heart's not open.
Her shadow takes life and snakes across the ground to her, and she takes it up and makes it her cape.	You're so consumed with how much you get, You waste your time with hate and regret. You're broken When your heart's not open.
She falls like a tower and breaks into pieces. The fragments turn	

(cont.)

Images	*Lyrics*
into crows and fly off over her as she rises unharmed from the ground.	If I could melt your heart, We'd never be apart.
Her hands weave as if performing magic, and we see that her	Give yourself to me. You are *the key*.
fingers are painted with leaves. When she next moves we see three images of her – a coven. A single crow flies over, keeping low.	Now there's no point in placing the blame, And you should know I suffer the same – If I lose you My heart will be broken.
As she dances, the black cape flies around her and she wraps herself in it, shrinks down to the ground and metamorphoses into a black dog. Yet we cut back to Madonna who is still singing.	Love is a bird. She needs to fly. Let all the hurt inside of you die. You're frozen When your heart's not open.
The dog runs past.	
Madonna continues an involved dance with the cape which winds around her in impossible shapes.	If I could melt your heart, We'd never be apart. Give yourself to me – You are *the key*."
She beckons. Clouds gather in a backlit sky which mixes through to a starlit night sky.	

Listen to the lyrics alone, and *Frozen* can be heard as a love song in which the singer calls on her cold lover to unfreeze by giving less devotion to material wealth (a nice reversal this for a one-time Material Girl) and more to love. But the pictures have nothing to do with such a scenario, and they make such a dramatic claim on the viewer's attention in their own right that they pull the words into a different frame. Madonna plays a witch or shaman, able to transform herself at will. The associations of the imagery are as dark as the robes that clothe her. She is still in a muted sense the seductress (the back of her bodice is cut in bands that bring to mind bondage costume), but she seems to invite her viewers to partake of something darker than sexual passion. The black dog and the black crow are the familiar harbingers in folklore of despair and death. Yet, having noted that, we must accept that the lyrics prevent the thought which the unaccompanied imagery alone might otherwise license – that she is acting as death's temptress.

From women's perspective it is no accident that the most potent symbol systems, of which religions are a prime example, vest power in the masculine, giving it a sacred cast. Writing in 1987, Demaris Wehr said,

As long as we live with masculine symbols for the Divine intact, we avoid the discomfiture that feminine symbols of the Divine tend to evoke. If we allow ourselves to change our religious language to feminine language, and to experience fully all the ambivalent feelings that change elicits, we can begin to comprehend the ambivalence we have toward the full power and authority of female being in general. We will begin to see the degree to which our feelings have been conditioned by the dearth of symbols of female authority in our society. (Wehr 1987: 24)

Wehr's insights enable us to go beyond the notion that the individual's self-regulating feedback is channelled through the symbol in order to implicate the social. In fact Jung himself demonstrated how the unconscious stands in compensatory relation to the conscious not only in relation to the individual but also on a collective basis. In the work he did on the great European upheavals in the first half of the twentieth century, he revealed how the propagation of archetypal images of terror led to the direct stimulation of unconscious energies through the collective unconscious. For her part, Wehr demonstrates that symbols impact on the psychology and behaviour of all sectors of our communities, and do so even when society is on the surface of things quiescent, that is, at a time when the collective unconscious does not appear to be aroused. Not only that, but when social pressures intersect with libidinous energies, they take part in shaping the archetypal images that result. The social, the cultural and the collective unconscious are linked together in a system in which each influences and interacts with the other.

The tricksters and jesters of the past were almost always male. For this reason alone the female trickster has an especial importance for women. Previously, men rather than women could violate society's norms, acting the awkward prankster, behaving unpredictably or even in a downright malevolent way, and get away with it. But women who did so would have risked being excoriated and labelled as witches. It is significant that, no matter how much Madonna has aroused anger and vilification, she has (occasional short-term banning of videos aside) neither been silenced nor pilloried. She has not suffered the witch's fate. On the contrary, in playing the trickster she has empowered herself, and now the archetype she has activated is available to help other women take first the psychological and then the socio-cultural powers they need.

Madonna's work in *Frozen* illustrates this. Her cultural allure as a media star helped to thrust the video up to the top of the popular music charts within days of its release. That fact clearly demonstrated its efficacy as a cultural symbol, and in turn makes it possible to speculate that some at least of those who were excited by it felt in it a potential to satisfy needs which they may not fully have articulated – that is of which they were by no means fully conscious. The videotape does present itself as dealing in mystery both because of the magical nature of the imagery and because lyrics and imagery interfere with each other, as we saw, in such a way that the easy explicit reading of either is made impossible by the other. And this is the point. As trickster Madonna offers her audiences, and particularly the women among them, what in earlier times saviours brought – the promise of revelations to come. But these revelations are not to be brought by an external goddess of whose coming Madonna is the advance messenger. Rather they are to come to those who respond to the invitation to look at the source of the mystery – the unconscious.

> 'Give yourself to me –
> You are *the key*.'

6 The quest of a female hero: *The Silence of the Lambs*

The mythological journey of the hero as recognised by classical Jungians represents a pattern of transformation long since rendered familiar by repetition in numerous guises across many forms of narrative art. (We took a preliminary look at a variant upon the theme in chapter 2 when we discussed Jules' progress as he first gained access to and then learnt more fully to know the Diva.) The complete journey of a hero entails a process of separation, initiation and return. The hero leaves the daylight world of ego to descend into the dark underworld, which is for Jungians the symbolic realm of the unconscious. There he faces extreme danger or defies a monster, typically suffering an injury in the process. Some would-be victors fail, or allow themselves to be seduced into staying among the shadowy forms beneath ground. But to finally claim his place as a hero he must return to the world, bringing with him the fruits of his conquest. In the *locus classicus* of this particular *topos*, the hero returns carrying the grail.

Jung describes the hero's transformation as symbolising his separation from his earlier state of consciousness. To complete the process he has to confront and break the mould of the unconscious dispositions inherited from his parents (and in particular from the mother). He does so with the intuitive goal of emerging renewed from this encounter with his innermost self. If he does so he is likely to be marked by suffering inflicted by the split from his old self, but he has his reward in bringing back either the grail itself or some knowledge of it derived from his experiences. In other words, he has made an entry into and been altered by his own unconscious psyche, in the process becoming more his own person. Joseph Campbell interprets the process in a fashion complementary to Jung in describing it as signalling a personal transformation from egoism to self-willed submission, from arrogance to humility (Campbell 1973: 30, 391).

As almost everything about this short summary declares, heroes have traditionally been male. As Mara E. Donaldson says, they have had the active role, while heroines (by equally compelling tradition) play supportive roles. They are defined either in relation to the hero or in terms of sex roles, while the hero is defined in terms of his quest (Donaldson 1987: 102). But where a woman is the hero in her own right, rather than playing the mirror to the adventures of a man, she may have to take quite another route from his, though the processes of separation, initiation and return may still mark important stages on the journey. The difference occurs because her starting-point is likely to be so different from a man's. Donaldson observes that the female hero often transforms from a position of self-negation to one of self-affirmation, and escapes from lack of self-respect to enjoy a proper self-pride. This may entail a personal development that is either primarily a spiritual quest (Donaldson and Carol P. Christ have both described that as the purpose of the woman protagonist in Margaret Atwood's *Surfacing*) or one which is predominantly social (as in Maxine Hong Kingston's *The Woman Warrior*) (Donaldson 1987: 102, 104; Christ 1976: 316–17). According to Christ the social quest more obviously embodies feminist ideals, because it entails 'a search for self in which the protagonist begins in alienation and seeks integration into a human community where... she can develop more fully'. Christ argues, however, that the spiritual quest is equally important to feminism because the latter challenges not only traditional social and political structures, but also the perception of reality that underlies and legitimates them. Fictions representing female quests have the potential to become fundamental stories with the power to create new ways of being for women in worlds newly made (Christ 1976: 317–18).

Jonathan Demme's *The Silence of the Lambs* (1990) features a trainee FBI agent as female hero. Clarice Starling (Jodie Foster) is assigned to a case which so tests her that it not only draws on all her skills as a detective, but also forces her into self-exploration to discover the reserves of strength from which to function. This search for self is social in that she seeks to establish a place in her own right as a woman in a community governed exclusively by male values. But it is rooted in the spiritual in that it brings about the awakening of a young woman who has hitherto suppressed her own feelings in order to comply with male value systems. Such acquiescence, as Christ and many other writers remark, has long typified a large number of women. Clarice is also representative of other women in that her awakening brings knowledge of her own female powers, of which she was previously not fully aware (ibid.: 325).

When we first see her, Clarice has set herself the task of competing on equal terms with the men in her squad of trainees. Whether she knows it or not, she is following the example of her father, a widowed cop who was himself killed while making an arrest before Clarice reached adolescence. An adoring daughter, she is now trying to redeem what she feels she owes him. In practice this means that she tries to do everything on terms set by men – whether it be surmounting an assault course, practising unarmed combat or disarming criminals. Labouring to perfect the physical and intellectual skills of the complete agent, the only successes Clarice recognises entail achieving the FBI's male-oriented goals on its macho terms, or, as the slogans on the assault course have it: HURT/ PAIN/ AGONY/ LOVE IT/ PRIDE. If she fails in any task, she uses that failure as the goad to intensify her efforts, just as the men do.

Her training programme is interrupted by her superior officer and mentor, Jack Crawford (Scott Glenn). He wants to make use both of her new skills and her good looks to assist him with a difficult case. She is to help capture a serial killer by teasing information about his psychology from a man uniquely placed to understand his motivation. This, her immediate target, is Dr Hannibal Lecter (Anthony Hopkins), a former psychiatrist convicted of a series of crimes so terrible that for years he has been mured up under the tightest imaginable security. Crawford's cold-blooded analysis leads him to believe that this monster may reveal more to a pretty young woman than the FBI's more experienced male behavioural scientists like himself.

From the start *The Silence of the Lambs* works hard to persuade audiences that they are watching a realistic film; and many people seem to experience the film's 'naturalism' as adding to its impact. But (as comparison of the film's events with press reports of serial killings reveals) the sense of truth that it generates does not spring from connections with actual homicides. Rather, its plausibility springs from what Todorov calls generic verisimilitude, the way the narrative conforms to the conventions of its genre – as it must if we are to find it probable. Thus in the first instance it is plausible because, as the detectives begin their investigations and the FBI trainees suffer the pains and humiliations of their initiation, the strands of well-loved plot threads seem to be weaving together. As spectators we are led in, undisturbed in our expectations of rediscovering the familiar until we come face to face with a full-blown and distressing symbol. For even in the grisly ranks of serial killers, Dr. Hannibal Lecter is a rare monster: slaughter alone does not sate him, and he eats the flesh of those he kills.

Hannibal the Cannibal becomes a symbol (in Jung's definition of the term) because he arouses intense emotions both in the other characters and the audience, and yet is so difficult to understand. His social manner is quite at odds with his deeds, and he seems in every way the highly educated man of exquisitely refined sensibilities who might otherwise represent the acme of western culture. However, far from confessing a sense of shame over his murderous pathology, he mockingly terrorises his young visitor with memories of victims relished as elegant meals.

When she visits Lecter, Clarice has to descend into the depths of the highest security wing of the prison, past guards and through a succession of locked grilles that keep her ordinary life apart from the dark and unknown world she must now explore. These are just some of the elements that lift naturalism into a symbolic reality and show that she has completed the first stage of the hero's journey – separation from her usual milieu. Meanwhile what we hear is also heightened far beyond the naturalistic, confirming that we should look to the imagination for meaning. In cinemas with Dolby sound, the auditorium itself fills with a disturbing hollow sound. Part a dull electronic music, part melancholy noise, it produces an emptiness filled by ceaseless, inhuman stirrings. In terms of genre, this susurration belongs fittingly to the horror movie (which should warn us not to place too much trust in generic verisimilitude), and it recurs whenever Clarice braves acute crisis. All these effects indicate that her entry into the basement underworld starts her on the symbolic journey into the depths of that unknown world, the unconscious, that so many heroes endure. It is a motif which will recur throughout the film on each occasion that she is forced to look into the darkness within the human soul.

On her way down to the cell, Clarice has to face increasingly brutal affronts. First she has to shake off the hospital's chief medical officer, who makes a cold-blooded pass at her. Then a psychotic killer (Miggs) insults her with grossly sexual language. However, even in this dark place she is not entirely without help. A black psychiatric nurse gently assures her that she will do well, and that he will use the security cameras to keep watch for her. He resembles the guides to the underworld who crop up in many myths, perhaps standing for the benign side of her shadow – a sign that she has unknown resources upon which she can draw for strength.

Immediately beyond Miggs' cell, in a cage of glass and steel from which he has not seen the light of day for years, is locked the monster who will become Clarice's demon. Their first exchange prepares us for the way their relationship will form. Lecter asks her what Miggs said, thus brutalising her hardly less than Miggs. Even though prepared to meet an ogre, she could hardly have expected their first meeting to inflict such personal humiliation. Yet she acts courageously and, perhaps guessing that he has overheard and is testing her (which he is), tells him, uttering the vile words. She does this despite Jack Crawford's warning not to allow Lecter into her head on the grounds that the latter's psychiatric experience would enable him to damage her. Lecter, however, knows that Crawford is trying to use him, and he requires an equal exchange before telling her anything. His price is that Clarice gives him power over herself by revealing her deepest secrets; and he enforces this exchange every time she interrogates him. He not only gets into her head immediately, but forges deeper each time they meet. His seemingly uncanny knowledge of her darkest secrets terrorises her because she can conceal nothing from him, not even the shabbiest and most sensitive memories and dreams buried so deep that she has forgotten she ever knew them. By forcing her to produce these lost shreds and tatters so that they can both see them, he hurts her. Thus begins Clarice's initiation. And as she suffers the return of repressed emotions, Lecter adds to her discomfort by the combination of his lust for her innocence of body and mind, and his open contempt for her ignorance of the darkness that engulfs him. In short, he presents himself as her nightmare shadow, compelled to compensate for her conscious biases.

It is now time to say rather more about this, one of the most common archetypal images, which we have already encountered on a number of occasions without giving a full account of it. When Jung and his followers refer to the *shadow*, they have in mind

the 'negative' side of the personality, the sum of all those unpleasant qualities we like to hide, together with the insufficiently developed functions and the contents of the personal unconscious. (Jung 1943: 66)

It follows that duality forms an essential part of all human perceptions, and is integral to Jungian thought. Good can only be perceived against a ground of evil, just as light has to be seen against a background of darkness. So in the psyche that which is conscious (is in the light) has to be seen against the background of the shadow. And the object is not to destroy the shadow and the evil it holds, but to recognise it as a necessary part of the whole. Thus to know good and evil more completely, Jung found he had to see them in the context of an image of a higher totality, the self.

To confront a person with his shadow is to show him his own light. Once one has experienced a few times what it is like to stand judgingly between the opposites, one begins to understand what is meant by the self. Anyone who perceives his shadow and his light simultaneously sees himself from two sides and thus gets in the middle. (Jung 1959b: 463)

This is the function that Lecter will perform for Clarice as the principal constellation of her shadow. (We shall see that her shadow also mantles characters no less evil than he, but who are so far below the surface of Clarice's consciousness that she can only reach them through him. These figures lurking in the inner depths of her psyche are all but mute. Lecter surfacing into her conscious mind is disturbingly eloquent.) His uncanny power over her is indicated by a number of factors. In their interviews, he is often framed in tight, full-face close ups got with a long focus lens so that his face is broadened and flattened while his unblinking eyes bore mercilessly into hers. As might be expected, he at first (though not later when they move onto less unequal terms) sees through her crude ruses. But, most tellingly, even though he gets some of the facts of her biography wrong, he diagnoses with razor-sharp precision the drives that motivate her and of which she is largely unconscious.

You're so ambitious. You know what you look like to me, with your good bag and your cheap shoes? You look like a rube, a well-scrubbed, hustling rube with a little taste. But you're not more than a generation from pure white trash, are you? . . .

Although she is not, as he guesses, the child of a coal miner or a farmer, her stricken face confesses he has intuited exactly the drive behind her dream of 'getting out . . . and going all the way to the FBI'.

Having dissected her motives, Lecter sends her away empty-handed. This would have been the end of Clarice's inquiry but for Miggs's depravity. To celebrate his first sight of a woman in years, he has been masturbating, and now ejaculates as she passes his cell, throwing his seed into her face. Lecter calls her back to make amends for the insult, and gives her a single clue to the case. Significantly he links it to advice she look deep within herself – advice more familiar in the therapist's consulting room than the jail cell. It links the professional search to the psychological quest.

That night Lecter kills Miggs, and (since he cannot reach him in the flesh) does so by means of what he says to him. Miggs dies with his tongue jammed into his throat, a death that symbolically reverses the talking cure of the psychoanalyst. From Clarice's perspective, this might signal the 'extinguishing' of one evil part of the shadow (perhaps her woman's fear of gross sexual assault) by another. However, as Jung warns us, autonomous complexes do not die (though they may be at least temporarily discharged). And, having only just faced it for the first time, Clarice has not yet dealt with this complex. As the story unfolds, we realise that the aspect of her shadow represented by Miggs has transferred on to yet another monster. This character turns out to be the target of her murder hunt, Buffalo Bill, whose deeds are no less extreme than those of the other two killers: he skins the corpses of the women who fall victim to him. Clarice has not only to look deep into the dark, but also to recognise that the shadow menaces her as much as anybody else – and in ways which are distinctive because of her womanhood.

She has a number of strengths to assist her, not least resilience. Despite the painful humiliations suffered during her visit to Lecter, she is not deterred, and while still surfacing from his autopsy on her personality, she courageously reverses the knife by challenging him to use his fine perceptions on himself. However, she faces an opponent who has the tactical advantage in knowing who the killer is and what motivates him. Lecter wants to see the light of day for the first time in eight years – a motif that complements the thought that the shadow is surfacing. In order to bargain for improved conditions of imprisonment, he withholds most of the relevant information while from time to time giving Clarice riddling hints in return for the promise of concessions. These clues advance her search for Buffalo Bill only in so far as her faltering insight into her own nature develops. So Lecter deals with her (judging rightly, from what we see) as one incapable of looking into the deepest dark until her capacity for insight has been improved. In effect he commences with her a quasi-therapeutic programme in which she experiences the full horror of the evil that is in human nature. The shadow is initiating her into its ways.

Why is this young woman's search into the nature of her own psyche connected to her need to understand the mad cravings of a serial murderer who mutilates his victims? Because at root both characters are facing crises of gender urged on them by motivations of which they are unconscious. Buffalo Bill lacks all control over his drives; but while Clarice has an altogether more contained (even repressed) personality, she has little self-regard as a woman, and her ambition to excel in a man's world – in compensation for the loss of her father – is not under control. It threatens to distort her personality with an excessively dominant animus complex. Looking back to chapter 4, we can see that she is an instance of the personality type which Ulanov describes as deflated by insufficient differentiation of her own ego (her 'I') from the paternal animus (Ulanov 1971: 42). Thus Clarice is exposed to dangers similar to those that, in *The Piano*, engulfed Ada before she knew Baines.

Clarice's authorised guru, the coolly intellectual Crawford, lets her follow up the one clue Lecter has let fall. It leads her to a furniture lock-up where she has to force an entry. A repeating pattern is developing in which Clarice makes dangerous entry into dark places, a recurring metaphor for her exposure to the dark side of the unconscious. Here the risk to which she is exposed shows when the lock-up door injures her leg. Although nothing in comparison with the psychological blows that fall on her, it fits the pattern according to which the hero suffers injury during the quest. And the blood on her inner thigh recalls the woman's wound, a reminder to her not to ignore her gender.

In the lock-up she finds, splendidly hearsed in an old car and under the American flag, the embalmed head of Buffalo Bill's first victim, a young man who has been elaborately made up in death to look like a woman. When she reports back to Lecter, he tells her to think of the victim as 'a fledgling killer's first effort at transformation'. But although this means nothing to her, he refuses to give more than indecipherable hints until he gets the improved accommodation he wants. Meanwhile he says just enough to leave Clarice certain he knows the killer's true identity.

Clarice returns to her training programme, but is pulled out once more when the corpse of another of Buffalo Bill's victims is discovered. She flies with Jack Crawford to do the preliminary autopsy in a backwoods county of West Virginia. As they travel, Crawford quizzes her on what she has worked out about the killer. She reckons that he must be a strong white male in his thirties or forties who has his own house where he can work on his victims. He is likely to have acquired a taste for what he does, and will therefore strike again. In making these deductions Clarice is operating in the coolly rational manner Crawford himself favours, and he compliments her on her methodical acumen. But it is a quite different method of searching from that which Lecter requires.

Despite his kind words, Crawford does not trust her to the full, merely because she is a woman. To add to the injury, he refuses her request for the information he is withholding, arguing that if he gave her an agenda, Lecter would know it and would toy with her. Thus there is more than a hint of muddied libido in the way both Crawford and Lecter deal with her. This complements the way each governs one aspect of her psyche. Lecter has already asked whether Crawford is advancing her career because he wants to seduce her. It is characteristic of him that he inquires gloatingly but nakedly about her emotions. By contrast, Crawford's cold rationality has allowed him to use Clarice without much concern for the damage he might do to her feelings.

When they reach the mortuary where the girl's corpse lies, gender discrimination continues. Clarice has to face both the resentment of the local sheriff's men at the intrusion of Federal Agents and their mute bonding against her presence as a woman. Nonetheless, she shares the hardest trial with her male FBI colleagues as they examine the decaying body. While the men use their professionalism to repress emotion, Clarice acts with equal competence (it is she who notices something stuffed into the dead girl's throat) but does not totally suppress her feelings in the process. Significantly, she is beginning to find ways of doing her work on her own terms.

What Clarice has found turns out to be the pupa of a large moth; but the entomologists who identify it as an exotic species which would have to be bred in hot-house conditions in the USA cannot say what it means. Lecter tutors her in this. It is the second symbol of transformation that Clarice has uncovered (the first body being the other, in whose severed head the FBI now discover a similar moth). Lecter tells her that, because they mutate from caterpillars to pupae and eventually become winged creatures (like some other metaphors for the psyche), butterflies are ancient images of rebirth into beauty. We can add to this that they are also symbols of rebirth from the life of the body to that of the soul. In the Jungian context, the butterfly can connote the renewal of psyche that occurs when an old form of existence is sacrificed for a new one. However, Clarice has discovered that the murderer's signature is a Death's Head moth. It is associated with night and hence reverses the usual significance of the butterfly: indeed, Buffalo Bill's attempts at transformation lead only to death. We shall see later how his case illustrates Clarice's psyche.

Buffalo Bill next captures the daughter of a senator, and the FBI comes under intense political pressure to find him before he kills the girl. Lecter's bargaining power is suddenly much increased. Crawford and Clarice seem to accept the logic of the new circumstances and make him an offer of better prison accommodation. However, the offer is actually bogus, a fact exposed by the hospital's director who (resentful because Clarice has refused him sexual favours, and the FBI has bypassed him in dealing with his star prisoner) has bugged her interview with Lecter. As a consequence the case is taken out of their hands, and Lecter is moved out of his jail, having convinced the Justice Department that he will help find the killer.

In her last interview with him in his old cell, Clarice has persuaded Lecter to give her a fuller psychological profile of Buffalo Bill. But he exacts a high price, and insists she tell him her worst memory of childhood. Once again he obliges Clarice to examine things she has locked away in the depths. His reflected face hovers over her shoulder, a visible reminder that he has infiltrated her mind like a demon. Each time he probes he goes deeper and takes her nearer to recognising the shadowy images that people her unconscious. On this occasion she recalls with desperate honesty the loss of her whole world when she was 10, through her father's slow death from gunshot wounds. As an orphan, she was then sent to live on a sheep farm with distant relatives, but had run away because she could not get on with her new 'father', the rancher. This information redoubles the emphasis on the absence of a father as a basic complex in her psychological make-up. However, Lecter senses that there is more to discover, and has by no means done with her yet.

Meanwhile, in recompense for her willingness to look frankly into herself, he hints that Billy has adopted his trademark because he wishes to change like a moth. This information does not resolve the puzzle for Clarice because she has already found out that he cannot be a transsexual. However, Lecter urges her on into the unknown: Billy thinks he is a transsexual because systematic abuse through childhood has pathologised him, but he is mistaken. His desire to metamorphose has found another form of expression which makes him a thousand times more terrifying.

And now for the first time we see Billy's basement lair. The camera slides around sinister rooms in one of which Death's Head moths are incubating. Tailor's dummies occupy floor space in another and Billy himself (Ted Levine) sits naked at a sewing machine. But before we can register what he is making, the camera glides forward, drawn on by muffled cries for help. We are led to a deep well at the bottom of which, like an animal caught in a trap, the senator's daughter Catherine is imprisoned. The basement motif recurs here to emphasise the diseased anima contents of Billy's psyche. His sickness also shows in his elated mimicry of his captive's screams, and in the way he commands her in a contemptuous monotone that dehumanises her: 'It rubs the lotion on its skin – it does this whenever it's told.' Incongruously, this ghoulish figure has a little lamb-like dog which he cuddles to his huge body: he has displaced the gentle side of his feminine being, the only spark of tenderness in him, on to the animal. The resemblance between Precious, the dog, and a lamb strikes us because of the film's title; and it forms a weird link between Buffalo Bill and Clarice.

Although off the case, Clarice sneaks one final meeting with Lecter in the Memphis courthouse where he is temporarily jailed in a gigantic steel birdcage. One last time, the malign doctor exacts the deepest pain from her in return for his riddles. This time he makes Clarice go to the core of her anguish. She tells how as a 10-year old she ran away from the ranch because she could not bear to listen to the lambs screaming before slaughter. Although she tried her utmost, even attempting to run away with one animal in her arms, she had not been able to save any of them. Instead she had lost her own home because the enraged rancher placed her in an orphanage. She admits that she still wakes in the night hearing the screaming, and that she hopes by rescuing Catherine to silence it.

After she has left him, Lecter draws her as the Virgin, with a Lamb in place of the Child. His parody of a familiar iconography draws attention to the associations of lambs with both innocence and slaughter in the Christian myth. But, even though her passionate desire to put an end to suffering is clear, we still have to discover fully how this bears on Clarice's innermost fears and needs.

In fact the figure of Christ is invoked again almost immediately. Lecter, while serenely listening to Bach's *Goldberg Variations* on tape, springs a coldly planned ambush on his new guards. He skins the face of one to make a bloody mask for himself and takes his clothes. When the rescue teams come they carry him to the ambulance (whence he escapes) in the belief that he is their colleague. But before their arrival he has eaten some of the flesh of the other guard, and hung the body on the bars of his cage. There the corpse, lit by misty rays from above, looks unforgettably like both Christ crucified and a winged god ascending.

Potent themes are in play here, bound together by the rituals of masking, eating and sacrifice; and they in turn are contrasted with motifs of containment and repression of evil. Lecter's acts in eating the flesh of an enemy and decking himself in his accoutrements resemble ceremonies that confer on the celebrant the power of the sacrificed victim. And the display of the Christ-like corpse brings to mind another familiar meaning of sacrifice. In order to enjoy rebirth, one must die to one's old self as a prerequisite to entering a new state of consciousness infused with energies freshly drawn from the unconscious (Hillman 1988: 68).

The ruthless slaughter that Lecter wreaks (he also murders the ambulance crew and, for his identity, money and clothes, a tourist) once again demonstrates the threat of the shadow that is not accommodated. The more it is restrained, the more it tends to build up energy and break out. It fits with this psychoanalytical observation that after her shadow breaks out, Clarice actually knows that things have changed for her and she is not in danger. She intuitively senses she can reach an accommodation with it provided she can deal with its demonic aspect through the split-off image represented by Buffalo Bill. And indeed after she has done so, she finds she can 'talk' to her shadow without being threatened with destruction. In other words, Lecter's escape (a kind of rebirth from jail) correlates with a stirring of Clarice's unconscious that will work through to consciousness in her own rebirth.

Appropriately, Clarice soon finds Buffalo Bill, and does so with the assistance not only of Lecter, but also of another female trainee. Previously seen working almost always with men, that Clarice's eventual success comes with a woman's help fits well with her increasing reliance on her own female experience and psychology. Her friend notices one last riddle Lecter has written in Clarice's case file, and helps to interpret it. They realise that the doctor has drawn their attention to the significance of the first victim, and remember that he has advised Clarice to think of Billy killing neither for sexual nor for other pleasures, but to gain something he covets. 'We covet what we see every day', he insisted. So Clarice decides to visit the first victim's home in a drab part of Belvedere, Ohio, in case Billy was her friend or neighbour.

When she gets there, the girl's father tells Clarice that the bedroom has been searched many times by police. We can safely assume that they were men, because Clarice easily finds secrets they have missed. In the lid of the girl's music box are Polaroid shots of her posing coyly in her underwear. And Clarice's next discovery (also unremarked by male eyes) makes it seem likely she was photographed by her covetous killer looking at the flesh he desired for himself. An unfinished dress hangs in the wardrobe. The diamond shaped panels inserted in its back exactly match the cuts made in her flesh by her murderer. The grim truth dawns on Clarice that Buffalo Bill is trying to turn himself into a woman by clothing himself in the skins of his victims.

She phones her report to Crawford, but he is flying into Chicago expecting to make an arrest and close the case. Some while earlier, Lecter had advised Clarice to check patients' lists at leading hospitals in the treatment of transsexuals, and this line of inquiry has yielded information about a Jame Gumb which matches what the FBI have on Buffalo Bill, and produced an address in the Chicago area. Crawford thanks Clarice for the vital work she has done, but in order to plan storming Gumb's house, he cuts the conversation short without fully weighing her words. Instead he instructs her to continue collecting evidence to prove Gumb guilty of murder as well as kidnap.

The narrative climax deceives the audience and augments terror through one of cinema's oldest and most potent aesthetic devices. In a succession of intercut scenes we move between the monster's basement, Crawford and his assault force preparing their attack on him, and (400 miles away) Clarice following up inquiries. Our knowledge of editing rhythms and relations firmly imprints us with the expectation that the FBI are about to break into the house where Gumb is holding his victim. Of course if we gave it due recognition our knowledge of cinema's generic norms would disturb this certainty, since we should expect Clarice to be in at the kill; but the action is so suspenseful and grim that we take as literal what we are shown.

With each return to Gumb's lair, we see its horrors more fully. At his sewing machine he stitches together carefully cured and tailored pieces of his victims' skin. The woman's head of hair he wears is exactly that, not a wig. And looking with fascination at the reflection of his changing persona, the painted lips, pierced nipples and tattooed razor cuts, he models himself as a woman, imitating a mannequin's hip sway with his genitals tucked back out of sight. But while he is thus preoccupied with his incomplete metamorphosis, Catherine traps Precious and torments the little dog, threatening to do worse if her captor does not lower a phone into the well. Her ruthlessness in extremity makes an instructive contrast with Clarice's grief over the screaming lambs.

Meanwhile armed police are gathering in the street, and the pace of intercutting between them and the stand-off in the basement increases. At the same time Clarice is about to make further inquiries at the house in Belvedere of a woman for whom the first victim did some sewing. As Catherine's conflict with Gumb boils to a climax, they are interrupted by the door bell. But the house into which Crawford's men burst is empty, and it is Clarice, not at first aware of the fact, who has entered the very place where they should be. Our disorientation and that of Clarice (who has not doubted Crawford's assertion that their man is in Illinois) are comparable as she notices spools of yarn and a Death's Head moth that has escaped its incubator below stairs, and realises whom she is facing. We share her rising terror the more painfully because we have been mis-led. Our confusion parallels the bewilderment of the conscious mind confronted by the unwelcome intrusion of unconscious contents.

Gumb dodges away from her, and to pursue him Clarice has to make one more entry into a basement. This time her search through the under-world develops into an extended metaphor for her own spiritual quest. At first consciously following police procedure quite efficiently, she moves through the gloomy cellars, and finds Catherine screaming in fear and rage over the dog/lamb. This image of Catherine informs Clarice's future as well as her past, providing her with an altered reflection of her own childhood anguish. Force of circumstance requires the young detective now to see that she must sometimes push beyond anguish in order to fight for survival. Terror makes this difficult (Catherine's shrieks, like a displacement of Clarice's own dread, make it hard for her to hear Gumb's movements) but no less vital. As she enters ever darker chambers, her con-scious self-control (though not her courage) begins to fail. She catches a glimpse of something in a rancid bath that might be the dissolved corpse of a long-deceased woman. Perhaps there is here a suggestion of the dead mother Clarice has virtually obliterated from memory, but we cannot tell because Gumb kills the lights. In effect, she has to deal with the out-of-control shadow before she can get to anything else. Searching for him in total darkness, she looks like a child in the extremity of fear, almost all physical co-ordination gone.

Gumb has the tactical advantage because he can see her by means of image-enhancing binoculars. It adds to our fright and guilt that, while identifying with her, we see through his eyes. As she flails around, he reaches out as if to touch her. We too seem both to feel and be felt, and, when he draws his weapon, to menace and be menaced. At one level it reminds us of the conflicting currents of power and vulnerability in the human mind. At another, as Gumb prowls around in this ghostly way with Clarice's life in his sights, he provides what might be called, for the purposes of a psychoanalytical reading, the point of view of the autonomous archetypal complex.

Jung described Jame Gumb's psychology almost perfectly in this passage about psychosis.

> If there is already a predisposition to psychosis, it may even happen that the archetypal figures, which are endowed with a certain autonomy anyway on account of their natural numinosity, will escape from conscious control altogether and become completely independent, thus producing the phenomena of possession. In the case of an anima-possession, for instance, the patient will want to change himself into a woman through self-castration, or he is afraid that something of the sort will be done to him by force. (1954a: 39)

If for a moment we take Gumb as the central figure, then his death at Clarice's hands represents the revenge of his anima that has been repressed until it has become pathologised.

Switching our point of view back to Clarice, we need to ask what is Gumb's significance as an *imago* – that is, as if he were a subjectively generated image within her psyche. As a split-off component of her shadow, he like Lecter acts as a kind of inverted mirror to her gender drives. As David Sundelson says, Lecter's cannibalism expresses a wish to do what only women can do – have another's life inside his body. Gumb has tried physically to do something comparable, and stitch himself into a woman's persona (Sundelson 1993: 16). In an analogous way, but psychologically, Clarice has sought to straitjacket herself into a man's role. While the attempts of the two men to attain enforced transformation can only be achieved by murder, her forcing herself into a man's role can only be done if Clarice kills off the woman in her – a kind of self-slaughter. So in retrospect the image of Clarice at the autopsy working sorrowfully on the dead girl's body becomes a displaced figure for her grief over the death of her own anima.

The notion that individuals may experience not only contrasexual archetypal figures, but also powerful same-sex images, is a recent development in post-Jungian circles. Generally among heterosexuals the contrasexual archetype is likely to predominate, while the same-sex archetype will be subordinate. None the less, it must be present in an individual as a reflection (even a constellation) of proper self-love. Homosexuals may experience the same-sex archetypal image as dominant. Meanwhile, heterosexuals may be seeking the completion of the androgyne in the psyche in their search for a partner (see Hopcke 1991: 130–5). In Clarice's case, the feminine in the unconscious (which her libido should foster and love) appears to have been all but obliterated upon the death of her mother. As we have seen, it is in need of restoration.

Unsighted by darkness in the final pursuit, Clarice focuses like a trapped animal on sound, and when she hears Gumb cocking his weapon she aims at the noise and empties her magazine, killing him outright. One of the bullets shatters a blacked-out window above the corpse, and light returns. In the current of fresh air that now flows into the dungeon, a mobile turns; it is painted not with a moth but a butterfly, an emblem of Clarice's transformation and rebirth.

She emerges from her ordeal changed. Although she suffers no worse than a powder burn, she now bears the physical mark of psychic suffering that distinguishes most successful heroes and signifies her rebirth into a new orientation on the Self. It rounds out this theme that Catherine, Gumb's last captive, lives; not only that, but she leaves her prison cradling Precious, the very creature whose life she had been threatening. She simply accepts the contradictory attitudes in herself to her innocent 'lamb'. Hitherto, Clarice has not understood that there is a psychological necessity implicit in the slaughter of the lambs: that the individual has to sacrifice her innocence in order to transform. Jesus as the Lamb of God who through sacrifice attained the transformation of apotheosis is the obvious mythological model for this process. But Jesus was far from silent, though he did not scream until the hour of his torment. It is a reminder that lambs which are silent are not full of joy, they are inanimate.

This brings us to the significance of Lecter. What is the difference between him and Jame Gumb? Both are multiple murderers. Both perform on their victims ritual acts of extreme horror. And both bring to the cinema screen something that television fiction seldom presents – an intense, emotionally palpable evil that stalks not only the other characters but also the audience. The difference is implicit in their names. 'Lecter' comes from lector – one who reads and obtains knowledge; also, interestingly, an ecclesiastic in the minor orders who reads the lessons. 'Hannibal' indicates the commanding power which enables him to do the unthinkable.[7] We should not miss the fact that sacrificial acts he performs are public, so that anyone who wishes can learn from them. By contrast, 'Gumb' is an unpromising name, implicates the mouth rather than the brain, and also rhymes with dumb and numb; fittingly, 'Jame' means one who supplants others. He deals in the dark, secretively

---

[7] According to Malcolm Bowie (1991: 46), Freud had imagined himself a new Hannibal entering Rome, for him a city where fantasies of omniscience and omnipotence could be freely entertained.

and pathologically. By contrast, Lecter knows his own nature and relishes it.

Incidentally, while we are thinking of these things, we should add that Clarice's first name means 'brilliant'. Her second name obviously brings to mind the messy bird with its coarse manners that overcrowds so many cities. Before she has to face Lecter, she is the very mix of brilliance and coarseness that he quickly perceives. However, there is a second, less familiar term, 'starling', which refers to the outwork of piles that protects a bridge against damage from fast-flowing currents or floating objects. In solving the case, Clarice shows herself to be Crawford's starling.

With the case file closed, Clarice graduates as FBI Special Agent. After her terrible initiation, the return. The way she receives Crawford's and Lecter's congratulations confirms her newly matured relationship with both aspects of her animus. They are reduced to a proper proportion and no longer dominate her psyche. No more the over-awed disciple, she calmly accepts Crawford's shy excuses as he leaves the celebratory party early. He speaks sincerely of the pride her father would have felt, and she has the presence of mind to offer her hand in friendship. Lecter (who is in the Bahamas in full pursuit of his former gaoler, the hospital director) interrupts the hunt to telephone his congratulations to her. Since the shadow does not die when we know its contents (though it is likely for a time to be less menacing) it is psychologically right that Hannibal Lecter should still be at large at the end. He remains a plausible, if for the moment remote, threat to Clarice, and their mutual though wary fascination still resonates through their short conversation. The shadow may change its form, or it may temporarily lose its energy charge when it has been recognised and its contents integrated into consciousness; but it usually returns sooner or later when the unconscious requires to disturb the ego in order to compensate for the biases that consciousness inevitably imposes on the psyche.[8] More than most box-office successes, *The Silence of the Lambs* merited its sequel, *Hannibal* (Ridley Scott, USA, 2001).

By the time of her graduation, Clarice has also made a warm friend of her fellow trainee Ardelia. Their comfortable amity implies a new enjoyment of her own femininity and suggests that she has restored her anima figure to a healthy level of activity. She has brought her social quest to a triumphant resolution and has won the respect of both her peers and

---

[8] Failure to concede the durability of the shadow dissipated the otherwise harsh drama of *The Fisher King* (Terry Gilliam, USA, 1991). It begins with powerful images of cruelty, madness and despair and ends up with lovable cuddliness as the two leading men celebrate victory over their demons by lying naked in Central Park and singing, 'I Like New York in June, How About You?'

superiors. No less important, her spiritual quest has greatly enhanced her self-knowledge, and has given her respect for the positive and negative powers within her of which she was previously unconscious.

Clarice is the third female hero whom we have analysed in detail. There are likenesses among the three, most evidently their courage in asserting their own needs; but the differences are more informative and they represent three different manifestations of the feminine. Prior to her initiation, Clarice was at much the same risk of animus domination as Ada. On their return to the world each has her animus in manageable proportion. However, Clarice does not emerge from her initiation with the equivalent of Ada's Baines, and appears to have no need of a lover at this stage in her life. She is self-contained; sufficient for the present unto herself.

This quality is seen the more clearly when she is compared with the public image of Madonna. The differences between them are self-evident. The fledging Agent is not remotely a shape-shifting trickster. Her constancy of purpose makes that obvious. Nor do either Aphrodite or Artemis govern her. However, she resembles Madonna in being ruled by the head. Also like Madonna, she is ambitious. These characteristics declare the influence of Athena upon both women. In Clarice's case it is stronger because, unlike the pop star, she lives mainly in her mind and is not in close touch with her body. Like many other Athena women, she focuses on her career, content to remain celibate for a long period (Bolen 1985: 93).

With its heroine in mind, *The Silence of the Lambs* was greeted on its release as a profoundly feminist film, as exhilarating as it was harrowing to many women (Taubin 1991: 18). Their exhilaration arose not just from sharing Clarice's triumphant quest, but from doing so in a best-seller. As Carol Christ says,

There is a dialectic between story and experience. Stories shape experience; experience shapes stories . . . In a sense, without stories there is no experience . . .

Men have actively shaped their experiences of self and world by creating the stories they have told . . . Because women's stories have not been told, women's experiences have not shaped the spoken language of cultural myths and sacred stories. (1975: 4–5)

Thus the telling of new myths through women's stories may invoke a new social and spiritual order. And, as we shall see, this project harmonises with the film's thematic as expressed through the other leading character.

I wish to turn now, however, to the attraction of terror in this film, which certainly played a part in its drawing a large audience. We may recall that Jung described visionary art as an expression presenting a compensatory adjustment to the conscious outlook of the period. It arises from the collective unconscious, and is expressed regardless of whether or not the blind collective need results in good or evil, the salvation of an epoch or its destruction (Jung 1950: 98). The attraction of this film arises in large measure from the power of Hannibal Lecter as the *collective* shadow. He is a celebrant of destructive evil, and his compensatory nature can be seen in two salient features. First, his split nature: in one aspect he is a sympathetic character demonstrating much that is admirable and attractive in mankind so that the spectator is tempted to identify with him. He is a psychoanalyst whose voice we want to trust when he speaks intimately. These things make his evil acts, which stand far beyond the limits of what spectators can comprehend in terms of what they themselves could possibly do, all the more terrifying. Second, there are the horrible masks in which his face is caged. They are intended to make safe his mouth, and incidentally to dehumanise him; but they fail to bridle that scourge of hypocrisy, his tongue. And the hypocrisy he lashes is exactly the obverse of the horror which the masks represent – namely, the orthodox belief that the democratic USA (and beyond it the democracies of the western world) have contained naked evil in a benign secular social order. Lecter compensates for the over-valuation of consciousness in our culture, and our continuing indifference towards the unconscious. As a cannibalistic shadow, his presence suggests that by way of compensation the unconscious might in its return devour the fruits of consciousness.

This leads the discussion directly to Lecter as a politicised representation of the collective shadow. For Amy Taubin, serial killers can be shown to be potent figures in the popular imagination because the horror they generate far outstrips the number of deaths they cause. She remarks on the peculiarly American nature of the phenomenon. The USA has only 5 per cent of the world's population but 75 per cent of its multiple murderers, almost all male. *The Silence of the Lambs* underlines the point, packed as it is with 300 years of relics of white America, including, in at least three scenes, the Stars and Stripes. For these reasons Taubin argues that the serial killers in this film (and in others released at the same time) can conveniently stand in for institutionalised violence that is otherwise difficult to represent in mainstream fiction (Taubin 1991: 16, 18). Lecter's elegant language that frankly declares his rank deeds mocks the politician's speech polished by party managers, as we hear when he meets Catherine's mother, the senator. His clamped mouth speaks the bloody undercurrent beneath the hygienic flow of public relations communications.

With memories of American-led killings in Iraq fresh in her mind, Taubin describes the final image of Lecter sauntering along a main street in Haiti as deeply disturbing: 'the serial killer, an American gift to the third world, a fragmentation bomb, ready to explode' (ibid.: 18). The argument can be generalised, since Lecter displays the shadow image of state or corporate institutionalised power as apprehended not just in the USA but also throughout the western democratic world. There is an ironic footnote to this which neatly doubles our sense of Lecter's compensatory nature. With the exception of an unfortunate tourist who happened to be in the wrong place at the wrong time, we have neither evidence for, nor a confession of, his ever having killed anyone who was not a government official or a public servant.

7   Television sport and the sacrificial hero

It is rare for the television coverage of sporting heroes to be concerned with aspects of their behaviour and thoughts beyond matters strictly relating to their physical performance. Sometimes sports reports also refer to the psychological preparations which enable athletes to improve that performance, but there is very little else. The main exception to these constraints is found in interviews with sports personalities in which the hopes and fears of the heroes are discussed. Often this format masks a somewhat prurient interest in the emotions experienced by winners and losers. Only very occasionally in the television sports calendar does the commentator's near total concern with physical achievements give way to an uneasy sense that something might be left out by so fixated an approach. However, mainly because a compulsory cultural element accompanies the Olympic Games, such doubts do regularly surface in coverage of their opening and closing ceremonies. On these occasions, broadcasters find themselves obliged to join with the Games' organisers to make much of the supposed connections between sport and culture. It certainly does disturb momentarily the usually complacent routines of sports reporting.

This chapter takes the ceremonies that bracketed the 1992 Barcelona Olympics as the stimulus prompting a re-examination of the television sporting hero. It begins with a short account of the nature of modern competitive sports and the values typically inherent in television coverage of them. It considers briefly the pressures that encourage broadcasters to build the most successful athletes into stars, and addresses some of the main elements propagated in the mythic figure of the sporting hero on the small screen. Turning to the 1992 Olympics, the chapter continues by offering a speculative reading of the myths presented to spectators in the Barcelona stadium during the opening and closing ceremonies. It then shows what happened to those myths (and the image of a legendary sporting hero) when they were passed through the filters of live coverage to the British television audience. It demonstrates plainly that the attempt by the on-site organisers to bring traditional mythic stories and images alive for the late-twentieth-century audience did not weather intact the dominant values of television sports reporting. The perspective alters in the final section to focus on a Jungian analysis of the sporting hero's image. This suggests that, notwithstanding the findings concerning coverage of the Olympic ceremonies, the dominant mode of sports reporting does in its own right throw up myths around the athletic hero. These mythic images, far from being unknown to history, actually renew certain ancient uses to which such idolised figures were always put.

Before speculating on how sport transfers to the small screen, we need to consider briefly its nature. We may begin by noting that participation in sports differs from the behaviour of the individual playing alone. This is because in the latter case the person playing can choose either to observe, or to break, the rules. Furthermore, the rules do not have to be pre-existent but may be made up on the spot. Andrew Samuels extrapolates from this idea the thought that 'the essence of [solitary] play is that the rules of the ego may be broken'. Where norms, hierarchies and clarity can be ignored, the unconscious rather than the ego system is dominant (Samuels 1990: 130). As Jung recognised from his own experience, the instinct to play is closely linked to the drive towards self-discovery and exploration of the unconscious. In this respect it has a religious quality (Jung 1961: 197–8).

The case is rather different with games. They resemble play in being non-utilitarian, but differ, as Allen Guttmann says, in that they are regulated and rule-bound. 'Games symbolise the willing surrender of absolute spontaneity for the sake of playful order. One remains outside the sphere of material necessity, but one must obey the rules one imposes on oneself.' The unconscious yields in part to a greater intensity of conscious control precisely because most games are social, wherein the players submit to rules that the group or community imposes. Such rules often function in a technically inefficient manner (like the off-side rule in soccer) because they are designed actually to make it harder to achieve the goal, and thus prolong the play itself (Guttmann 1978: 4–5).

Although many games (such as leapfrog) are not competitive and players neither win nor lose, modern sports belong to a wider class of activity that is normally rule-bound. This is the contest, which apart from sport includes such things as elections, legal proceedings and war.

We can ... define sports as 'playful' physical contests, that is, as non-utilitarian contests which include an important measure of physical as well as intellectual skill. (Guttmann 1978: 5–7)

Triumph through contest or conflict is a pre-requisite to becoming a hero.

Several writers show how the history of sport can be traced not only in terms of the progression from play to contest, but also (among other factors) through shifts in the values that dominated it. There is abundant evidence that, although not all sports of every nation were once dominated by religious significance, a great many were. Some were part of a yearly fertility right (Guttmann cites the sports of the Jicarilla Apaches of the Southwest Plains). Others enacted rites of passage from puberty to adulthood. Yet others, such as the ball game of the Mayans and Aztecs which celebrated the birth of sun and moon, appear to have invoked creation myths (Guttmann 1978: 17–20). Jung cites mediaeval records of ball games such as the pelota basque which were played in churches across Europe. In them the ball is associated with the annual renewal of the sun at Eastertide and, through that symbolism, with the yearly cycle of the godhead (Jung 1938: 32–4). The Ancient Olympic Games were thus not unusual in celebrating the sacred. However, after a long period of evolution, sport ceased to be consecrated and became predominantly secular in nature.

Modern sports are activities partly pursued for their own sake, partly for other ends which are equally secular. We do not run in order that the earth be more fertile. We till the earth, or work in our factories and offices, so that we can have time to play. (Guttmann 1978: 25–6)

As sports evolved, so did their rules. Eric Dunning and Norbert Elias demonstrate that the characteristics of sports, including the degree to which they were governed by rules, should be viewed in the context of the kind of society that fostered them. For example, the pancration, a form of wrestling that was popular in the Ancient Olympic Games, was both far less rule bound and far more physically violent than the make-believe and theatrical televised wrestling contests of the late twentieth century: 'To be killed or to be very severely wounded and perhaps incapacitated for life was a risk a fighter in the pancration had to take' (Elias 1971: 99). Elias endorses an idea in circulation among the Ancient Greeks that such contests were a training for war, and, conversely, war prepared men for victory in the Games. In that context, and in a society where the transformation of private conscience into general social principles of justice was still the exception rather than the norm, regulation of physical contests was of less importance than their execution with honour. (Elias 1971: 98–101)

Games still were expressive of social custom and ritual in mediaeval Britain when an early and riotous form of football was played by whole communities in frank defiance of the authorities. The organisation of the game was much looser than it is today, and a good deal more dangerous.

People did not play according to nationally agreed rules (which did not yet exist), but rather contested the issue in the light of local customs. Yet, in many places, this wild form of play formed part of annually observed and solemn folk rituals. Nothing was seen to be incongruous in the conjunction of riot and ritual (Elias and Dunning 1971: 116–26).

Today's sports are no less firmly embedded in their social structures, as Lipsky has observed: 'Sport is the symbolic expression of the values of the larger political and social milieu' (1975: 351). One indicative factor is the quantifying of performance through the recording of data. Another is the burning ambition of athletes to break records by exceeding the achievements of the past. Both objectives have become obsessive foci for those interested in sports. Yet Guttmann shows that this was not always so: measurement was once almost irrelevant to the reckoning of sporting success. Today, quantification of sporting achievements is ideologically of a piece with the dominant work practices of late-twentieth-century economies. The latter depended for survival upon recording and calculation. Few people employed in the industrialised nations in the 1980s and 1990s escaped the constant pressure to perform their tasks faster or more efficiently than before. Arguably, our 'Faustian lust for the absolutely unprecedented athletic achievement' (Guttmann 1978: 54) stands in compensatory relation to the daily experience of millions of workers. The obsession with quantifying sporting achievement indicates a massive investment of psychic energy. Thus we express through statistics, a language we have endowed with magical power, a new way of attaining an ancient goal.

Once the gods have vanished from Mount Olympus or from Dante's paradise, we can no longer run to appease them or to save our souls, but we can set a new record. It is a uniquely modern form of immortality. (Guttmann 1978: 55)

A number of converging factors encourages television sports programmes to build star players into heroes. We may begin with what Alan Clarke and John Clarke describe as apparently the most natural characteristic of contemporary sport.

Sport provides the opportunity for individuals to pit themselves against others, and be judged by their competitive performance. It appears as the most primitive and natural form of interaction between humans. This may seem 'self-evident', but it is connected to propositions about this as the natural state of society – that social life is 'competitive individualism'. From this standpoint, it is possible to see the cross-connections that are constructed between sport and social images. (Clarke and Clarke 1982: 63)

It follows that images drawn from the sports field serve to affirm that competitive individualism, which is in fact a cultural and political ideology, is the natural human condition. Therefore the strongest, fittest and (above all) most successful athletes are lionised as exemplars. Among them, the most outstanding become media personalities, and as such they reveal their hopes and fears, as well as their thoughts about their game, to the viewer. The process is not restricted to the cultivation of personality, however, because these heroes are usually cast as individuals who have succeeded while obeying the rules. Meanwhile those who are perceived to be bending or breaking them become stereotyped as villains. Thus, on the face of things, television sport shows a pronounced moralising tendency in its construction of heroes, although some villains may be sneakingly admired for challenging authority (Clarke and Clarke 1982: 72; Hargreaves 1986: 147).

As is well known, television stations use sport as a means of enhancing their power by increasing their audience share, income and status. Broadcasters have to appeal to an audience far larger than the numbers of fans for each specific sport in order to gain these ends. In creating heroes, sports programmes satisfy what appears to be an incessant audience appetite. That is one reason why broadcasters lionise stars. Another is that the practice marries with the sports reporter's need to create a story.

Although the forms of narrative employed in the coverage of sporting events are rather different from fiction, commentators still need to create 'characters' to people them. This is another reason why today's sporting heroes are required to have distinctively marked individual personalities. But even so, their production as images has to conform with the requirements of routinised, cost-effective television production. This economic factor, together with the desire of audiences to get to know personalities with easily recognised qualities, exerts a strong stereotyping force on the construction of sporting heroes. Their images are turned into vehicles for a cluster of culturally acceptable values.

One symptom of this is the fact that the characters most frequently discovered through sports coverage are winners. Winners rather than losers receive most attention because, as we have said, the constant pressure to compete in most twentieth-century societies encourages the adulation of victors. Those who come in second or after do not arouse the same media interest unless they represent the viewer's nation. But if they happen to be doing so, a distorting effect can result as conflicting stereotypes collide. For example, after the World Cup of 1990, Paul Gascoigne became famous in the United Kingdom not only for his soccer-playing skills but also for what was in fact a momentary outbreak of tears at being shown the yellow card. He had committed a foul which would have kept him out of England's next game – hence his disappointment. In fact England lost and was knocked out of the competition. The tabloid press and television worked on the episode for several days, after which the tears came to signify something else altogether, Gascoigne's devout patriotism – the sorrow of a man who cannot bear to see his country lose. In this case, a member of the losing team was turned into a national hero.

Because most sporting contests result in triumph for an individual or a team, there is a constant stream of winners. This feeds television's need for the predictable occurrence. Of course, it is seldom possible to foretell the outcome of any particular contest. Despite this, commentators and experts constantly try to do so as a means of giving continuity to the 'characters' in the event by drawing on their athletic history. However, the difficulty of foretelling results is actually welcome since it feeds television's equally strong need for the unpredictable – for the dramatic surprise. It follows that the institution of sports broadcasting is indifferent to the fact that individual heroes may come and go because, just as in pop music or the movie business, there are always new stars to replace those that disappear. In the end the cultural phenomenon of the sporting hero matters no less than the personality and success of the individual.

All these factors provide a framework for the emergence of sports heroes in routine television coverage. Before we consider their nature from a Jungian perspective, let us turn to one of the comparatively rare instances when mythology has been consciously promoted in the context of televised sport.

The opening and closing ceremonies of the Olympic Games have for some years been conspicuously costly spectacles. Designed to entertain a vast global television audience, they both celebrate the Games themselves and promote the venue that is hosting them. During the days leading up to the event, some of the attractions that the city elders want shown to the world (as well as others that they would prefer were not publicised) are communicated by a variety of programmes. These include sports features; documentaries on the history, culture and life of the locality; and holiday programmes exploring the promise the locale holds for tourists.

During the actual ceremonies, the city's marketable qualities are depicted through a display of performing and other arts associated with the region, presented with entertaining panache in order to attract an international television audience. In the Olympic Games in Los Angeles (1984), the opening ceremony exploited the city's close associations with Hollywood. Similarly, performances based in local culture that showcased both the host cities and nations were mounted in Seoul (1988) and Barcelona (1992). However, the organisers in both the latter venues did much more than market their region to potential tourists. They exploited the antiquity of their civilisations in a way that Californians had not found possible. And they introduced a new element to the ceremonial by entwining certain ancient myths of the regions into their dances and spectacles.

What follows is a two-part analysis centring on the episodes in the opening ceremony that featured Hercules. The first part represents a speculative attempt to interpret the mythology in the way the Catalan organisers appear to have wanted television audiences to perceive the performances in the Montjuic stadium. The second part gives an account of the way the myths became obscured in coverage provided by the two channels that transmitted the ceremony to the United Kingdom.

A tentative interpretation of the themes governing the performances in the stadium can be drawn from two sources. First are the live images fed to participating networks by the television company set up in Barcelona specifically to cover the Games. The networks were entitled to add their own live or pre-recorded images; but a comparison of BBC coverage with that of the satellite channel Eurosport shows that for the duration of the opening and closing ceremonies both took the feed without interruptions other than for commercial breaks on Eurosport. The second source is fragments of the narration. Careful attention to the verbal texture of the commentaries on both these channels suggests that in places the scripts were not written by the reporters. It seems reasonable to deduce the existence of an official, explanatory text designed by the authorities in Barcelona to help sports commentators to explain what they were witnessing. Commentary teams appear to have sampled this text with varying degrees of success.

The dramatists and choreographers in Barcelona took advantage of their Mediterranean site to recall not so much the history of the ancient Olympic Games (which is obscure) as the mythology surrounding their origins. In the opening ceremony, they made Hercules the main protagonist of a vast theatrical production. The mythical inaugurator of the Games, he was represented as a gigantic, god-like figure – literally a hero made of steel who towered metres above the human operator who was working him. In metaphoric terms it created an image in which the myth was larger than the man beneath, but intriguingly also dependent upon him.

In this rendering of a fragment of Hercules' ninth labour, the founding of the Olympic Games was shown to be integral to his creation of Mediterranean civilisation. In the first place, he challenged the sun by running a race through its gorgeous but dangerous flames, accompanied by his team of athletes. This test was said (by the BBC's commentator) to have made it possible for him to divide the column of civilisation. The idea seems to be a double reference both to his erecting the Pillars of Hercules at the Straits of Gibraltar, and (as the Eurosport commentary team mentioned) to his parting good from evil. These events were seen as both the source of and model for the Olympic Games.

Hercules' heroic powers were called on again as a ship laden with Greek mariners sailed across the arena, now transformed into the Mediterranean sea. Presently the ocean grew hostile and great waves hurled monsters up from the deep. (The imagination of Barcelona's artists and designers showed itself to brilliant effect with sun and sea represented by hundreds of costumed dancers. The ship resembled an iron relic of the industrial age, its attackers a rabble of sea demons, among them animated claws and knives, a nightmarish globe of corpses and weaponry, and an aetiolated black octopus.) When the vessel broke and the demons threatened to overwhelm them, the crew prayed to the gods for help. And they were answered when, under the tutelage of Hercules, the sun returned and the waves lost their force. Guided by the sun, the ship then reached the shore where, offering the gods thanks for their salvation, the voyagers built an altar with a flame like the Olympic beacon. There they settled and established a community – the future Barcelona.

The spectator in 1992 seems, then, to have been invited by these performances to recall the long-forgotten ritualistic celebrations of the Ancient Games. They were encouraged by the narrative to use them as a mental backdrop to the modern Games, the televised rituals of which would otherwise have centred almost exclusively on the athletes' physical prowess. Thus, despite its surface appearance as an opulent and startlingly original performance (features which television extravaganzas require in order to attract a vast audience), the spectacle allowed one to see that beyond the exuberant blend of modernist Catalan imagination, artifice, and high technology, there were connections to be drawn to an older tradition of drama. This was not just a matter of the story's antiquity, but also its structure.

First, the characters and story line functioned in an allegorical mode comparable to that of the Renaissance masque. They existed not only in their own right but also as keys to an interpretive text. For example, in addition to being a striking visual representation of a man of iron, Hercules acted as mediator in the age-old conflict between the elements. Neither the sun nor the sea alone was shown to be a benign influence. In isolation either could destroy humanity; in co-operation they brought peace and new life, so that Hercules' labour symbolically defeated the forces of death and fostered life. Taken a step further, the peaceable resolution of elemental battle was shown to be a model for the Games. This reading is confirmed by the perilous voyage of the ship which (as the commentators for Eurosport explained) represented in dramatic form the long and difficult journey of Olympism from ancient Greece to Barcelona.

Like the allegories of old, this narrative was also intended to function on a less abstract level. This became evident when, in his welcoming speech, the Mayor of Barcelona expressed the hope that the Olympic spirit could expand across the world and help bring an end to conflict in the war-torn states of the former Yugoslavia.

The theme of conflict was worked through a number of segments in both the opening and closing ceremonies. So too was another, related, theme, the invocation of fertility. Hercules' own mythological line of descent is strongly marked with this association. Although he had been demoted to the rank of hero by the Greeks, in his prior incarnation he had been a Minoan fertility god. In addition, as Guttmann shows, the theme provided the common thread linking every version of the Games' origins. And a ritual intended to assure continued fertility constituted an integral element of the Ancient Games, a sacrifice being made to Zeus to persuade him to return from the dead 'in the form of a new shoot emerging from the dark womb of the earth into the light of day'. Looking at the obverse of this, defeat in an athletic contest was regarded as the symbolic equivalent of death (Guttmann 1978: 21–2).

This theme extended into the closing ceremony in which fertility myths were again invoked. This time fire was used to extend the elemental imagery that in the opening ceremony had been provided by the sun. Fire now became a unifying motif signifying both creation and rebirth. In this register, it fused together the symbolism of many elements in the final show. These included a performance of De Falla's *Fire Dance*; the extinguishing of the Olympic flame; and a festival of fire in which, while the sun gambolled among the planets in a universal dance, flames blazed in the bowels of the universe where cheerful devils worked the smithy of creation. In the end, something with a new and benign purity sprang from the raw energy of these demons' unexpurgated flames. An aerial ship of shining steel, a refulgent creation forged in the fire, arose from the stadium floor. A massive fireworks display coincided with its launch and carried it high on the updraught of a hundred thousand rockets. It was said to take with it an invisible flame, the spirit of the Olympics, bound for the 1996 Games in Atlanta. The rebirth motif could hardly have been more clearly stated.

The themes remarked upon above – the god-like stature of Hercules; his achievement of heroism through conflict; and the links between his acts, sporting rituals and ideas of fertility and rebirth – were plainly indicated in the dramaturgy in Barcelona. The question is, why did they not penetrate the UK television coverage more effectively?

Whether or not the reading offered above might find favour with the producers of the ceremonies or the Catalan television directors, it is not one which many UK viewers of the ceremonies could have made. It would be an exaggeration to suggest that the BBC and Eurosport commentaries did not aid my understanding in any way; but they did leave large gaps and serious confusion. So the interpretation sketched out above also required careful consideration of the images' potential meanings. This was augmented with readings in mythology, and with Allen Guttmann's history of early sports.

When we listen to the commentaries at leisure, it sounds as though the reporters are editing the script as they go along. They seem to do this in part to fit it to events on screen, but mainly because too much explanation of the spectacle is thought likely to bore many viewers. For example, Archie MacPherson in his live commentary on the closing ceremony for Eurosport felt that at times the ceremonies were 'a little bit heavy'. From this perspective, the good side of the elaborate rituals in the arena was found in the entertainment and emotional pleasure they gave. Meanwhile, the bad aspect was anything that was 'pompous', which it was if it contained 'a good deal of symbolism'. That seemed to refer to anything outside the routine experience of the commentator in his familiar role as the representative of the British television viewer.

Thus, for MacPherson, there developed a split view in which the closing ceremony was both pleasing and dull, simultaneously joyous and pompous. Conceivably, this view arose simply from his own predilections. Since he had taken up a similar no-nonsense attitude in his sports reporting for BBC Scotland over many years, this thought is not implausible. He may equally well, however, have been reflecting an institutional rather than a personal set of values. That is, his attitude may have been intended to meet the supposed preferences of the majority in the audience – those alleged to dislike anything not obvious to the uninitiated. Since an average of more than 11 million people in the United Kingdom were estimated to have been watching each ceremony (about 20 per cent of the population), the producers' concern for the mass audience is understandable. It was, and remains, the always compelling justification for domesticating anything foreign in order to render it recognisable and comfortable to the home audience.

As a consequence of the commentators cutting down explanation of the spectacle to less than the bare bones, the information actually given was so fragmentary as to be incomprehensible. There were even occasions during coverage of the ceremonies when the British presenters appeared not to understand the words they were uttering. No surprise then that they were unable to clinch meaning for the viewer.

Far from being an exception, incidentally, the presentation at Barcelona conformed to the usual pattern of coverage of Olympic ceremonies on

British television. For example, Hugh O'Donnell and Raymond Boyle show how David Coleman's BBC commentary on the opening ceremony of the Norwegian Winter Olympics used text much of which was locally inspired (O'Donnell and Boyle 1997: 100–1). Coleman did not appear entirely comfortable with it.

Something more than the protection of the audience from boredom is at work here. It relates to the well-documented fact that television coverage of the Olympics is dominated by the entertainment requirements of the world's richest nations. A ceremony of this kind is designed to depend on extravagant spectacle in order to guarantee the mass audience in these countries, and thus it inevitably solemnises conspicuous wealth. Sporting and other myths become subsumed to a dominant idea of market-oriented capitalism, namely the myth that we find our main pleasure in consumption to excess – be it of goods, or of orchestras and choruses supported by casts of thousands dressed in all the colours of the rainbow. Thus a principal object of television presentation of the ceremonies is to give the viewer satisfaction through the richest sensuous pleasures that aesthetic plenitude can offer in the spectacle. This practice has certain consequences.

As John J. MacAloon argues, the aggrandising ethos of spectacle that is designed to reach a mass audience has licensed passive watching. This undermines the requirement of all rituals that those who watch them be engaged. He finds that games, in so far as they are embedded within a spectacle, tend to be taken as 'mere games', or 'mere entertainments', rather than as 'metaphors that are meant' (MacAloon 1984: 263).[9]

Jung commented on this kind of tendency in connection with drama and painting. It amounted to taking art as if it were merely an aesthetic exercise. The consequences of such a tendency were not far to seek.

The aesthetic approach immediately converts the problem into a picture which the spectator can contemplate at his ease, admiring both its beauty and its ugliness, merely re-experiencing its passions at a safe distance, with no danger of becoming involved in them. The aesthetic attitude guards against any real participation, prevents one from being personally implicated, which is what a religious understanding . . . would mean. (Jung 1921: 142)

---

[9] A further diffusion takes place in countries such as the USA, where NBC interrupts coverage with not only commercials but a great deal of material that lionises US national heroes. James F. Larson and Nancy Rivenburgh record that when covering the Seoul Olympics, NBC interrupted the opening ceremony twenty-five times for nearly 52 minutes of commercials, and another twenty-one times for news breaks, interviews and background segments averaging more than 3 minutes in length. Most of the inserted material cut into coverage of the cultural performances in the stadium. (Larson & Rivenburgh 1991: 75–94)

That is exactly the way that British coverage of the Olympic ceremonies functioned for its viewers.

What happened to Hercules, the bionic hero, in the British commentaries? The short answer is of course that he was treated as a colourful component of the vivid spectacle, but nothing more. His image was not used to augment our understanding of today's sporting heroes. At first glance, this slighting of a heroic figure might seem strange, since, in the abstract, the parallels with the modern athletic hero are clearly marked. Both test themselves through contests. Both have something superhuman about them. And both offer the commentator lively stories.

When one considers the routine naturalisation of sports reporting, however, it is not so surprising that Hercules was ignored despite the seductive appeal of spectacle. He was neither predictable in terms of television routine, nor readily conformable to its realist register. He was a figure from the distant past who could not be interviewed. And although constructed as a character in a narrative, he was given no personality. More significantly, allegory is not a mode to which sports commentators are accustomed, as MacPherson's unease with the idea of symbolism showed. Finally, the Olympic Games are now heavily marketed as gatherings for peace, so the ancient association with warfare was an alien concept. Thus, from the perspective of the sports reporter, the differences between Hercules and the athletes gathered round him would have been more striking than the likenesses. Not only have the gods vanished from Mount Olympus, but we have lost the habit of thinking about human activities as shadowing their deeds.

Our loss may seem trivial, but from the perspective of Jungian analytical psychology the gods and heroes aided not only individuals but also communities to gain a better intuitive understanding of their predispositions and needs. We can see this by looking both at what might have been made of the Barcelona spectacle, and at the values which attach to the sporting hero in routine television coverage.

The Barcelona Hercules could have been the mythical hero embarked on a journey of self-discovery such as we described in chapters 2 and 6. Starting with his separation from the familiar and progressing through painful initiation, it concluded with his eventual return, bringing with him the great gift of the Games. Embedded as he was in conflict, exposed to monsters and other dangers, Hercules had potent associations with the kind of rebirth motifs that often express the renewal of the psyche. But these quasi-religious associations latent in the performance in the stadium were exactly what television's concentration upon spectacle ensured most spectators would overlook. The organisers' attempt to offer a spiritually or psychologically regenerative hero for our time did not succeed.

Accepting that many of the mythological elements embedded in Olympics ceremonies were ignored or suppressed in the process of mediation to television audiences is one thing. Finding traces of ancient myths in the routine coverage of sporting activities is a rather different challenge, because their presence is not consciously indicated in any way, whereas it was signalled boldly by the organisers in Barcelona.

Consider, for instance, the forming of heroes. As with all popular media icons, the public – in this case a large sector of the audience for television sports – choose their own heroes from the many candidates offered them. The process, though fostered knowingly by broadcasters and marketing departments, depends only to some extent upon their activities, and far more upon the devotion of fans and the demand of the television audience. It is clear that many spectators (for example, the Welsh with rugby and Australians with all sport) devote themselves to their sports with passionate enthusiasm. As Guttmann says, sports have become for some people religions in themselves, with the best practitioners heroes who are worshipped (1978: 25–6). Heroes are not created without a surge of popular desire for what they represent.

The adulation of sporting heroes arises therefore in large part from unconscious desires and impulses that are collective. However, the fact that people buy clothing and equipment merchandised by sports stars and enjoy the association with the image they market implies that while the creation of heroes is urged by the libido, it is directed in the cultural unconscious towards its object. The specific images of both the heroes and their fans are embedded in the cultural, and never more plainly so than when they wear the same team strip in the way that, to take an obvious example, football supporters do. Libido, stirred from the collective unconscious by the common desire to find a hero as a role model, discriminates between one potential form for its expression rather than another through the cultural unconscious. Influenced by the latter, it projects on to one individual rather than another, or one team (by no means invariably the local lot) in preference to their rivals.

Because the search for personal power through identification with the image of a hero is often led by the libido in this way (no less in the twenty-first century than other eras), it could be described as a quasi-religious activity. The description fits when the activity has the devotion of very large numbers of people, for where a psychological search through mythologised experience becomes a collective enterprise, it embodies significant elements of popular intuitive needs.

And this indeed is the point. Whereas Guttmann is plainly correct in asserting that all the surface signs demonstrate the evacuation of the sacred from twentieth-century sport, we can also detect exceedingly strong contra-indications. The latter are sufficiently strong to suggest that the psychological law which Jung derived from Heraclitus is functioning. This posits the idea that sooner or later everything runs to its opposite. Jung called it *enantiodromia*, and we saw it embodied in the behaviour of the trickster in chapter 5.

As we have seen, the great tasks of the contemporary sporting hero are against all odds to win contests, and to strive to break records. In some sports physical danger has to be confronted, and in all of them athletes have to face painful difficulties. These include lack of physical or mental fitness; the technical difficulties of the sport, and rules that often make the task harder; and the strength of the competition. Equally devastating are private hells of self-doubt, and the public hell of failure and humiliation.

The sportsman or woman, as opposed to the solitary games-player, acts in a rule-bound world – the world of the ego where will and consciousness dominate. It is that which allows such an individual to gain recognition as a hero – something which the solitary games-player who has ready access to the personal unconscious can never be. Like every other hero, the sporting hero has to be seen to have confronted not only every conceivable external hardship, but also all his or her deepest fears and doubts.

In the first half of the 1990s, Linford Christie was a British national sporting hero much lauded on television. He captained the men's team of track athletes. There was no question that he had completed all the external tasks of the athletic hero, winning countless sprint championships (including the 100 metres sprint in the Barcelona Olympics) and breaking world records. When he ran, his face became a totally focused mask. This expression, often featured in slow-motion close up recordings of his races, could be read as the haunting sign of his knowledge of the internal hells through which the supreme champion must pass. Thus he was an obvious repository of the heroic archetype.

The television sporting hero differs from those whose triumph seems eternal. We have seen ample evidence of the way television practice invites the sports spectator to celebrate the increase of human vitality. But time has another inescapable dimension in sports aside from the measuring of speed and records – namely, the short professional life-cycle of most athletes. Indeed, few sports commentators omit to mention whether an athlete is still improving, has reached his or her peak, or is in decline. So the waning of human energies is simultaneously implicated in every celebration of their waxing. In 1995, Christie announced his immediate retirement in a fit of pique; and although he later changed his mind, it was impossible not to be aware, with the champion in his early thirties, that his top-level running career must be nearly over.

The fact that our sporting idols rise and fall across the screen in swift succession makes them resemble in some ways the archetypal image of the year king or sacrificial hero. As such, they belong to a line that reaches back to the vegetative gods and goddesses. Their intense but brief lives are dedicated to us as spectators and invested with our libido, as the inflated fees they earn demonstrate. We accept their heroic feats as our due, and they celebrate for us the triumph of our desire for strength and vitality. They also mark the years' passage. Therefore, to some degree they perform a function like that of the dying kings and heroes of old whose sacrifice was intended to assure the harvest's fertility. However, today's sporting heroes do not wax and wane in accordance with the year's farming seasons, but do so in a rhythm that embodies in stark miniature the rising and ebbing of life. At one fairly obvious level, then, they hallow human fertility and vitality; and this is confirmed by the way in which sportswear designed for a number of activities (swimming, tennis, gymnastics and track events, for example) shows off the physique of the athletes who help to market it. Not only does such clothing display athletes' strength, but it also often enhances the sexuality of their images. Christie, for example, started wearing a new style of Lycra running suit in the early 1990s that did just this. The effectiveness of this appeal is evidenced by the numbers of people who seek to empower themselves vicariously by copying their heroes' appearance. Thereby, incidentally, they signal the way that products of the cultural unconscious seep into cultural and collective consciousness.

The special quality of television sporting heroes is confirmed and complemented by the magical nature of the space they occupy. Contrary to MacAloon's belief that the loss of frame boundaries blurs the impact of the Olympic ceremonies (1984: 263), it can be argued that conditions for the production of myth are met in televised sporting events in that they are often carefully set up to prepare audiences for their quasi-religious significance. On the sports field itself, as Guttmann observes, the progression from play through games and contests to sports seems to involve an increasing degree of spatio-temporal separateness from ordinary space and time (1978: 5–7). Thus, in the minds of many fans, their home stadium becomes a sacred place, no matter whether it be a national monument or an almost unknown venue. This is true of many sports on both sides of the Atlantic (Bale 1991: 131; Trujillo and Krizek 1994).

The kind of separation to which Guttmann refers is typically developed further in television coverage of sporting events. The viewer is introduced to a place and time analogous to a magical zone. Everything, including the scheduling of programmes into clearly demarcated slots, the glamour of their title sequences, their modes of address, and the lionising of star performers, lets the audience know that the televised arena is a place in which the extraordinary can almost always be anticipated and is often delivered by heroes with seemingly superhuman qualities (see Clarke and Clarke 1982: 70–2).

This is clearly demonstrated when the magical arena is violated. When, early in 1995, Eric Cantona responded to provocation during a game in the English soccer league by jumping into the terraces and kicking a fan, it was more than just the assault which shocked television audiences. He had breached the frame boundaries surrounding the sacred, and in so doing cast off the hero's invisible mantle. Because it entailed the descent of a hero, it was a desecration more abhorrent than that of the fans who from time to time run the other way on to the pitch in the vain hope that entering the sacred space will enable them to touch the glory of their heroes.

Jung reminds us that images which seem to have magical qualities are invested with energies rising from the unconscious. Finding their archetypal sources helps us perceive more clearly the values which the present-day myth expresses. The year gods were sacrificed to assure human survival and the continuity of the seasons. In this function they clearly differed from today's sporting heroes, even though the lives of the latter as television performers are short. How, then, can the myth of sporting heroes be read? There seem to be at least two opposing ways in which television spectators might understand the myths projected by their athletic heroes, depending upon the stage in life and personal development of the individual viewer.[10]

The first is found where recognition of the inevitable decline in athletes' sporting prowess furnishes people with a psychological role model. It could conceivably support them through a time of crisis brought on by the changes with which the ageing process inevitably confronts the individual. Instances of athletes providing such a role model include some of those former sporting heroes who have a continuing screen life as commentators or experts. At their best, they recall the archetypal image of the wise old person. Jung said of such figures that they represent knowledge, reflection, insight, wisdom, cleverness, intuition, and positive moral qualities

---

[10] Although gratifications research into the pleasures people take from televised sports is still in the early stages of exploration, we know from the work of Lawrence A. Wenner and Walter Gantz that audience experiences are diverse. They tend to vary according to the sport watched and the social position of the viewer. As it happens, Wenner's and Gantz's research demonstrated that viewers experienced the strongest feelings when their favourites did well (Wenner and Gantz 1989: 266). But while this conclusion complements my account of the sporting hero's significance, it needs to be emphasised that what follow here are speculative readings which have not been tested by audience research. If, as Sut Jhally says, images of competition are appropriated differently by groups in different social positions (Jhally 1989: 88), many more readings of the sporting hero will be possible than those spelled out below.

(Jung 1948b: 219–30). They may occur in dreams as psychopompi – guides offering the dreamer hints, clues or even direct instruction concerning the nature of the inner life. In life the archetype might attach to an image of an older doctor, teacher, or spiritual leader.

In general, however, it has to be said that the archetypal image of the wise old person does not fit the case of most television sports personalities particularly well. Whatever their private off-screen qualities, it is rare for them to express wisdom reaching beyond the technicalities and occasionally the morality of sporting practice. A few do play this role; but of course most sporting heroes do not 'survive' on television at all after their athletic careers have ended. Some are lionised in a final, valedictory appearance; some join the developing professional circuits for veterans; but many simply slip off the screen into obscurity. Their going hardly troubles the ceaseless celebration of the young in the televising of sport.

This observation indicates the second, dominant way in which such mythic figures may be used by viewers. The glorious eternal youth of the endless stream of sporting heroes will be what makes them the cynosure of most spectators' eyes – not the grace and wisdom of their ageing. Such a reading of the heroic image fits with the expression of the desire for power often associated with sport. Freud noticed that the playing of sports can represent the desire to achieve mastery through more than just the physical contest, because a wish to gain the upper hand through psychological conflict may also be acted out. Meanwhile, televised sport offers viewers role models for their own psychological exploration of power relations in society. (If it did not, there would not be the need for sports commentators to scourge foul play as obsessively as they do.) John M. Roberts and Brian Sutton-Smith argue that 'Games are ... models of ways of succeeding over others, by magical power (as in games of chance), by force (as in physical skill games), or by cleverness (as in games of strategy)' (Cited by Guttmann 1978: 9).

But what does fixation upon youth imply for the culture that is locked into it? One answer is prompted by the main factor that all sports seem to have in common: the requirement that participants exercise the will and focus it intensely upon their goal. Jung said of the will:

It is of the greatest importance for the young person, who is still unadapted and has as yet achieved nothing, to shape his conscious ego as effectively as possible, that is, to educate his will ... He must feel himself a man of will, and may safely depreciate everything else in him and deem it subject to his will, for without this illusion he could not succeed in adapting himself socially.

It is otherwise with a person in the second half of life who no longer needs to educate his conscious will, but who, to understand the meaning of his individual life, needs to experience his own inner being. (Jung 1929: 50)

Jung often focused his readers' attention on the second half of life because he saw it as the time when the well-rounded person needed to get in touch with and respond to the unconscious. Not so long ago, religion (and to a lesser degree myths) initiated people in the second half of their lives into an awareness and understanding of the archetypal images as the symbols older than the individual which make up the groundwork of the human psyche, and give access to the unconscious. Through the religious archetypes people were once able to reach a measure of intuitive knowledge of their inner lives. However, for most people religion has now lost that important cultural function (Jung 1931b: 396–403).

Therefore, contemporary propagators of myths and enduring symbols (among which the media are probably the most powerful) carry the burden of this work, whether they know it or not. The significance of routine television programming is that it can relay myths and images which resonate in tune with the ancient archetypes (such as that of the athletic hero). It then reworks them into symbols that convey variations upon those older values in forms adapted to today's needs.

What then of our cultural fixation upon youthful heroes? We have already met this phenomenon (in chapter 5) in Michael Jackson's cultivation of the pseudo-child. As we saw then, in Jung's experience the desire of people in the second half of life to hold on to youth frequently indicated a failure to look towards the unconscious and acknowledge the prompting of primordial images. He also thought it was caused by a fear of facing the inevitable decline of physical energies and a reluctance to prepare for the eventual approach of death (Jung 1931b: 396–403). Thus the ceaseless collective celebration of youth in television sport seems to exalt the triumph of physicality and will. Read metaphorically, it claims the victory of consciousness over the unconscious, and covers a marked collective fear of the inner life.

That is the dominant perspective; but a thorough Jungian analysis will respect the principle of enantiodromia – the idea that all things carry within them the seeds of their opposites and eventually run to them. In this case, it has a bearing on the nature of the hero as a mythical image. As we have seen, the distinctive characteristics of heroes are locked into their classic narrative. They regress, they battle with their dark side, and in the process they may suffer injury. If they succeed they emerge changed by the encounter with the opposites, and are more completely adapted to their present stage in life. What is more, they have to expose themselves to the danger not once but many times. It is a lifelong process. 'What we seek in visible human form is not man, but the superman, the hero or god, that *quasi-human* being who symbolises the ideas, forms, and forces which grip and mould the soul' (Jung 1956a: 178).

As a figure who represents the willingness to undergo repeated trans-formations to explore wholeness, the hero is analogous to the priest (Samuels, Shorter and Plaut 1986: 66). Thus, masked beneath our over-riding absorption with the youthfulness of television's sporting super-stars, there lie concealed the seeds of a rather different desire. Perhaps one day televised sports will provide a platform for heroes with the potential to offer viewers a role model for more challenging explorations of the self than those restricted to developing physical power and the control of will.

8   The polycentred self: *The Passion of Darkly Noon*

This chapter derived much of its shape and several of its core ideas from work done by my former research student Catriona Miller, for whose generous input I am most grateful.

This and the following two chapters examine films that present the spectator with images of the archetype of wholeness, the self. The followers of Jung, in the course of their ruminations about the nature and functioning of the psyche, developed two distinct models of the self. Although they are not irreconcilable, they do have a different basis. The older model, originally delineated by Jung himself, is the Classical configuration. It characterises psychological development as progress towards an individuation in which unity is achieved through the balancing out of opposites. The many are contained within the one: the entire pantheon of archetypal energies is held in balance within the one overarching dominant, the self. It goes with this that the Classical model often features the self though a single godhead, and is for that reason described as monotheistic. Given the dominance in Western cultures of belief in the individual as a unique personality, it is not surprising that our screen fictions often feature monotheistic models of the self. We shall analyse examples of such fictions in the two chapters that follow this.

The Classical model has limitations which inhibit good therapeutic practice, in the opinion of some Jungian psychoanalysts. They point out that where the unified self is seen as the ultimate goal of analysis, everything else in the psyche and in therapeutic analysis is relegated to second place (Samuels 1990: 107). The Archetypal school of Jungians (among whom James Hillman is a leading figure) therefore give priority to deepening consciousness and integrating each of the images that derive from the deep unconscious separately. Archetypal analysts think it preferable to attend to all the voices and images that emerge from the psyche, integrating each in its own right. The resultant picture favours a polycentred (or, where the archetypes are represented by types of god, polytheistic) image where the self is de-emphasised in favour of better insights into emotions and relationships between the parts (Samuels 1990: 107–8). It is with just such a polycentred image of the self that *The Passion of Darkly Noon* concludes, and it is to this film that we turn now.

A young, Bible-fearing man, Darkly Noon (Brendan Fraser) stumbles through a forest escaping from the mob who have slaughtered his parents and members of their religious cult. After he collapses, he is found by Jude (Loren Dean) and taken to recover in a house deep in the forest where a young woman, Callie (Ashley Judd), lives. When she has nursed him back to health, she asks Darkly Noon to stay as part of the family, and the young man finds himself increasingly attracted to the beautiful young blonde. However, the third member of the group is her unwed lover Clay (Viggo Mortensen). Jealousy vitiated by fundamentalist biblical bigotry begins to grip Darkly's soul.

Soon he meets an angry old woman who lives alone in the forest. Roxy (Grace Zabriskie) tells him that Callie has taken over the home that used to be her own, first seducing her husband and killing him before taking her son Clay as lover. Persuaded by Roxy, and a vision of his dead parents, that Callie is a witch, Darkly is convinced he must destroy her and Clay to eradicate their sins. He mounts a ritual assault on the house, injures Clay severely and sets the place on fire. But Darkly himself is gunned down by Jude as he is about to kill Callie.

The film's director–scriptwriter, Philip Ridley, and some commentators have remarked that *The Passion of Darkly Noon* draws on both the fairy-tale and the horror film. It forces tropes and devices lifted from these genres into deliberate conflict with each other (Macnab 1996: 49; McLeish 1996: 16). Parody and overstatement often, as here, characterise the work of artists who do not want to represent the real physical or social worlds. Rather, they signal by this means an engagement with ideas beneath the surface that may deal with other arenas of experience – in this case, the psychological.

The stylistic register is distinctly mannered. The director's description of the conflagration that ends the film could account for its style throughout: 'In terms of realism, it's completely nonsensical, but on an emotional level . . . it works absolutely. It's meant to be over the top' (cited by McLeish 1996: 17). Although the style does not interfere with the narrative line, many of the images and events have a surreal quality. For example, in one riverside scene a silver boot the size of a barge drifts into vision out of nowhere and floats downstream before Darkly Noon's (and our) disbelieving eyes. Other occurrences draw attention to their non-naturalism by going far beyond the conventions of realism. A case in point is the filming of the final scenes of destruction where the timescale of the attack and the conflagration it starts is drawn out by a battery of cinematic devices to delay the action well beyond the bounds of realism. Yet another stylistic device centres on the editing, which is often obtrusive, and tends to become increasingly visible as the film progresses to heighten the viewer's sense of the main character's impending madness. But even at the beginning there is an obvious example. When Darkly Noon staggers and falls as he flees in panic through the forest, the film is edited harshly to the irregular stresses of the music's pounding so that, what with hard cuts and elisions that are unexpected (because they jar with the visual rhythm of the action), the mind of the viewer experiences a series of small shocks.

Ridley remarked that he consciously dressed his characters not only in costume but also in make-up and light to make them part of the landscape and use them as images at least as much as fictional personalities (McLeish 1996: 16). So they, too, no less than the plot and its attendant imagery, are abstracted from realism in some way. Their visual construction sometimes recalls cardboard cut-outs saturated with colour. Thematically, too, several characters resemble cut-outs in that they have two faces. Only Clay and Jude have constant natures. Darkly Noon first loves Callie, then hates her and tries to exterminate her. And Callie is framed in deliberate ambivalence so that we are never quite sure whether she is a sensual angel or a witch. Her pink perfection (a sweetness of the flesh which seems to imply a sweetness of the heart also) dissolves instantly into focused and aggressive rage when Roxy shoots up her house. The ambivalence of both characters provides good illustrations of enantiodromia.

Imagery is therefore of such significance in this film that it invites analysis in its own right. There are various image clusters that are held in thematic tension with each other: principal among the explicit images are the forest and the house in the sunlit clearing. Both are placed in iconic juxtaposition not only to each other but also to the outside world (which we hear about but do not see). In addition, the contrast between day and night is heavily marked. To some extent the characters have associations with particular elements of these clusters – Clay with the forest and the wood that he cuts and works; Callie with light and the clearing in the glade and also with the house, which is falling down; Darkly Noon with the tension between night and day.

Although we don't see Callie and Clay together before the arrival of Darkly Noon, we have plenty of evidence that their passionate relationship has been in place for some time. They are deeply involved. Callie seems totally wrapped up in him, yet when we first encounter her she is alone, sensually pining for his return. In terms of the mythological symbols that feed analytical psychology, their passion is so nearly complete that it almost makes them the perfect syzygy – but not quite.

In its perfected form the syzygy presents the linking of opposites in a pair. It sometimes occurs as an abstract interlinked symbol like

Yin and Yang but often as the male–female couple representing animus and anima who might be shown as lovers, the king and queen. The alchemists, to emphasise that they intended the syzygy to refer to abstract concepts, sometimes gathered both genders into one and depicted it as a hermaphrodite. Thus the syzygy reflects the ideal in which opposite elements held in balance comprise the differentiated *self*.

However, the Callie–Clay pairing, although close enough to completeness to draw our minds towards the image of the complex self as a symbol of totality, is not perfectly stable. The first symptom of imbalance shows when, despite his obvious passion for Callie, Clay from time to time leaves her and wanders off. And, in contrast to Darkly Noon, he is able to get in touch with himself when he gets confused. He does so by going into the forest 'for a walk in the dark' until he sorts things out. This implies an ability to look or listen for prompts from the unconscious. But although he is able to gain access to the unconscious, Clay does not have a highly developed conscious awareness. This is not to say that he lacks intelligence. On the contrary, he has the qualities of physis. He is a skilled joiner who can make anything work: under his hands wood takes on almost pliable form. And he is a magician who takes childlike pleasure in playing with Callie and pulling objects from her hair and breast. However, his consciousness is at best only partially formed. His other dominant characteristic, the inability to speak, underlines the idea of his inarticulate innocence. We may guess that when his bad temper shows (as Callie says it does) it is caused by frustration of the desire to escape his present condition. This is likely to be the driving force that urges him to return to the woods periodically. He remains tied to the Earth Mother, as the name Clay suggests; and as we shall see, his natural mother Roxy, who lives alone in the forest, exhibits certain characteristics of this archetypal figure.

In contrast, Callie once lived in the outside world but left it when brought into the forest with a broken ankle by Clay's father. This accident, the initiating event for the entire plot, occurred long before the action that we see begins. It is easy to see why the older man would have been attracted to Callie. He would have recognised her as anima: her name is derived from Greek Calista, whom Tennyson described as 'Daughter of the gods, divinely tall, and most divinely fair'. She is luminous, a blonde physically radiant in a golden light that endows her with a fairy-tale beauty of pinks, pastels and gold that is deeply seductive, if not quite natural. It is not hard to see that her intimate manner and free spirit might have seemed to all three men – the father, Clay, and Darkly Noon – to speak directly to their souls just as the anima can do.

Callie's broken ankle and the events which that accident precipitated make her a gender-reversed Oedipus figure. Two stories attach to her.

One treats her as malevolent, the other as a positive, loving figure. Both are roles which the anima can fill, but they reflect other people's take on her, rather than her own sense of what she is. According to Roxy, Callie seduced her husband and brought on his death through heart failure caused by excessive sexual exertion. She then seduced Clay. However, according to Callie herself, Clay's father tried to rape her and died from a heart attack in the attempt. She says that the love between herself and Clay is mutual – she has not played the dark seducer with him. Wherever truth lies between these stories, the fact of Callie's injury is not disputed. Its Oedipal associations bring the topic of incest to mind.

As we saw in chapter 2, Jung had different ideas concerning incest from Freud. Jung believed that this motif, far from always being the expression of a child's banned desire for sexual knowledge of the parent (as his mentor maintained inflexibly), could express a phase in a young person's routine development. Although, as we have had ample opportunity to see, Jung and Freud almost always thought in terms of the activity of the man's psyche, psychoanalytic theory and practice in the early twenty-first century is paralysed if it does not recognise that women experience similar realms of the psyche. We had occasion in chapter 6 to analyse Clarice Starling's encounter with images of the father and her triumph over the horrors that she met in her journey to the underworld. Callie's case differs because she has not prevailed over the parental imago.

Whatever the true nature of the sexual connection between Callie and Clay's father, he died as a consequence. Given their age difference, relations between them would have had overtones of symbolic father–daughter incest. But Callie's was not a face-off with the dark parent from which the daughter arises triumphant, exerting a new-found independence of spirit as Clarice Starling eventually did. After the older man's death, Callie simply shifted her projections, displacing them on to the much less threatening, but closely associated figure of his son, and lost all desire to leave the forest. Hers, then, was an encounter with the unconscious from which she did not emerge at all (either strengthened or wounded). When Darkly Noon bursts into the woods, she remains symbolically embedded in the unconscious, and the intense sexuality of her's and Clay's passion does not disguise its self-enclosed nature.

So as we get to know more about them, it becomes apparent that Callie and Clay together form not so much a syzygy as a uroboros. The difference is crucial. The syzygy represents the self in its most differentiated state. This is attained when both conscious knowledge and the awareness of the unconscious have been developed as fully as possible. In Jungian psychology the uroboros invokes the self before differentiation of ego consciousness from the unconscious has taken place. As Neumann says, it is a highly charged image because it constantly slays, weds and impregnates itself. In one aspect it is an image of perpetuity, and hence of eternity; but in its circularity it also signifies the germ cell of creativity. The round, self-contained uroboros is 'the symbolic self-representation of the dawn state, showing the infancy both of mankind and of the child' (Neumann 1954: 11). It signifies 'the unconscious state . . . the original, basic, psychic situation that is everywhere the rule' (ibid.: 271). Ego-consciousness normally develops only later as the infant grows.

In the Clay–Callie pairing, the green world state of the early unconscious is associated with him while Callie has the qualities of the immature ego. For Jungians, ego is the feeling-toned complex that consists of representations of oneself: it is the way one sees oneself (Hopcke 1992: 77). Ego should be concerned with mediation between the conscious and unconscious (Samuels, Shorter and Plaut 1986: 50). In Callie's case, for all its sweetness and light, ego is in danger of drowning because of her willingness to submit to the draw of the unconscious.

The uroboros with its completeness entire unto itself and its closure from the outer world is, therefore, a symbol that does not convey the idea of a mature self, but rather of origins. In its womb-like circularity, it has strong associations with the archetypal idea of the nurturing Great Mother who represents the primal sea of unconscious out of which consciousness has to struggle (Neumann 1954: 14–16). Where symbols implying uroboric incest occur, as they do in *The Passion of Darkly Noon*, they point to a regression – the surrender of ego-consciousness in whole or in part to the mothering unconscious which reabsorbs it. Neumann points out that such symbolism is always accompanied by the insignia of death to signify the abandonment and dissolution of consciousness before it has flourished completely (ibid.: 17). Note then that Clay's main source of income comes from supplying coffins to the flamboyant town undertaker, Quincy (Lou Myers), and that the latter, exulting in the sombre glories of his profession, visits Clay and Callie shortly after Darkly Noon has taken up residence with them.

As we have had occasion to see elsewhere in this book, the Great Mother has two faces – the loving, nurturing aspect to which we have been referring, and the fearful aspect of the Terrible Mother who fills her children with the (well-founded) terror that she will destroy them. This second side of the Primordial Mother's character is felt by the individual whose ego-consciousness has begun to emerge from the womb of the unconscious, but is experiencing a painful struggle in making the separation. The thrust to achieve maturity is dependent upon the evolution to the fullest capacity of consciousness, the distinguishing mark and *sine qua non* of the human species. However, the urge towards growth has to fight against the psychologically fatal attraction of continued submersion in the unconscious. That attraction is great because it holds out the illusion of a safe return to an earlier, known state, and escape from the fears which come with the enforced adventure into the developing world of consciousness (see Neumann 1954: 39–101). As we have seen – for example, in the case of Clarice Starling – a temporary regression can benefit the individual because it offers a way of revitalising consciousness by revisiting forgotten and repressed states of being in the unconscious and the chance to renew contact with the energies of the Primordial Mother. However, prolonged regression threatens psychological seizure in an earlier, childish state of mind – which can be a form of living death. This is the retrograde attraction which so deeply tempts Callie in her flight from the outer world. The precariousness of her desire for continued existence as a perpetual juvenile is framed by the overarching symbol with which she is linked: Callie realises that the house in which they live is decaying and will soon fall down, notwithstanding Clay's talent for fixing things.

There is indeed a Terrible Mother patrolling the forest in the person of Roxy. She takes pot-shots at the house to remind Callie of her desire for vengeance; and later she poisons Darkly Noon's mind against the young woman. One of the first things she tells him is that a monster lives in the woods. Actually, from the psychoanalytic perspective there are several potential candidates for that role. They include Roxy herself, her dog, her dead husband, Callie (in her witch aspect) and Darkly Noon. The fact that they are all thematically interlinked suggests that the archetypal image has fragmented. Splitting of this kind fits with the kind of psychological instability that the story events reveal.

We first see Roxy when her Rottweiler menaces Darkly Noon. The incident occurs as the latter wanders in the forest, bitten by his emerging feelings for Callie and his jealousy of Clay. As it happens, the savage animal is a recurrent symbol of repressed sexual appetite in mythology which surfaces often in both literature and film (see, for instance, *The Company of Wolves*). But it is not necessary to know the history of the image to appreciate the point: by this stage in the story we are well aware that Darkly's animal instincts are out of control. Deeply repressed, his sexual desires have not moved out of the ambit of the Mother into consciousness, as one incident in particular demonstrates. Before Clay returned from the woods, Darkly had been preparing to show Callie his feelings. He had picked a bunch of white Michaelmas daisies to give her.[11] At

---

[11] The name 'daisy' derives from the Old English equivalent of 'day's eye' to celebrate the way it opens with the sun and follows its progress through the day. The flower has strong associations with the sun, and hence with consciousness. In this context, the daisies imply that Darkly's love for Callie is about to draw him into new self-awareness.

that moment Clay makes his return from the forest carrying an identical gift for Callie. Catching sight of him, Callie runs, sensual, alluring and passionate, into her lover's arms. His hopes wrecked, Darkly crushes his daisies into a ball and drops them at his feet. But on the ground they metamorphose strangely, and when he picks up the ball to look at it, it pricks his thumb. It has turned into one of the dummy birds which Roxy makes from feathers and barbed wire to train her dog not to eat the birds she shoots. Just as pain has curbed the dog's natural appetite and re-directed it, so it does in a most sinister way with Darkly's. He places the barbed-wire bird in the tin where he keeps the icons that excite him most – as if the container holds the formative contents of his mind.

Her black dog is Roxy's only companion, and when it dies her grief is boundless. Their closeness is apparent when, not long after its death, Roxy kills herself. But although the animal and the woman are close, they are not identical. The Terrible Mother has greater power, resisting not only the bringing to consciousness of sexual (animal) desires, but *all* forms of feeling and experience. Roxy's suicide is by no means typical of the Terrible Mother, who does not usually abrogate her own power. In considering its meaning, it is essential to keep in mind the fundamental axiom of Jungian psychology that whatever happens to the images that are the vehicles by which they find expression, the archetypes themselves are not destroyed. They merely go underground and surface again in another form. Where they have been repressed, they resurface with energy at least equivalent to the force with which they were pushed under. Roxy's suicide would therefore lead a Jungian to suspect that the unconscious energies she embodied would reappear, probably demonically augmented, in one of the split-off images with which she was associated. This turns out to be the case when, immediately after her death, Roxy's vengeful aspect transfers on to the addled faces of Darkly's dead parents and they speed his descent into madness.

We first see Darkly Noon at the start of the film while he is blundering through the forest having lost his way. Eventually he collapses and loses consciousness. This is one of several occasions when a character becomes lost in the forest. The dark woods, as in *The Piano* and the chronicles of human imagination since Dante wrote *L'Inferno*, evoke the confusion and obscurity that lies beyond the limits of consciousness. They are fertile and self-sustaining, but although they contain both much that is beautiful and much that inflicts terror, they display few map points to help unwary walkers find their bearings. Darkly's fall therefore symbolically submerges him in the green half-light of the unconscious.

If we accept that the forest can be interpreted as the (endless) un-conscious where people get lost, then the outside world from which

Callie fled and Darkly Noon has been driven is consciousness. Although the film does not take the audience to this world, we find out enough about it to perceive that, whereas the ways of the forest are mazy and hard to discern, life in the outer world is focused with crystal clarity. But the common factor that gives the conscious world its sharp but narrow focus is bigotry. The members of Darkly Noon's community, including his parents, have been murdered by a mob resentful of their enclosed, Bible-fearing cult. Yet the prejudices of Darkly and his parents against Callie and Clay make it plain that the zealots themselves are no less bigoted. As with many cults, the Bible is deployed as if it were a weapon to destroy enemies – not as a record of myths that trace the attempts of a substantial sector of humanity to come to grips with its religiosity.

Symptomatic of Darkly Noon's misuse of the Bible is his imperfect knowledge of it. Despite his unquestioning reverence for its words as the revelation of God's truth, he gets them wrong in a matter no less significant than explaining his own name. The name was chosen by his parents who stuck a pin in the Bible. The pin settled, he says, on the second epistle to the Corinthians, 13, 12, 'For now we see each other through a glass darkly.' However, his quotation is wrong. The verse (which actually comes from the first epistle) does not refer to our power to perceive *each other*, but to look with clarity at the end of time upon the ultimate mystery, the Godhead.

For now we see through a glass, darkly; but then face to face: now I know in part; but then shall I know even as also I am known.

Darkly does not comment on the conjunction of his first and second names; but the idea of darkness at noon resonates with the imagery of the terrible prophecies of the Revelation of St John. When the Lamb of God opens the sixth seal, 'the sun became black as sackcloth of hair, and the moon became as blood' (6, 12). And after the opening of the seventh seal, the sun is darkened for one-third of the day (8, 12). Revelation's portents of calamities to be visited upon the damned reverberate through both the plot and the dialogue of this film. And just as St John's rhetoric relies upon the duality of the themes associated with darkness and light, so too does the film: its dénouement will be neither wholly benign nor wholly evil, but vested with both qualities.

Incidentally, Darkly Noon seems ignorant of the well-known verse following the one from which his name comes: 'And now abideth faith, hope, charity, these three; but the greatest of these is charity' (I Corinthians 13, 13). The quality of disinterested spiritual love which the archaic use of the word charity or *caritas* refers to is entirely foreign to Darkly Noon. On the contrary, his name underlines his starkly oppositional nature; Callie finds it intolerable and calls him Lee, perhaps intuitively attempting to draw him away from the apocalyptic. However, his new name emphasises how the two men are bound to her since her own name is almost an anagram of theirs taken together: Clay/Lee/Callie.

All these factors confirm that the dominant aspect of Darkly's personality represents the archetypal shadow. We have seen before that the shadow is

the 'negative' side of the personality, the sum of all those unpleasant qualities we like to hide, together with the insufficiently developed functions and the contents of the personal unconscious. (Jung 1943: 66)

It will also be recalled that that which is conscious (is in the light) has to be seen against the background of the shadow. The well-rounded personality is not achieved by destroying the shadow and the evil it holds, but by recognising it as a necessary part of the whole. As the shadow, Darkly lives a kind of half-life, catatonically repressed and erratic in purpose – except in twisting down towards the dark. He is not mute, but his mumbling and stuttering make him nearly so. He changes constantly: at one point, before commencing the walk in the dark that culminates in his attempt to murder Callie and Clay, he adopts the broken-machine stance made into an unmistakable icon by Boris Karloff as Frankenstein's monster. It fits with the half-life of the shadow. A type of Caliban, he never anticipates, nor shows any sign of understanding, the impulses that move him.

That said, it seems like a paradox to assert that Darkly is the main source of dynamic energy in the plot. But without his intrusion into the forest, nothing in the lives of the other characters would change. Indeed he is like the obverse face of Clay, arriving and moving in while the other man is away. Clay soothes Callie, but Darkly disturbs her. Clay is 'the only one who can fix anything around here' and Darkly is the one who destroys. This observation conforms well with the nature of the shadow, whose painful entry into lives which may be superficially stable can start an enantiodromian process and introduce necessary psychological adaptation to the changing circumstances – either of the individual or the group. As we shall see, Darkly Noon exerts what is in the end a positive though painful force on Callie and Clay; but only at the very last moment, as Darkly is on the point of striking her down, does Callie see him for what he is.

The dramatic terrain of the film is like a negative image of that in *The Silence of the Lambs*. There, Clarice Starling descends into the underworld and allows her conscious mind to experience the monster held underground – a classic hero's journey. In *The Passion of Darkly Noon* the shadow figure visits the light and brings the terror of the individuation process and the negative unconscious to a heroine who previously had little experience of either.

As the drama unfolds, associations attach to each of the three principal characters which link them with the four prime elements recognised in mediaeval scholarship. Clay, obviously enough, has connections with earth through his name, his nature, and his woodwork with coffins as well as fittings for the home. Darkly Noon's rage burns with red heat, and he destroys the house with fire. But Callie is the figure hardest to understand at first, because her characteristics are only half formed. As we saw earlier, the male characters (and men in the audience) will be drawn by her sensuality to perceiving her as an anima figure. She also has strong associations with air, visually represented in light. When, at the start of the film, Jude drives up to the house and calls for her to help with the young man he has rescued, she is nowhere to be seen. A moment passes and – our first sight of her – she emerges silently from the black forest into the sun-flecked glade as if Jude's call had brought her into being.

The other element with which Callie is repeatedly linked is water. On Darkly's fourth day in the forest, she leads him to a spa spring. Darkly refuses to follow her into the water to escape from the heat of the day; and he tries to cool the rising heat of his interest in her by stopping her from casting off her clothes. Callie bathes, sensually submerging herself in the soothing waters, surrendering herself to the urges of libido. She is intuitively in touch with her desires as they form (and hence open to the primal unconscious) even to the point of being ready to allow herself to drown in these pleasures. However, she rises from the water like a reborn naiad, and (seemingly unaware in her childlike primal innocence of her allure) seductively asks Darkly to remove the dragonfly that has become tangled in her hair. Incapable of delicacy in anything he does, he crushes the tiny form. Like its symbolic cousin the butterfly, the dragonfly may signify metamorphosis into maturity. Callie wants rid of it, and Darkly cannot handle it in the way she asks. It is an early sign that he cannot act in the way she requires, which is that he should be a part of the family, but should not spoil (that is, change) anything. We may recall that those who caught sight of the naiads bathing risked being 'possessed' by these anima figures and driven mad (Grimal 1986: 285).

Presently Callie leads Darkly Noon to the heart of the forest, a grotto with a pool that reflects a magical, undulating light on to the walls and ceiling and the two visitors. The dimensions of time dissolve here: a handprint made thousands of years earlier decorates the wall. For Callie, murmuring her assent to its claims on her feelings, it is a holy place. Water and the underground cavern bear well-established associations in myths and dreams with the feminine, implying entry into the collective unconscious. The centrality for Callie of this secret place brings home the point that the conjunction of her elements (light, air and water) enriches the symbolism of a delicate consciousness barely beginning to emerge from the uroboric union with the unconscious.

When Clay returns, the family of three which Callie naively wants to put together is at once put to the test when Darkly finds himself excluded. Locked out but jealously fascinated, he spies on the lovers in their bedroom. Unable to reconcile himself, he flees the household, stalking the woods in mad moonlight, the tree trunks lit like the steel bars of a monumental jail. Having spent a night of despair in the open, he wakes to the sight of a silver boot the size of a ferry floating down river past him. The vision of the boot, at once grotesque and magical, hints at Darkly's encroaching madness. Coarse in its gross exaggeration of the dumbly physical (the foot, so distant from the head, seemingly alien to the soul) it also calls to mind the outsized boot, the ineluctable guilt, of lame Oedipus. The sense of magic arises, besides the incongruity of its presence, from its size and shining colour. It carries a passenger, a bird that looks very small perched on this huge vessel, another flying creature that has well-attested symbolic connections with the idea of soul. And although the possible spirituality of the bird is far outweighed by the mass of the boot, the idea that spirit invests even the most doltish body will later be reinforced when Roxy's dog dies. Roxy and Darkly then turn the boot into a funeral vessel to ferry the beast to the other world, setting the bizarre boat on fire to ensure the animal's soul reaches its final destination.

Darkly returns to the house and retreats to his room, obsessed like a Peeping Tom with stolen glimpses of the lovers' naked passion. His jealousy, already fanned by Roxy into hatred, pushes him to project his distorted feelings on to Callie as an evil witch. But his blocked sexual desires soon develop into a drive that embraces a broader range of passions. Binding himself in barbed wire so tightly that it cuts his flesh and he bleeds, he makes himself into a type of barbed-wire bird. As he lashes the steel thorns to his body, Nick Bicât's and Philip Ridley's stream-of-consciousness song 'Look What You've Done to My Skin' betrays his awareness (at some level of his being) that he is preparing an evil act.

> This feeling is scary, like sparks on the skin.
> How it excites me is like a sin.
> Pray for forgiveness, this feeling is wrong,
> But while I'm praying, the feeling goes on.

Darkly wears his vest of thorns until he dies, his mortification having strong visual links with the Christian iconography of sacrifice. Although the obverse of the Christ-type, he is now moving towards fulfilling the prophetic aspect of his name and nature – bringing light through darkness. The paradox implicit in this is that out of the evil that Darkly brings as the shadow, good will come: his murderous deeds will have the purging power of the angels' apocalyptic destruction in the Book of Revelation.

Darkly's parents appear to him in a vision shortly after he has discovered Roxy's suicide. Adopting the role of Terrible Parent that her death has left vacant, they rant at their son, urging him to wreak destruction on Callie. As they hector him, their wounds putrefy, an effective metaphor for the psychological corruption caused by an excessively close connection between an adult and his or her parents. Callie is not the only character dominated by the parental imago.

Finally ejected from the house by Callie because the jealous anger between himself and Clay has become uncontainable, Darkly carries his few belongings to the cavern deep in the woods and prepares for revenge. He dresses himself for war in scarlet paint which, while working for Clay, he had applied to an infant's cradle. Now blood leaking from his wounds mixes with the paint. Thus Ridley forges an image cluster worthy of Nicolas Roeg: scarlet paint/blood/flame/passion/death/rebirth. Backing this, the red handprint on the wall (against which Darkly measures his own hand), invokes the archetypal via the mute presence of the ancient generations.

Intercut with his preparations for war, Clay and Callie are seen making love with tender ferocity. The camera eroticises the lovers in glowing light as they fling themselves at each other; but it also shows Callie wearing both a filmy skirt and solid walking boots. The imagery conjoins the magical and the corporeal: their love, no matter how ethereal to them, has to remain lodged in the body. It is a plausible metaphor for the necessity of living consciously as well as through the unconscious. Yet their mutual self-absorption is once again total: they are unconscious of Darkly Noon's murderous advance on the house until he bursts in on them.

Darkly's attack is literally electrifying as he searches for the couple to cleanse their sinning by slaughter. While a thunderstorm gathers, he launches himself against them in mad rage, stalking the house like an incarnation of lightning. The long steel gouge that he wields grounds his pent-up energy in the building where streams of sparks and flame burst in succulent slow motion out of every skirting-board and light-fitting. He confronts Clay, wounds him with the heavy gouge, and hurls him from the house. The injuries to his leg turn Clay into another Oedipal figure wounded so severely in the confrontation with the shadow that he cannot protect Callie. Darkly now goes after her. An endless primal scream (far beyond the capacity of mortal lungs) rips out of his body. Around him the house bursts into flame as if fired by his yowl; and when he corners Callie, his focused intensity terrifies her. Yet, at the very last moment before he swings the gouge at her, she cries out, 'I love you!' It is as though she finally recognises only at the point of death that she has to embrace the shadow. It is the turning-point for her, and the instant at which she is saved from extinction by Jude. He had been searching for Darkly to take him out of the forest and save him from his own passions; but now, in the extremity of the moment, Jude has to shoot Darkly to save the young woman. Jude pulls Callie from the conflagration, the house becomes a second funeral pyre and cremates Darkly Noon's corpse.

Why is it Jude who kills Darkly Noon? We have mentioned plot motivation, but his action fits the psychological design too. His name recalls the apostle who castigated people for pursuing ungodly lusts, warning that they would be 'set forth for an example, suffering the vengeance of eternal fire' (Jude 7). Just as his namesake sought to guard against errors brought about by unbridled passion, Jude has tried to do the same for Darkly Noon. He lives in the shadow of exultant death, residing with and working for the local undertaker Quincy who, like an enthusiastic preacher, portrays death as a magisterial event that enriches him and fills him with delight. However, as a young man, untouched by its poetry, Jude merely accepts death as a matter of fact.

All the elements of Jude's personality suggest that his psychological function is to represent ego-consciousness. Thoroughly practical, he possesses a commonsense approach to life based on the application of observed actuality. He has an active morality: he befriends Darkly, and advises people to avoid the extremes of passion. Although he and Quincy are the only characters who dwell outside the forest and travel in and out of it at will, he is not a free man, being held like the others in the forest's ambit. He often says he wants to move away but is unable to. In comparable fashion, ego-consciousness cannot escape the pull of the unconscious, try though it may. The action of the film takes place in unmapped landscape where Jude and Quincy are the only characters from the outside world who can find their way. So, to extend this line of thought, it is as a particular inflection of consciousness, insight or self-consciousness that Jude destroys the rampant shadow, Darkly Noon, and reduces it to manageable forms assimilable at least in part to the ego.

The events of the final morning allow us to pull this high melodrama into meaning. No title card opens this section, unlike all the others which have been numbered with the twelve days since Darkly's entry to the forest. The omission of a title for the last chapter licenses the inference that we have entered a new time. It is a new beginning. Although the forest still engulfs the stunned survivors, everything else has changed with the house burnt, Darkly Noon dead and Clay lying injured. No longer luminous, Callie is grubby, spattered with Darkly's dried blood and burdened with sorrow for his death. Remembering that archetypal energies are not discharged when the images that bear them are destroyed, we can interpret the change in her to mean that she has assimilated the shadow formerly lodged in him. The fire Darkly brought into her house has burnt her. This is the first change that suggests a reorganisation of the psyche.

Without warning, a family of circus artistes with an elephant wander out of the dark forest and into the glade's exhausted dawn. They make a fine visual impact, though the effect is somewhat marred by wooden dialogue. Unfortunately the script obliges these characters to explain their presence and how the silver boot came to be in the river. Better if these things had been left mysterious, for the troupe, both in their sudden materialisation from nowhere (like Callie at the start of the film) and in their professional work, once again connect us to the theme of magic.

For the Jungian, the magical expresses unconscious energies, as we saw in chapter 7. The more limited an individual's field of consciousness, the more he or she encounters the contents of the psyche projected on to exterior objects. The latter, because they are invested with this internal energy, seem not quite settled in their usual frame, bounded by the laws of cause and effect. Rather, they are perceived as having magical powers which can affect the life of the perceiving subject either for good or ill. Indeed, 'the effect does not proceed via the object but via the subject. The magical rite, like all magic . . . acts upon the subject who practises [it] . . . ' (Neumann 1954: 209). In the context of analytical psychology, the magician (like the shaman or priest) is understood as intervening in order to restore a balance between consciousness and the potentiated unconscious contents (see also Samuels, Shorter and Plaut 1986: 88–9; Jung 1957: 44–5).

Here the role of magician or minister is played by the leader of the troupe. However, he does not address the survivors of the fire in the charismatic fashion of the shaman, who reveals numinous energies to people who need to be persuaded the unconscious exists. Rather, because all those present are in danger of being stuck in the forest (i.e. are exposed to the risk of an unconscious inflation that threatens to overwhelm the psyche), he speaks softly of his own error in supposing that it would be easy to find a way through the forest. He and his family offer a corrective to the excesses of the unconscious and allow the claims of moral consciousness to be heard. The troupe are peaceable and embrace the others with charity – the antique term we parsed earlier as referring to disinterested compassion and love. The young son confirms this when he gives Callie his prized possession, a model of the silver boot. Meanwhile, the tame elephant that accompanies them could hardly be more different from Roxy's dog. Animal nature holds no perils for this family, but is accepted as natural – a fact registered in that the parents are fertile. Not only do they have children, but they accommodate without difficulty the more animalistic (and less differentiated) personalities of young people.[12] The family offer to help the devastated group of survivors in the glade and their offer is accepted. Significantly, each group will have to help the other, since only the forest-dwellers know the way out.

The Passion of Darkly Noon is yet another drama in which sacrifice represents the destruction of the old and makes way for psychological rebirth. Callie and Clay have suffered the Oedipal wounding that will precede their rebirth, and the destruction of their shaky house means that they now have to find a new home. However, we have here a reverse progression from that of the familiar journey of the hero. In this instance the main storyline does not include a hero testing his consciousness against the forces of the dark. A minor character whom we do not see often, Jude's infrequent presence is significant if we accept that he stands for the counterbalance of conscious insight. His function in the culmination of the drama does not take the form of an arduous long struggle to close in on the monster. Rather, he bursts in and ends a confrontation that he has been powerless to prevent. What precedes that sudden irruption of consciousness has resolved itself into open warfare conducted by more-or-less unconscious energies (Roxy, her husband, and her dog, Clay and Darkly Noon) in an attempt to submerge in the forest the under-developed ego (Callie). The chaos of unconscious forces out of control drives the narrative. The young couple are saved only by the final awakening of Jude (representing a more advanced stage of socialised moral consciousness) to the nature of the crisis.

The film concludes with the disparate group of survivors slowly winding their way out of the forest. The reading that we have been developing allows us to perceive that the group represents an image of the self. But this is an image very different from that in which most journeys of heroes culminate, and which we shall see played out against dreadful odds in Dennis Potter's TV film *Cold Lazarus*. Here we have no lasting union of opposites characteristic of the classical idea of the self as a balanced totality. Rather, these characters suggest an association of components of the psyche in a balance that is provisional and temporary. Two related points bear on this. First, in the course of the movie we have seen how certain archetypal energies have become displaced from one character on to others. There is no reason to suppose that the process will end when

---

[12] Roxy says that Callie is barren. It is a motif which complements the idea of the uroboric sexual relation between herself and Clay.

the characters leave the forest and a new environment envelopes them. Secondly, the archetypal energies (represented through the characters) alter in dominance and influence within the self relative to each other as the story progresses. Although the present resolution of tension brings a sense of exhaustion, and with it release, the dynamic energy of the characters will recover. They are not at the end of their existences, and the flux of energies among and around the archetypes will continue and may well lead to renewed conflicts and liaisons. The film concludes, then, with an image that can be read as a metaphor for the polycentred, provisionally balanced self. But it is plainly a balance that will not hold for long after the characters emerge from the forest into the community.

9   Haunted: searching for the whole self

In the 1990s, British and North American audiences were once again being invaded by a wave of phantoms and aliens. Some of them travelled in on the Ultra High Frequency wave band. Others, like their predecessors in the 1950s and 1970s, came in on beams of light.

From the perspective of analytical psychology, ghosts can be seen as representations of half-formed impressions generated in or released after suppression from the unconscious. It hardly needs adding that they are often regarded as hostile and the cause of deep distress. But one of the interesting features of the 1990s invasion was that a high proportion of the visitors were more or less friendly.

Take, for example, a series transmitted in 1996 on the mainline commercial channel in the UK under the title *Strange But True*. This found its material in the reconstruction of all manner of strange encounters. It could be described as reality programming focusing on the occult world. As such it shared with other reality programming (such as documentary) a marked tendency to favour tabloid journalism – the kind of thing previously located in programmes about the activities of the emergency services – such as the BBC's *999* and CBS's *Rescue 911*. The reality TV format imported several features into *Strange but True*: reconstructions, eye-witness accounts to verify extraordinary events and the rhetoric of immediacy, with the whole thing being played at a crisp pace. The short segments – perhaps four 'happenings' crammed into each half-hour programme (which made for about 6 minutes running time per segment) – kept the frissons coming fast. Before all else, the reality programme has to be a market-oriented entertainment package (Kilborn and Izod 1997: 157–61).

Strange But True presented its viewers with recorded instances of everything from psychic dogs to sightings of aliens – with a good number of benign ghosts and vicious poltergeists to fill the measure. Particularly significant was the way the programme addressed the viewer. The show was hosted by Michael Aspel. No presenter working in British television at the time more perfectly personified a smooth and cozy urbanity.

Nobody could do more to reassure and domesticate, guaranteeing the underlying friendly ethos of the show. His scripts were devised so as to perform a calculated double act. On the one hand they were written to placate, with their mild scepticism, those who doubted the occult. So, for example, Aspel would ask periodically whether the manifestation of some phenomenon or other could be the result of a clever fraud. But, on the other hand, the programme's reconstructions often favoured occult explanations and were invariably accompanied by comfortingly eerie music, so we would know that the weird truly was in front of our eyes – 'strange but true' indeed, the reassuring frisson. These were ghosts and aliens perfectly served up to feed conversation at the office coffee-break the next morning. Sometimes they had the power to distress, but always pleasingly so. Viewers could be secure in the knowledge that their world view would not be shaken. There could be no better demonstration of just how familiar and unthreatening, at the domesticated end of the scale of fear, such minor manifestations of the demonic had become in popular screen fiction. But precisely because these domesticated phantoms accommodated the audience with so little disturbance, the cultural unconscious did not seem to have had much to do with their advent.

Two films that moved large audiences during this decade were *Truly, Madly, Deeply* (Anthony Minghella, 1991, UK), featuring Juliet Stevenson and Alan Rickman in the lead roles, and *Ghost* (Jerry Zucker, 1990, USA) with Demi Moore and Patrick Swayze as principal protagonists. In each film an early death claims the male partner, breaking a loving union. Soon afterwards each grieving woman is visited by the ghost of her dead man. Both phantoms account for their return by saying that their love for their woman is so strong it makes them incapable of leaving her. Alan Rickman's ghost, Jamie, hovers deliciously between the intensely sweet (he continues to play the cello to delight Nina when he returns) and, at the opposite extreme, the annoying (in that he brings back to his former home a growing band of vagabond wraiths with whom he has made friends since his death). In due course, however, he has to learn how to respond to Nina's entanglement with another man. In the American film, Sam Wheat (Patrick Swayze) also suffers, like Jamie, the pain of a love that has become unattainable. Since Sam cannot be seen or heard by the other characters but is capable of observing that Molly Jensen (Demi Moore) is at risk of being harmed by a former friend and a gang of criminals, he has to learn new ways of communicating with her in order to save her.

Eventually, having solved a number of (more or less dramatic) problems for his woman, each ghost releases his former lover to commence a new life of her own free from the quasi-living presence of the past. In psychological terms, therefore, it is not difficult to see both Jamie's and Sam's ghosts as projections of the surviving partner's emotions. Each ghost functions as a kind of fantasy mirror which, in the lineaments of the beloved man, actually reflects back at the woman a portrayal of her own feelings at a time when they are too painful to absorb. It is possible to describe a kind of dynamic plot line in respect of both films. To over-simplify, each ghost cleaves despairingly to his partner when he first returns – just as she does to the memory of him. With the passage of time, however, other men appear on the far horizons of the woman's awareness of a world which at first seemed to have been left utterly void by the death of her lover. As the living begin to claim more of her attention, disturbances involving the ghost and the newcomer ensue. These tribulations can be read as projections of the doubts of the bereaved woman, and of her guilty fears that she is betraying the deceased, even if only in memory. In the end, the ghost releases her at the very moment that she is ready to return to the world of the living and take a new lover. It is not hard to see the final farewell of both Jamie and Sam (which occurs only when the women are reconciled to the necessity of parting from their wraiths) as the withdrawal of Nina and Molly's animus projections upon their dead partners. New lovers take the place of the dead, and in turn become the vessels for the women's amorous projections.

So while each of the two films is dominated by the narrative motif of the ghost whose loss is so great that he struggles to return to material existence, it has its psychological antithesis in the passionate desire of the survivor to rejoin her lover and escape the bonds of the flesh. The question remaining for us to answer is what might be the attractions of this trope for the twentieth-century movie-going audience.

I want to suggest a parallel with a set of frequently reiterated themes (that is, a topos) that at first sight has no obvious link to the subject-matter with which we have been dealing. The connection is to the ancient convention in which the celebration of humankind's sacred love for the divinity finds an outlet through verse that takes an erotic form. The *locus classicus* for this topos is 'The Song of Solomon'. A pair of lovers sing verses that celebrate the beauty of their love and their desire for each other. Each describes the other in richly sensual terms, but does so using language that registers a desire for more than the flesh alone.

Thy navel is like a round goblet, which wanteth not liquor: thy belly is like an heap of wheat set about with lilies.

Thy two breasts are like two young roes that are twins.

Thy neck is a tower of ivory; thine eyes like the fishpools in Heshbon, by the gate of Bath-rabbim: thy nose is as the tower of Lebanon which looketh toward Damascus. (7:2–4)

The many lush images in 'The Song' redolent of the enclosed garden and the City of Jerusalem were interpreted in the Christian era by textual exegetes eager to read Old Testament writings as prophetic of the new epoch to come after Christ. They constructed around these images and those of the ecstatic lovers a complex allegory which was buttressed by and in turn reinforced authorised Christian iconography. Not to go into the fine filigree of detail, the garden was held to embody the idea of the soul, and (in a reading for which the verses themselves give some fairly direct grounding) the City of Jerusalem stood for the Church itself. The bride sighing for her bridegroom came to be perceived as representing the yearning of the soul for Christ. Conversely, Christ yearns for the love of the human soul.

As it happens, there is an episode in 'The Song of Solomon' which is comparable in its feeling tone to Nina's and Molly's experience of the loss of Jamie and Sam.

> By night on my bed I sought him whom my soul loveth: I sought him, but I found him not.
> I will rise now, and go about the city in the streets, and in the broad ways I will seek him whom my soul loveth: I sought him, but I found him not.
> The watchmen that go about the city found me: to whom I said, Saw ye him whom my soul loveth?
> It was but a little that I passed from them, but I found him whom my soul loveth: I held him, and would not let him go, until I had brought him into my mother's house . . . (3:1–4).

Described in a different way, the idea that runs through 'The Song of Solomon' and turns up in much erotic sacred poetry through to the seventeenth century is that passionate desire for the beauty of another human being can lead a lover to knowledge of the godhead. Through the eye, the lover delights in the lineaments of the beloved, and remembers that humanity is made in the image of its maker; meditation leads the mind to the spiritual and devotion frees the soul.

Converting this trope into the language of analytical psychology, we can recognise a certain mythological pattern generated when anima and animus shape the expression of libido. (Some variants of these patterns were examined in earlier chapters.) In particular the mutual yearning of animus and anima for each other seems to find expression in the syzygy comprising the interlocked images of the two partners, male and female. As we observed in chapter 8, in its perfected form it may occur as an abstract interlinked symbol such the Yin and Yang. But often it presents as the male–female couple representing animus and anima who might be shown as lovers, the king and queen. The syzygy represents the completion of the *self* through love in the perfect, balanced conjunction of opposites. It is a beautiful, static image of perfection but hard to attain because the pressures of everyday life – the sense that eventually comes to most mourners that life must go on – make it impossible to lock the psyche indefinitely to the symbolism of the syzygy. This is what quite rightly presses on the women in these two films. They give way to life. Attainment of the quasi-divine union and fulfilment of the self has to give way to more pressing and mundane needs.

Apparitions are by no means inevitably vehicles for the expression of anima and animus. They are just as liable to figure in screen fictions for their property of having escaped, so to speak, from their own time. This is true of one episode, 'Paranormal Activity', in the cult series *The X-Files*.

The stories in this series update and fuse three genres, making of them something new and exceptionally subtle. They borrow on a grand scale from police/detective television series and emphasise the identification and pursuit of dangerous targets. This component gives *The X-Files* much of their structure. To add to this, they lift from science fiction and horror films the shades, phantasmagoria and aliens (both real and phony) that haunt many episodes. Their plot lines are also often drenched in the paranoia which has saturated all three genres since the release of Don Siegel's *Invasion of the Body Snatchers* in the 1950s at the height of the Cold War. Ever since, it has been a commonplace that screen aliens have represented the projection of deeply internalised fears experienced by an entire culture. Numerous episodes of *The X-Files* are laden with the virtually universal belief in malign conspiracy that so afflicted the peoples of both the USA and the UK subsequent to the Nixon–Watergate revelations of the early 1970s. Because similar fears were still being stoked a quarter of a century later by revelations of government and big business intrigues, the evocation of conspiracy fostered by *The X-Files* fitted the ethos of the late 1990s all too comfortably. Throughout this period, the great power-players were frequently perceived to be acting systematically against the interests of the people.

The fictional society in which Mulder and Scully operate is deeply penetrated by corruption (often metaphorically represented by the ghastly creatures and phantoms which they have to investigate). Each episode opens with a montage title sequence which reminds us of the series' provenance: a UFO skids across blue skies; the words 'Government Denies Knowledge' occupy a headline; a distorted face is locked into a grimace resembling 'The Scream' in Edvard Munch's painting; and (reminiscent of Saul Bass's title sequence for Hitchcock's *Vertigo*) a graphic representation of a corpse spins down into the void. In the classic formulation which derives from *film noir*, the investigators cannot always trust even the FBI colleagues with whom they work. Mulder and Scully therefore depend heavily on each other, and the relationship between them has developed into something more than a strong bond of professional loyalty. Although the latter quality remains dominant, deep personal regard and affection underpin it. The importance of this regard is made clear in the episode we shall consider.

Another factor which makes *The X-Files* distinctive is the skilled realisation of slow-moving scripts. Contrary to the boisterous style of most American televised drama, episodes of *The X-Files* often display (whatever the underlying turmoil) a surface quietness that comports well with the bearing of the two principal characters. Written as a plausible pair of middle-class professionals in their thirties, FBI agents Fox Mulder (David Duchovny) and Dana Scully (Gillian Anderson) go about their business softly, deploying their well-honed expertise in a manner that does not draw attention to itself – as befits the managerial and professional style of the 1990s. The realisation of the programmes (as in the story we shall analyse, with its noirish shadows on the faces of the police, its muted lighting and its consistently low-level sound mix), frequently draws out these qualities. The subdued style has the effect of making the phenomena which its lead characters investigate all the more scary.

'Paranormal Activity' is an episode from the series 'The Truth is Out There' (1997).[13] The combination of ingenious scripting and the characteristic understatement of the roles make for an emotionally powerful drama. Its power is not diminished by the fact that Mulder and Scully discuss openly the nature and meaning of the events with which they are concerned, in effect offering a running interpretation. Although they do not use the Jungian term 'synchronicity', that is what they have encountered.

A serial killer is slitting the throats of young women who shared only one thing in life, their liking for a relaxing game at Angie's Bowling Alley. However, they have another, ghostly characteristic in common. Each makes an appearance at about the time of her death as an apparition. Each ghost tries, despite her appalling throat wound, to speak to the person she is visiting, and the words 'SHE IS ME' are scrawled where she is sighted.

Mulder and Scully are put on the case because it concerns the paranormal, and the police are handling it ineptly. The FBI agents have therefore not only to find the meaning of the occult apparitions, but also to catch the murderer. The police suspect Harold Speuler (Alex Bruhanski), a mentally damaged patient who is granted day release from his care home to work in the bowling alley. While the cops woodenly mistake his guilty

---

[13] The episode was listed in *The Radio Times* prior to UK transmission by the BBC on 18 February 1998 under the title 'Elegy', which catches its mood exactly.

behaviour for a sign that he is the killer, Mulder swiftly perceives that Harold is innocent but does have information pertaining to the case. By disproving the crass allegations of the police against Harold, Mulder deals with the rampant (and corrupting) paranoia of the outer, social world. And subsequent detailed inquiries do in due time wrap up the murder plot and satisfy the demands of the world of law and social action. At the end of the screenplay Scully is confronted by the true killer, and succeeds in disarming her. However, although the pursuit is an essential part of the bait by which the programme hooks its viewers, it is by no means its centre of interest.

It is an essential principle upon which the series depends that the two agents are effective in the final showdown through their courage in exposing themselves to not only physical risk but also the occult forces that they are investigating. In some instances they consciously allow the invasion of their own inner beings by alien phenomena. In other circumstances they do not have the power to resist these phenomena, which simply take them over. Typically they are saved by a combination of research-based knowledge and intuitive insight into what is happening to them. This blending of deeply worked rationality with irrational responses prompted by the unconscious is a particular marker of *The X-Files*. It is a feature of the programme's assured endeavour to seduce audiences into complicity. Not only does it characterise Mulder's and Scully's *modus operandi*, it also draws the audience into a world where stimuli arising from the unconscious are valued.

As Scully pores over the documentation relating to Harold, a drop of blood falls from her nose on to the papers. The small shock of this incident for the viewer establishes a link between the investigator and the victims, a connection to which the development of the plot immediately gives several painful twists in a way that deepens our involvement with her and our readiness (for the purposes of the programme) to accept the paranormal on the same terms as she learns to do. To check that her nose has ceased to bleed, she uses a mirror in the women's washroom. But the words 'SHE IS ME' suddenly appear scrawled in blood on the glass. When she turns away, the ghost of a young student with her throat cut (unknown to Scully, the fourth victim) stands before her. Scully is so shocked that she cannot speak to Mulder about the vision – and since he has just been told about the killing of the same girl, he is too preoccupied to notice her distress, although it deepens visibly when she examines the body.

Scully visits her doctor and we discover that she and Mulder have known for some time that the condition which has caused her nose to bleed is a cancerous growth for which there is no cure. But this is not all she has to endure because Mulder is sharing with her thoughts about the nature of the apparitions, and his ideas have dire implications for her. He believes them to be disembodied souls, spirit beings who visit as harbingers those to whom they are most closely tied – in most cases people who are themselves about to die. It is not long before he gets the evidence to back up his theory when Mr Angie Pintero (Steven M. Porter), the operator of the bowling alley and the one who saw the first of the ghosts, dies suddenly of heart disease. As a consequence the viewer has to accept that Scully is likely to die – and that she herself is digesting the revelation that the message from the revenants, 'SHE IS ME', directly implicates her. Confirmation of the apparent sentence of death comes all too soon when Harold himself (who has seen all the ghosts) dies as a consequence of the murderer having stolen his drugs for her own use.

We have already remarked on the way the plot's orientation towards the thematic material results in the treatment of the detection of the murderess (one of the nurses at the mental home) almost as a side issue. The obvious opportunity for ironic play on the nurse's mental derangement is not exploited. Nor is the motivation for her deeds explored. Instead we are left with Scully, utterly desolate, not only facing the prospect of her death, but also doubting whether she still has the trust of the partner whom she values so highly. Although Mulder knows about the cancer, and has given her staunch support throughout, he rebukes her for keeping hidden from him her sighting of the ghost of the fourth victim, telling her that anything less than total openness between them threatens the partnership.

Certain that her early death is fated, late in the night Scully quits the mental home where the investigation has culminated. Seeking a moment of privacy after the horrors she has been through, she rests in the driving seat of her parked car and weeps quietly in the dark. Then something catches her eye in the rear-view mirror. There in the back of the car sits the wraith of Harold. But when she turns to face him, he is gone.

The undisputed popularity of *The X-Files* indicates, given the arguments advanced in earlier chapters, that such an episode can claim an engagement with the cultural unconscious. This is not least because, as we have said, the themes of the series are deeply imbued with the social paranoia augmented by widely publicised political betrayals and financial scandals in several western nations. It is therefore particularly curious that Scully's sighting of the two apparitions that convey so intense and bleak a message to her is utterly private. Indeed, although her personal isolation is doubly marked on this occasion because she has not been able to tell Mulder about the dead girl's ghost, the two FBI agents are frequently scripted as almost the only believers in a sceptical and uncaring world. Very few other characters share either their knowledge or experience of the paranormal; and those who do, like Harold Speuler, are often shown as marginalised by society.

Thus if (as seems likely from the intensity with which its fans followed *The X-Files*)[14] the series does resonate with energies having their roots in the cultural unconscious, the programmes show the self (conscious and unconscious) as the primary resource and refuge in a time of advanced social paranoia. This reading is only strengthened by the discovery in a later episode that Scully's cancer has been planted by a state agency. Yet if we interpret the manifestations of the paranormal seen on the screen as images having their sources in the the unconscious, the ignorance of the unconscious that typifies the social world within the series implies that the self is largely unknown. Only a handful of people – the two heroes of *The X-Files* among them – seek a fuller understanding and experience of it. The activity of reclaiming the self – not only for the individual but also for the collective – is seen as the core from which resistance could commence to the corruptions that late twentieth-century history has imposed on the western world. The episode 'Paranormal Activity' quietly presents through a topos long valued in conservative tradition the means by which the individual can start the process of personal and social recovery. It centres on *caritas*, the deep but disinterested love of one's fellow beings which we found so lacking in Darkly Noon. Neither sexual desire nor thirst for personal advantage motivate the person experiencing the passion of *caritas*, rather it is driven by the want for the other person's good. In 'Paranormal Activity' it is carefully established that Harold's unspoken love for the young women who have been murdered has this kind of purity. *Caritas* is also the shaping force in the mutual affection between Harold and his boss Angie Pintero. And, lastly, Mulder and Scully have this most civilised of emotions in abundance – for each other, of course, but also for many of the victims and unjustly accused people whom they encounter in their work. It is the deep passion that organises their lives.

In the episode 'Paranormal Activity', anima and animus are by no means the dominant archetypal images they were in *Ghost* and *Truly, Madly, Deeply*. Rather, Scully's suffering is caused by coming face to face with the wraiths. Mulder might refer to them as spirit guides, but the Jungian term for these figures would be psychopompi. In myth the psychopomp is a figure that leads souls down to the underworld; in analytical psychology, as we saw in chapter 3, it acts as a symbol of interchange

---

[14] The popularity of the series encouraged the sale through retail video outlets of many episodes. It is relatively unusual for television programmes to achieve this kind of post-transmission marketability and thereafter to provide the matrix for a theatrically released feature film.

between the unconscious and consciousness. Scully, in beginning to accept the meaning of the apparitions for herself, is recognising the significance of what Jung referred to as synchronicitous experience. Through this (although much more consciously) she undergoes a private trial not unlike that suffered by Dennis Potter's hero Daniel Feeld. So we shall discuss this phenomenon further after describing the predicament of the latter.

The last two television dramas written by Dennis Potter are crowded with ghosts. Linked to each other in plot and theme, *Karaoke* and *Cold Lazarus* (Renny Rye, BBC and C4, 1996) both comprise four one-hour episodes. Because finishing the scripts was barely possible in the time left to him before his death, the plays were always intended for posthumous production. Through them Potter summoned as principal phantom his own authorial ghost, Daniel Feeld (Albert Finney). The latter is a successful but irascible screenwriter who in *Karaoke* battles, just as Potter did, to complete two screenplays before cancer kills him.

The scenario is deliberately complicated by the fact that Feeld's first play (currently in post-production) is also called *Karaoke*, a play remarkably similar to the one we are watching. It too has as one of its main protagonists a cantankerous writer, in this case Oliver Morse (Ian McDiarmid) a look-alike for Potter himself. We find ourselves peering into Chinese boxes of the imagination containing many phantoms within their multi-dimensional mazes. To add to the in-weaving of the text, Feeld and Morse both like to dine in the same restaurant (so it is used as a location in Feeld's production), and this is the place where chronologically both plays begin. From the start it is clear that, far from enjoying their meal, both writers are enduring a writer's nightmare, continually hearing people around them speaking lines that they themselves previously wrote for characters in their plays. We too hear these voices, a factor which adds to our uncertainty (if we allow ourselves to play with the thought that Potter may have been going through a similar experience) as to just how many Chinese boxes we are opening.

Both writers overhear a young woman at another table in the restaurant uttering lines from their scripts. Feeld becomes ever more agitated by the experience when the woman he overhears, Sandra (Saffron Burrows), speaks in synchronisation with him as he mouths the same lines, while Linda does the same with Oliver Morse's (which are almost identical to Feeld's). The involuntary two-way current that starts to flow between the writers and their characters distresses them all. Both young women take the writers for dirty old men and rail at them. But, undeterred by the brush-off, Feeld's memories and dreams quickly fasten upon Sandra and she becomes the vehicle for recollections that arise unbidden of women for whom he has yearned. In this respect Sandra is, so to speak, the ghostly sister of many of the young women in Potter's screenplays. They are reflections of passionately loved anima figures on to whom, as living women, Potter's male characters never quite manage to hold. And they all leave behind them images which burn ardently in the men's memories.

The attractive Sandra, although unknown to Feeld when he first sees her in the restaurant, not only becomes the bearer of his projected anima memories, but soon takes on another role, which recurs in many of Potter's plays, as Feeld's muse – a function that the anima often performs. However, Feeld cannot stop his mind overlaying on her the lineaments of the girl in his play. This alarms him because Linda is a young woman on the fringes of the sex industry, exploited by her boss, a grotesque gangland figure who operates a sleazy karaoke club. Feeld discovers that Sandra too works for a karaoke club-owner – a seedy criminal who has the same name as his own pernicious villain, Pig Mailion (Hywel Bennet). Dread suffuses Feeld's mind, convinced by this series of coincidences that Sandra is condemned to live out the scenes of his play: and Linda has already been filmed as the victim of a sex murder, strangled by her boss. Feeld decides that the only way he can save Sandra from Pig Mailion is by rewriting the end of his plot.

It may sound on the basis of the foregoing as though viewers, in common with some of the characters around Feeld, might deduce that he is suffering from gross delusions, possibly brought on by severe paranoia aggravated by the pain in his gut and excessive drinking. But Potter gives us enough information to allow us to see his hero as a man of quicksilver but sound temperament. Frequently irascible, sometimes twitched by the tail of his own memories, often in pain and much put upon by idiots, he is (notwithstanding his emotional outbursts) sane, albeit highly sensitive.

The many coincidences to which we have referred have a powerful emotional impact on Feeld. Viewers are cued by them to share his feeling of foreboding. The ordeal that he suffers when he hears his scripts echoed falls into a wide category of experience that Jung referred to under the term *synchronicity*. It covers the popular understanding of *déjà-vu*, extra-sensory perception, telepathy, clairvoyance, psychokinesis and the like occurrences. Broadly speaking, Jung used the word to express his perception that certain events that appear to be related are connected without necessarily obeying the rules of space, time and causality (Jung 1952a). A commonplace example is the experience of receiving a letter the morning after dreaming that it is on the way. The fact that the dream precedes the letter's arrival is felt by the dreamer to have significant meaning.

The overarching concept of synchronicity is that it constitutes 'an acausal connecting principle'. Within that category it covers, as Samuels indicates, two kinds of occurrence. One class encompasses events that are meaningfully but not causally related – that is, events that do not coincide in time and space. The advance knowledge received through dreams would fall into this category. So does Dana Scully's apperception of the two ghosts whose visitation is to her so momentous. The other class gathers together events that do coincide in time and space but are perceived as having other, more meaningful psychological connections (Samuels 1990: 101). Daniel Feeld's experience of overhearing strangers speaking lines from his scripts is of this second type.

Although such theoretical mapping out of the ground makes it seem a dry business, the experience of synchronicity is far from arid. As Jung observed, synchronicity coincides with feeling heightened emotions (as with Scully's suffering). The impact of such affect on the psyche of the person undergoing synchronicity is of equal significance with the coincidence of events which appears to trigger it. This heightening of emotions occurs (as so often) in conjunction with the lowering of the level of conscious control and the strengthening of the unconscious.

The conscious then comes under the influence of unconscious instinctual impulses and contents. These are as a rule complexes whose ultimate basis is the archetype, the 'instinctual pattern'. (Jung 1952a: 446)

The synchronistic experience occurs where two forms of reality – those of the inner and outer worlds – intersect. It postulates a meaning that exists both a priori in relation to human consciousness and apparently outside the perceiver (Jung 1952a: 501–2). These factors, together with the heightened emotion associated with synchronicity, have the consequence that the experience often has a numinous quality, and appears to present the recipient with an 'absolute' knowledge not mediated by the sense organs (ibid.: 506). This is true for both Dana Scully and Daniel Feeld. In turn such a response suggests that archetypal energies have been stirred.

All of this makes it possible to interpret synchronistic experience as if it were symbolic and had the power to expose unconscious drives to conscious scrutiny. For example, Scully's unwelcome psychopompi do just such service for her, bringing her consciously to face what she has already registered unconsciously – the need to contemplate the prospect of her death. Because it has this potentially symbolic function, synchronistic experience may be of therapeutic value in analysis of patients (Samuels, Shorter and Plaut 1986: 147).[15] In the analysis of screen fiction, it can

---

[15] Jung cites the celebrated case of his patient who was recounting her dream of a scarab beetle when a similar-looking insect flew in through the consulting room window as an instance where a synchronistic event advanced an analysis. (Jung 1952a: 525–6)

effect an encounter in virtual reality between viewers and the potent archetypal structures underpinning the mythology which the text is representing – more of which in the Conclusion.

The occurrences of synchronicity that first impact on Daniel Feeld are, as we have noted, of the kind in which events that do coincide in time and space are seen to have meaningful connections. Whenever he hears his characters' lines in other people's mouths, this type of synchronicity is in play. Feeld tells his producer that the karaoke motif has not only provided the ruling metaphor for his play but lately has governed his sense of life's meaning. He is obsessed with an idea that could be the epigraph to much of Potter's work, as shown by their both putting popular songs of Tin Pan Alley in the 1930s and 1940s in the mouths of their characters. There they function as crude, ready-made encapsulations of the emotional traumas of the present. As Feeld puts it, 'The music's been written beforehand by someone else, and there's this piddling little space left for you to sing, but to their lyrics. The feeling that it's all been arranged beforehand.' His anxiety produces a nightmare vision in which the archetypes have complete power to determine the tenor of the individual's life and consciousness and experience count for almost nothing. In his terror, he does not give enough weight to the knowledge that he has the power to rewrite his own play. It is an early symptom that he has still to learn accurately to appreciate his unconscious.

Other instances of synchronicity in *Karaoke* fall within the class in which events are meaningfully but not causally connected. Specifically, Feeld experiences 'the coincidence of a psychic state with a corresponding, not yet existent future event that is distant in time and can . . . only be verified afterwards' (Jung 1952a, 526). Although he does not know it (and the viewer does not fully appreciate the fact until looking back at his life from the perspective of *Cold Lazarus*), Feeld is periodically given a nudge by the future. Some of these moments pass almost unnoticed. In the restaurant he remarks in the middle of a diatribe against the artistic arrogance of Nick Balmer, the play's upper-middle-class director, that he has no intention of being metaphorically 'run over by his bloody Rolls Royce'. A few minutes later he staggers out on to the street very drunk, and is almost knocked down by the very same car. Other, more troubling incidents give rise to spasms of fear in Feeld, although he does not truly understand why. For example, while still in the restaurant, he (like his *alter ego* Morse before him) is startled when, staring drunkenly into his wine glass, he glimpses a movement on the surface. The terrified feeling that a message is trying to break through grips him momentarily before he recognises the reflection of the fan and persuades himself that that is all there was. He does not fathom that the ceiling decoration, depicting a mock Elysium, might be a concealed (synchronistic) message. Decorated in a parodic baroque style, it is a veiled intimation of the future that awaits him. Not yet consciously aware that he is dying, Feeld just misses registering here a preview of a scene that will be not be played out in full until nearly four hundred years of story time and seven hours of screen time have passed.

Notwithstanding that we have the opportunity to pick up this hint, with so much else going on in the interlaced dramas of *Karaoke* we too miss reaching a complete understanding of what Feeld's synchronistic experiences might mean. But we are able to see that the doubling of characters' speeches functions like Potter's celebrated use of popular songs. He himself said two things about this device. The first was that they bring back remembered emotions, but through their coarseness give them a coating of irony. When lip-synched by characters, they are utterly direct and in-your-face (a point that Feeld makes about his screenplay); but at the same time they are held at a distance by our knowledge that they are neither an accurate nor a complete rendering of that person's feelings. Potter's second observation was that cheap songs have something about them of the Psalms of David (Dennis Potter, Channel 4 interview, 1994). In similar fashion, the doubling of Feeld's speeches through overheard conversations implies that dramatised speech too has about it something of the archetypal. However, it is not until we look back at this play from the point of view established by *Cold Lazarus* that we can appreciate the full force of Feeld's intuition.

In *Karaoke*, as Feeld faces the end of his life, he (like Potter himself) starts a new screenplay, devouring his remaining days to complete the work that so excites him – the script for *Cold Lazarus*. Meanwhile he settles with the ghosts of his immediate terrors, willing a large part of his substantial estate to Sandra and exacting as the price for his generosity the promise that she will not return to the karaoke bar. And he rewrites the end of his play with a vengeance, ensuring that she will never again be at risk from Pig Mailion. He makes certain by enacting one of Potter's own fantasies as a dying man, and shooting the villain himself (Potter, ibid.).

Dennis Potter made it clear that he enjoyed mixing some of his own traits into characters who in other ways were wholly different from him. One striking difference is Daniel Feeld's willingness to allow his corpse to be frozen. He does this to help his twin brother launch a business selling to wealthy individuals the prospect of immortality. They can have their heads frozen in order to be brought back to life when a cure for the disease from which they have died has been discovered. There is an interesting splitting here (signalled by the introduction of an otherwise peripheral twin brother). While on the one hand Daniel wants to attain a kind of immortality through his work, on the other he appears secretly to be tempted by a desire for some form of physical life hereafter. He pays a horrible price for this hubris.

At the start of *Cold Lazarus* 374 years later, his severed and frozen head has been installed in a laboratory to undergo experimental exploration. He is forced helplessly to play out the central role in the regurgitated drama of his own past as scientists try to plumb his most intimate secrets. The petrifying suspicion that everything had been arranged beforehand which haunted Feeld in the last weeks of his life can now be seen as a clairvoyant (synchronistic) forewarning of the anguished freak show that he has become. The irony double-folded in time is that he himself has written the words to which, suspended in icy limbo, his soul is forced by the laboratory staff to dance more than three centuries after his death. Thus the plot of *Cold Lazarus* presents the viewer with both an explanation of Feeld's past and an unusual variation on the idea of the writer in touch with the future. This is an idea to reprise later.

In *Cold Lazarus* the ghosts of Daniel Feeld and the other characters from *Karaoke* enter the world of 2368 AD at the summons of the investigative team. Their images are drawn via biochemical intervention from Feeld's reluctant psyche. They appear like wraiths on the laboratory's enormous virtual screen where their forms buckle and warp with the sway of emotion that drives Feeld's recollections. His memories are a mixture of what actually occurred, those moments his raddled mind chooses (or can bear) to recall, and some episodes which in the half light of this partial existence he rewrites in order to express himself to the unknown tormentors whom he cannot see but who are cruelly forcing him to relive his own life.

What is, as far as his gaolers are concerned, the most striking single fact about the memories they tap from Daniel Feeld's head? It is that they are all driven by and laden with his emotions (the importance of the latter emphasised by his punning name: feeled/felt). In the world of 2368, emotion deeper than irritated contempt and occasional trapped anger is not permitted. A young laboratory assistant Kaya (Claudia Malkovitch) dies, murdered by one of her superiors after she breaks ranks: she cannot conceal the pity she feels for Feeld nor her revulsion from the cruel torments that the team are causing him. Her death is accepted by the team without much dismay because it looks to them (although they are mistaken) as though she must have brought her fate upon herself by admitting her emotions. No accident that Potter builds in explicit reference to Aldous Huxley's *Brave New World*, and implicit links to George Orwell's *Nineteen-Eighty-Four*.

Potter's dystopia is governed by uncontrollable mega-corporations driven by the voracious greed of their owners. The contents of Feeld's frozen head are being probed in one of a world-wide network of laboratories owned by Martina Masdon (Diane Ladd). She rules her corporation tyrannically. For her the application of human intelligence in the service of rational scientific exploration and technological innovation has only one purpose – the pursuit of profit. When Professor Emma Porlock (Frances de la Tour), leader of the team delving into Feeld's mind, overspends her budget, Masdon responds by threatening the unit with closure. She has no regard for the nature of their research until its commercial worth is noticed by a rival.

It fits well with Potter's vision of this cold world that Emma Porlock's work – a highly specialised investigation of the memory function – has been commissioned from within a culture in which access to the inner life has atrophied. The thrust of this investigation is directed at piercing the inner life of one individual, but the scientists themselves speak as people ignorant of the possibility that they might have such a thing themselves. Needless to add, they lack the ability to see intuitively into other minds. Porlock exclaims with amazement when they first manage to screen some of Feeld's memories that their success on being able to reach into the mind of a human being who died so long ago is the pinnacle not only of her professional life but of 'my life in general'.[16] Intuition has been marginalised and love has been banned along with all forms of human contact other than passionless sex. The passions that rule here are cold: greed, cynicism and grudging admiration of the strategic skill to take advantage of a commercial opponent.

These values are enthusiastically propagated by the most sinister character in *Cold Lazarus*, Dave Siltz. A personality more evil because more powerful than Martina Masdon, he hungers beyond profit to seize global control of humanity by harnessing people's desires. He is a target for Potter's moral rage. In his last television interview, the latter mused on the mystery writer's stock question: given only three months to live, whom do you hate enough to murder, secure in the knowledge nothing could be done to you? Potter had no doubts. He even named his primary cancer Rupert out of cold loathing for the corruption which he believed Murdoch had visited upon the press and broadcast media via his News Corporation. Potter laid at his door, and those of like moguls, a large measure of

---

[16] The professor is linked by name with Coleridge's man from Porlock who interrupted the poet's dream of Xanadu. Here in a dystopic stately dome decreed by Masdon, she presides, albeit without much idea of what she is doing to a human being, over a kind of rediscovery of dreams. The unconscious of her specimen resurges despite her best efforts to control it.

culpability for the decay in English cultural and political values (Potter, Channel 4 interview, 1994).

Siltz (notice the values implicit in his name) is the foul heir, four hundred years further on, to the destructive tendencies with which Potter charged Murdoch. Siltz controls a multi-media empire with television and interactive video reaching eight hundred million people. His group possesses chains of hotels and also supplies consumers with food and drink, not to mention virtual-reality sex with anyone they choose. Social and economic corruption are universal both within and beyond the giant corporations. Siltz's and Masdon's vision of a perfectly run hierarchical society which they can control by shaping the desires and thought patterns of the population, does not actually hold sway over the entire twenty-fourth-century world. The two moguls' wealth has distanced them from ordinary people. Society is disintegrating despite the totalitarian powers that have been granted to the thuggish armed police (themselves hired servants of the corporations). Gangs of thieves roam the ruined streets despite the risk of being fired at on sight. Simultaneously the authorities are in a state of covert warfare with a guerrilla organisation. Corporate espionage and counter-espionage is pandemic, and employers try to enforce loyalty on their employees through fear. Masdon's organisation has its own police force, which resorts to psychological torture without hesitation. Yet its Chief Inspector is in actuality one of Siltz's more effective agents.

Despite his immense financial power, Siltz remains a slave to thieving ambitions to make his empire grow. He sees the prime-time transmission of Daniel Feeld's memories as his opportunity to pull in a multitude of new viewers – and he suborns Emma Porlock and her team with the offer not merely to restore the funding that Martina Masdon has cut, but to multiply it many times over. The team capitulates and steals Feeld's frozen head from Masdon's laboratory.

Again there is the doubling back on to old, but now strange, values. With the head in his possession, Siltz exults (like Emma Porlock) that never before has one person been able to enter another's mind. Siltz, however, has no wish to put anyone in touch with adult emotions so they can discover new maturity for themselves. He wants to make profit from Feeld's mind by luring people to plug into a new salacious virtual experience which will bring them in thrall to the Siltz empire. The contrast with Feeld, only half-alive, is sharp. We experience with the latter both some familiar and other new memories that did not surface in *Karaoke*. They have a direct emotional impact, whether they concern the devastating recollection of being raped in childhood by a tramp, or the sweet joy of his time with Beth, the first woman he loved. Potter scripts him (and Albert Finney plays him) as a writer whose command of felicitous language is always driven by, and is the vehicle for, inexhaustible passion. In this respect the emotionally atrophied Matilda Masdon, Dave Siltz and their minions (at least until some of the latter reassess their values) can be described as archetypal shadow figures in relation to Feeld. Barely visible to him, they are his constant tormentors. But their most pronounced features connect them with politically and culturally charged archetypes, a phenomenon which we shall account for when discussing the outcome of the drama.

At first, those who resurrect Feeld's inner life experience little more than salacious interest in his sex life and the risqué fact of his having lived and shared emotions deeply – for example, in the antique tribal passions aroused by watching soccer matches. But as their familiarity with Feeld's past and burgeoning memories grows, some of the laboratory crew are drawn to 'feel' him as a human being who may not be as reassuringly virtual as they had hoped. His emotions begin to stir their own.

When we first meet the team in Laboratory 16, they appear to be a homogeneous, if irritable group – a microcosm of their undifferentiated society. However, as the pressures on them grow, they reveal previously hidden characteristics. A pervasive set of variations on a single theme emerges. Blinda (Carmen Ejogo), until murdered by Fyodor, is Martina Masdon's spy, the traitor within – hers is professional betrayal. The conceited Tony Watson (Grant Master) experiences terror when Siltz's police persecute him and force him to spy on the team – the betrayal of a malleable coward. And although Emma Porlock begins to detect the stirrings of long outlawed feelings within herself, she betrays her employer and sells out to Siltz. Of them all, Fyodor is the most dangerous, being not only one of the principal scientific investigators but also secretly a member of a resistance group. Kaya, the team member with an embarrassing tendency to emotional outbursts, was actually murdered not for that reason but because she stumbled across this organisation.

In the true manner of a Huxleyan or Orwellian dystopia, the subversives are the truth-seekers. They run a highly effective guerrilla operation, RON, 'Reality Or Nothing'. The name refers first to the need for contact with nature. There are no trees, fields or animals in this world. Couples join together only for the momentary release of sex. There are no children – not even Huxley's clones. But it becomes apparent that the reality sought by the guerrillas runs even deeper than filling these lacks. Fyodor sees that Feeld has something to offer his generation that can be found in the past. It tempts him into a dangerous gamble. He decides to go along with Siltz's plan to broadcast Feeld's memories and dreams to a mass audience. But while Siltz plans to screen Feeld's memories for entertainment, Fyodor guesses that he would in fact unwittingly plant them in the collective consciousness. They should then supply archetypal images to a people who have cut themselves off from history, culture and knowledge of their inner lives. That in turn should cause the whole rotten system to explode as for the first time viewers encounter reality rather than its simulation.

In the event, the crisis Fyodor anticipates does not occur, mainly because he himself is swayed by compassion and brings the series of experiments forcibly to an end. For some time the scientists have observed that Feeld has been mixing occasional messages for them among the images of his past that they oblige him to revisit. However, they have for the most part repressed the suspicion that he might be experiencing some form of consciousness. Were they to face it, it would urge unwelcome ethical considerations on them. But once the head is installed in Siltz's labs, it sends an unmistakable message that obliges Fyodor to recognise that Feeld knows what is being done to him – and that the scientific team have been his torturers. At this point, Fyodor acts swiftly and shoots the head in its glass case. So at the conclusion of Potter's 8-hour diptych Feeld dies a second time. His frozen head explodes with a force far greater than would be caused by the impact of a bullet. The laboratory is engulfed in flame, Fyodor himself is caught by the blast and dies.

Something larger than one man's physical life is implicated in this. Until this moment, Feeld's great head has loomed over the laboratory like a ghostly moon. Its ancient associations with cold Luna and the unconscious bring to mind a somewhat threatening projection of the collective unconscious of the scientists (and, by extension, the entire society). Feeld himself is a turmoil of emotions to which he is well adjusted, but his captors have no experience of feelings. So the final explosion might be interpreted as a metaphor for the onrush of deeply repressed affect in which the unconscious contents overwhelm the ego with devastating consequences.

In fact, its impact is limited. It wipes out only Fyodor, the scientist with the strongest doubts about the laboratory programme, and *after* he has shot Siltz. The recordings of Feeld's memories are also destroyed and cannot now be broadcast to the millions. Therefore his second death does not have the miraculous power to reactivate the archetypes for which Fyodor had hoped. Potter, too much the political realist to countenance an easy resolution to societal ills, does not show his hero bringing about a collective transformation in the world of 2368.

Feeld himself, however, does experience final transformation. At the hour of his death his psyche is released and unites with the numinous and collective self. The moment reprises Feeld's memories of his first death. Once again, we see the visions his mind presented him with as life was sinking; but whereas on the first occasion the metamorphosis was aborted (Feeld wailing like one of the damned as the freezing of his body prevented the release of the psyche), this time his soul makes its escape triumphantly. We revisit his memories as he is sucked back down the twentieth century. Suffering and exultation pile one on the other. Beth, his first lover, muse and anima, calls to him. The exhilaration of his student years catches him up for an instant. Then his terrors are hinted at, including the childhood rape. Finally, rushing onwards down the long tube of time, he enters the empyrean. As he does so, we catch a glimpse of a Christ-like image. Of all the figures we might expect to see, this is the least likely because it resembles his tormentor Fyodor.[17] During his life the scientist-cum-revolutionary terrorist had killed three living people, culminating with Siltz, before finally releasing Feeld. Now an angel of death garbed in white, his image stands at the threshold of eternity to welcome Daniel.

This conjunction of dark and light reaffirms the theme of duality that recurs throughout Potter's work. That there exists a necessary and ulti-mately transformative relationship between perceived opposites – good and evil, conscious and unconscious energies – is also a basic principle in classical Jungian thought. As we saw in chapters 5 and 7, Jung observed that 'every psychological extreme secretly contains its own opposite or stands in some sort of intimate and essential relation to it' (Jung 1956a: 375). He named the phenomenon enantiodromia and argued that the more extreme a position is, the more easily it may be expected to run to its opposite. 'The best is the most threatened with some devilish perver-sion just because it has done the most to suppress evil' (ibid.). More than a moral law, it governs every cycle of natural life, both physical and men-tal (Samuels, Shorter, and Plaut 1986: 53). It is a fundamental principle, part of the compensatory process allowing the mind to regulate itself in a self-balancing system (see Stevens 1991: 47–52). When discussing the transcendent function of the symbol as mediator between conscious and unconscious, we were in effect describing an enantiodromian process.

The relevance of this topic to the final moments of *Cold Lazarus* is that classical Jungian theory holds the self to be profoundly enantiodromian. Jung postulated that it was the archetype of totality and the image of the entire personality, both circumference and centre, embracing not only conscious but also unconscious contents. Therefore it can only be partly knowable, remaining partly unknown and transcendental (Jung 1921: 460–1). It brings together the opposites – positive and negative energies,

---

[17] His name equates with 'Theodore', which means 'gift of God'.

life and death, and good and evil. The negative and positive energies vie in endless conflict, and Jung argued that if the individual is to be made whole, he or she must do everything possible to hold them in balance in a *conjunctio oppositorum*. As indicated in the last chapter, some therapists regard this as an endeavour impossible to achieve in life, and not an appropriate goal for most of their patients to aim at. Archetypalists, for example, see integration in a monistic image of the self as only one option. They regard this goal as better suited to introverted personalities with a deep need for theological solutions to life's mysteries – personalities like those of Daniel Feeld, Dennis Potter and Jung himself (Samuels 1990: 107–8). It follows, however, that the image of the self as wholeness *does* have a function as the focus for the end of life for the very reason given by the archetypal school, and that is how it features at the end of *Cold Lazarus*.

Since the image of the self is archetypal, it is also autonomous. Like all archetypal images it seems to be independent, following its own nature, beyond the control of the person experiencing it. Images of the self convey a numinous energy of overwhelming religious intensity, subsuming (but not obliterating) the individual's ego-consciousness to the totality. Jung identified the self with the image of the divine, but in a very specific sense as the god within us, a figure unlike the Christian deity in that it combines both good and evil.

[The self] might equally well be called the 'God within us.' The beginnings of our whole psychic life seem to be inextricably rooted in this point, and all our highest and ultimate purposes seem to be striving towards it . . . When, therefore, we make use of the concept of a God we are simply formulating a definite psychological fact, namely the independence and sovereignty of certain psychic contents which express themselves by their power to thwart our will, to obsess our consciousness and to influence our moods and actions. (Jung 1935a: 238)

Here too is a point of contact with Potter, since both prefer to represent god as both the creation and a natural activity of humanity (Cook 1995: 293). God and man are linked by the transcendent function of the symbol (Samuels, Shorter and Plaut 1986: 130–1).

By affixing the attribute 'divine' to the workings of autonomous contents, we are admitting their relatively superior force. And it is this superior force which has at all times constrained men to ponder the inconceivable, and even to impose the greatest sufferings upon themselves in order to give these workings their due. It is a force as real as hunger and the fear of death. (Jung 1935a: 239)

Therefore it is entirely fitting that as he nears his death Daniel Feeld, in common with many who have reported mystical experiences, should find his mind filled by archetypal images invoking the self with overwhelming power.

Potter always made his work run close alongside his life (and vice versa) to honour his sense of writing as a religious vocation expressing the spirit. Hinting at his own feelings was his usual practice, as Cook observes (1995: 292). The final scenes of *Cold Lazarus* give the viewer a sign that Dennis Potter aligned himself with Feeld's eagerness for release into the state where opposites unite. The scene in question is that in which Feeld makes his final direct appeal to Fyodor for release. He does so by transmitting via the laboratory's giant screen an image of himself in his study writing the words 'LET ME GO'. Believing his gesture has failed, he turns back to the desk, inconsolable; but as he does so a current of wind throws open his window. It is a moment that recalls similar interventions when disregarded spirits call attention to themselves in Nicolas Roeg's *Don't Look Now* and *Eureka*.[18] But instead of the barren London street on to which Feeld's window looks, we see a cherry tree in gorgeous pink bloom. This is an image imported from Potter's own life: in the interview with Melvyn Bragg, he recalled his vivid delight in the beauty of the tree that stood outside his own study window in Ross. It had come out into full blossom shortly after he had been told he did not have long to live, and while he was writing *Cold Lazarus*.

It is also in line with what Potter showed us of himself in that final televised interview that he should let us see his last hero (this bruised, cantankerous, yet wittily optimistic writer beset by unstoppable prophetic visions) as the Pilgrim of the end of the twentieth century. As Cook says, all Potter's work reveals his deep sense of the religious nature of authorship, with the artist already characterised in a poem he wrote while still at school as the pilgrim in search of the holy city.

> The Artist
> Beauty is like the transcendent God
> whom earthly pilgrims never attain . . .
> There lies the purpose and the tragedy
> of the artist who seeks mastery
> Pity him walking an endless road
> like a pilgrim to a holy city.
>   (Potter 1953, cited in Cook 1995: 7)

No accident, then, that Feeld's story is analogous to the long and often-mythologised journey of the hero battered by all forms of experience (inner and outer) as he strives to reach the ultimate goal. But where Bunyan's Pilgrim gave his devotion to the one-sided Christian god and fought to escape the clutches of the devil, Feeld's perseverance brings him in the end to what Jung described as both the centre-point and the circumference,

---

[18] Potter wrote the screenplay for the feature film *Track 29* which was directed by Roeg.

the individual's starting-point and goal where the opposites are held in conjunction. At the last we hear Daniel whisper ecstatically 'Yes, yes!' as he attains the long-desired goal, union with the self.

Feeld's psychological journey, as the play's title requires us to recognise, takes him through sacrifice and resurrection. Indeed, his frozen head, pinioned by pipes, cables and tubes, hangs in its glass box like a grotesque parody of a crucifixion. The comparison of his circumstances with those of Lazarus and Christ reveals enlightening points of likeness and difference with the biblical text. Christ raised his friend Lazarus from the grave in an event staged as an explicit preview of his own resurrection (John 11:1–44). The bringing of Lazarus back to life was a miracle in the old sense of an event inexplicable by natural laws which bore witness to the supernatural. From such an event there sprang a form of psychological rebirth in the renewal of religious faith among those who witnessed it. By contrast, the resurrection of Daniel Feeld in Laboratory 16 is a miracle in the restricted modern sense: it is something wonderful merely because beyond previous human experience. However, so far as those who precipitate it are concerned, it can ultimately be explained in terms of the scientific knowledge that they command. This Lazarus is cold, therefore, not only because his head has been frozen but also because the 'miracle' of his resurrection is intended to serve a banal end. Its purpose is to demean humanity, rather than augment and invite others to exult at what is mysterious and potent about the human imagination.

In psychoanalytic terms, it is significant that Feeld's attainment of union is postponed until after he has undergone sacrifice and resurrection since, as we have had abundant evidence to show, these themes comprise a no less common image cluster in the literature of analytical psychology than in religion and myth, and are frequently presented by patients undergoing a psychological rebirth. In terms of the psychology of the individual, the sacrificial element (which often includes powerful images of the patient's own death) expresses the anguish brought about by the dying of an old and outgrown set of personal values and predispositions. Such a dying is necessary before they can be replaced by a new psychological orientation better adapted to the present circumstances and emotional needs of the individual. The experience of psychological sacrifice can occur therefore at any stage in the life-cycle (not just on the point of death) where the unconscious insists upon fundamental change in the personality. It seems as if Feeld had such a goal intuitively in mind when he faced and resolved the contradictions in his personal unconscious during the last days of his life in the twentieth century. This was the main thrust of his labours throughout *Karaoke* when he dealt with characters who presented themselves to him like the phantoms of his unconscious – his anima (Sandra *et al.*), shadow (Pig Mailion), trickster (Nick Balmer), and guide (Ben Baglin).

His attainment of union at the moment of death is a genuinely mystical experience which gives retrospective meaning to the synchronicitous events of the last days of his twentieth-century existence. That meaning is reemphasised when we recall that the doubling of events upon him through time has all been filtered through his own mind as (also suitably doubled) the writer both of his own story and that of another writer, Oliver Morse. The search through the maze of ego, consciousness, memories and dreams reinforces the perception that the governing archetypal image throughout has been the self.

The merging of the personal in the transpersonal is not, however, the only aspect of the unconscious with which *Cold Lazarus* is concerned. Feeld is nothing if not a writer, and the fact that he (like Potter behind him) communicates to a wider audience his own experience of life gives his work a cultural and political dimension. This explains, in terms that implicate the cultural unconscious, why the symbolism of Feeld's suffering is necessary. He has to undergo sacrifice – crucifixion on frozen tubes – in order to allow society to purge its spiritual coldness. In effect, he cannot gain release before going through the purgatory of *Cold Lazarus*: his own peace cannot be made without addressing the cultural. The conflict that ensues between the resurrected values embodied in Feeld's head and those of his shadows Masdon and Siltz demonstrates this.

The most pronounced features of Martina Masdon and David Siltz connect them with politically and culturally charged archetypes. The society in which they are the governing policy-makers is devoid of emotional life. The freedom of people's imagination has been leeched away by the willing subservience of this society's dominant class, the intelligentsia. The connivance of the latter in the greed and cynicism through which the evil king and queen govern has allowed them to develop totalitarian authority. The political nature of their power is demonstrated by their unfettered ability to do whatever they wish with their corporations. But that power runs quite counter to all spirituality, witness the gross obscenity of their gratifications, their main pleasures consisting in the scatological coarseness of their speech, and domination of the sex servants they employ. As evil king and queen, Siltz and Masdon take on the negative archetypal qualities associated with the diabolical. And they are also tainted by cultural associations with the dark power of rampant chief executives whose corporations in late twentieth-century capitalist societies were too powerful for governments to bring under control.

As we have seen, Daniel Feeld's anguish runs so deep that it has the potential to stir the emotions and imagination of other characters and to reorient their psyches both unconscious and conscious. As for members of the audience, by engaging (even empathising) with the joys and traumas of Potter's hero, they too have the opportunity vicariously to experience the kind of emotional roller-coaster ride that may, in the safely dangerous environment that powerful fiction is capable of creating for most spectators, be conducive to psychic change.

The screen manifestations of ghosts discussed in the preceding pages engage with successively deeper levels of the psyche, moving from the merely trivial through the personal and on through the mordantly cultural and the passionately archetypal. We conclude this book's textual analyses with an examination of a rare film which makes the cycles of humanity, the rebirth and regeneration of the entire species its majestic theme.

10   Transforming the final ghost: the god within

In the iconography of myth, ghosts have interesting first and second cousins in UFOs (Unidentified Flying Objects) and fictional spaceships respectively. They are related, of course, through their signifieds rather than their signifiers (their connotations rather than their looks): and it was the mythological connections of flying saucers that engaged Jung's interest in the 1950s. During that decade many sightings were claimed and these phenomena attracted much public attention.

Jung argued that the UFOs of that era were a collective manifestation of the fears aroused in western nations by the Cold War. Indeed, although he did not use the term, he was in effect showing how the cultural unconscious could energise and launch a symbolic cluster with archetypal roots that responded to the pressures of the time. Demonstrating that such images have a history which at the very least reaches back to the sixteenth century, he wrote an *amplification* not only of reports of sightings but also of their images and associated ideas. He showed how, whatever other passengers they might be suspected of conveying, flying saucers were most certainly carriers of archetypal energies.

Among other factors, he considered the pervasive nature of geometric and numeric symbolism associated with the UFOs, and demonstrated how the same symbolism traditionally represented images of divinity (Jung 1959c: 406–7). He also found that the masculine–feminine antithesis occurred in some graphic descriptions of UFOs, with, in one case, cigar-shaped objects opposed to others that took a saucer or lens form (ibid.: 350). That kind of opposition, as we have observed in earlier chapters, characterises images of the unified, monotheistic self such as the syzygy. In addition, he observed that manifestations of UFOs took the form of revelations from heaven; as such, they often developed traditional representations of the divine. Not surprisingly, then, they also built upon and in turn heightened the familiar contrast between a higher world which is perceived as being the locus of the enigmatic, the fabulous, the mythological and the divine on the one hand, and the ordinary lower world on the other. When he took all the evidence into account, Jung found abundant reasons to associate UFOs with the central archetype of the self that his earlier work had differentiated (ibid.: 406–9). It follows that they are close to the idea of the divine.

We have mentioned that dreams occasionally take a predictive form, and certain visions may do the same when the contents irrupting from the unconscious indicate a coming change in disposition of which the dreamer is not yet consciously aware. In 1968, Arthur C. Clarke published *The Promise of Space*. There he advances the idea that there is a powerful interaction between science and literature – in both directions. From our perspective, it is particularly fruitful to recognise that the fiction of space travel did a great deal to draw humanity closer to the goal of interplanetary travel, which it only began to realise more than three hundred years after the first fictions were written. Clarke makes a persuasive case that from the second half of the nineteenth century onwards, the human hunger for space found expression in fictions and dreams. These in turn eventually excited interest in the great labour needed to convert dreams and aspirations into the intricate material technologies of actual space travel (Clarke 1968: 21–32).

The Promise of Space was published in the same year that the celebrated film *2001: A Space Odyssey* was released, the screenplay for which Clarke had written with its director Stanley Kubrick. The film's distribution was synchronised with a time when worldwide consciousness of space travel was acute. It was the period when the Cold War was at its most intense. The race for superiority in outer space between the then two superpowers, the Soviet Union and the USA, had been hard fought ever since the Soviets had launched the first artificial satellite Sputnik 1 in 1957. Hypnotised by the paranoid belief that control of space would lead to military superiority, the American government responded over the next decade with massive investment in a fast-track space programme. This phase of the race reached a dramatic culmination on 20 July 1969 when the American space team achieved the first landing of a human being on the moon. In the aftermath of this triumph the main themes celebrated by the popular media in the capitalist world were twofold. The first theme concerned the clear evidence of American technological superiority over the Soviet Union – a superiority which was widely understood to entail the reasonable certainty of safety from surprise nuclear attack by Inter-Continental Ballistic Missiles. The second was less xenophobic and imperialist, and centred on the prospects for humanity in the new era which this first step appeared to have opened.

Kubrick and Clarke alluded to the former and developed the latter theme in *2001: A Space Odyssey*, but did so in a manner which changed both themes and linked the film ideologically with records of UFO sightings and the associated literature cited by Jung.

The first thing to recall, for all those who did not have the opportunity to see the film in its original format, is that no screens in today's cinemas other than those in specialised IMAX venues (such as theme parks) can compete with Cinerama for size. On that giant screen Kubrick created vast empty zones to provide a visual simile for the idea of galactic space. The screen's sheer dimensions, together with the splendour of the images and music that filled it, endowed both the fictional odyssey and the film itself with a sense of majesty. In addition, the movie moves at a distinctively slow pace from start to finish. Its deliberate rhythm ensures that there is time for the extraordinary images, effects and sounds to register their points with audiences. The measured progress of the action adds to the sense of awe engendered by its scale.

All the above factors emphasised the epic nature of the action. However, because throughout much of their history until the end of the 1960s Hollywood studios tagged every lavish feature production with the slogan 'Epic' for publicity purposes, it is worth reminding ourselves what the term means when applied more stringently to narrative form. While a true epic is a narrative which may well have a large number of characters in it, the fundamental point is that its action should be on a grand scale, its themes involving the fate of an entire people, or indeed, as here, the entire human race. Nothing inhibits the presentation of large heroes and villains with strongly marked personalities, but such characters should in some way further the noble purposes of the epic as leaders of a people, or their all-too-threatening enemies. Characters are likely to be used as vehicles to convey substantial moral statements, whether by words or deeds. These observations, which fit the formal outlines of literary epics from Homer's *Odyssey* through Milton's *Paradise Lost* and on to Melville's *Moby Dick*, can be applied with equal accuracy to *2001*, vindicating its claim to present an epic odyssey for the twentieth century.

The narrative has an outer frame, opening and closing to the triumphant musical annunciation of Richard Strauss's 'Thus Spake Zarathustra'. As the film starts to this accompaniment, the Sun slowly rises over two aligned planets – Earth and Jupiter. The plot's ambitious claim to enter both universal space and time is immediately indicated.

The first of four distinct acts, 'The Dawn of Man' starts in the era of pre-consciousness. Family groups of large apes nose around looking for greenery to eat. They forage, having the capability neither to grow food nor decisively to defend their territory. What brings these creatures to the new consciousness that marks them out as prototypes of humanity is the advent of a sign, a black monolith that appears without forewarning in the territory of one of the groups. It stimulates in them an appetite for rudimentary knowledge and understanding. After touching and being touched by it, their leader works out how to use the bones of dead beasts as weapons. As he puzzles how to make inanimate objects work for him, Richard Strauss's 'Zarathustra' sounds once more and emphasises the high significance of the moment.

The leader soon arms his companions, and their new power enables them to kill for food and to drive aggressive rivals away from their waterhole on penalty of death. However, this is only one side of their story. The discovery by the emergent race of human beings that a bone can be an implement brings the ability not only to take up arms but also to use tools. Kubrick articulates visually the entire history of humanity's skill with implements in one of the most celebrated cuts in cinema. The leading ape-man hurls his bone hammer into the air, exulting in new power. The image cuts from the bone hovering at the zenith of its flight to a space ship approaching its docking zone millions of years later. This extraordinary juxtaposition leaves the audience recognising that, whilst the complexity of both weapons and tools has multiplied many times during the history of our species, the fundamental moral opposition remains unchanged. The nature of the power that distinguishes humanity – the capacity for constructive thought – brings with it the inescapable consequence that we can use it either for good or evil. Power itself is morally neutral; but the use of it always has moral repercussions.

The monolith can be interpreted as analogous to the presence and activation of an archetype in that it awakens latent capabilities. However, the range of archetypes that it might body into symbolic form is limited by its characteristics. This is obviously not one of the figures commonly found in both personal and collective psychologies that take a personalised form (as the anima, animus, shadow, trickster, wise old woman or man do). Rather its minimalist abstraction, the high seriousness and ascetic rigour of its signals, link it firmly with the transpersonal. One of the few clues to its function on this first appearance is the alignment of its vertical plane with the Sun and the Moon. It points metaphorically to something unknown, at a high level, and yet to be discovered. That the monolith is vertical implies, given that the ape-men have limited knowledge of their environment, the need for the species to stir out of uroboric pre-consciousness to deepen their conscious understanding of their world. And indeed the advent of this signal starts for humanity the long journey into the ever-more intense consciousness that the film charts.

In earlier factual records and fictional evocations of human experience, the coming down to earth of UFOs is typically presented as the arrival of the gods pressing in upon consciousness from a higher order of the archetypal unconscious. In *2001*, however, there is a double trajectory, the new element being that humans go out to meet the unknown. We shall return to this topic later.

Aeons after the awakening of humanity and at the end of the twentieth century, scientists discover a second monolith buried beneath the surface of the Moon where it has lain some four million years. The second act of *2001* is set in a time when global conflict (the Cold War between the superpowers still current at the time of the film's release) has been superseded by relatively cordial, if somewhat suspicious, political relations between the Earth's great powers, the USA and the Soviet Union. Lunar exploration has become routine and devoid of mystery, and international tensions are not the major issue for the space travellers; rather global terror, fear of the unknown, is. So the discovery of the monolith is not the source of awe that we might have expected from its previous manifestation. It causes instead acute anxiety in the top echelons of US scientists and bureaucrats who know of its existence. When a senior scientific administrator Dr Heyward Floyd (William Sylvester) goes on a fact-finding trip to the moon, his visit is conducted under conditions of the utmost secrecy to prevent word reaching Earth's populations.[19] His purpose is to advise the authorities when and how to break the news; but the ideological straitjacket within which he and his superiors have bound themselves is revealed when he addresses a meeting at the American Lunar base of the board of scientists who discovered the monolith. All are soberly suited, their formal language and the over-cautious atmosphere just like that of countless boardrooms on Earth in the second half of the twentieth century. One sentence from Floyd's speech gives the register:

I'm sure you're all aware of the extremely grave potential for cultural shock and social disorientation contained in this present situation if the facts were prematurely and suddenly made public without adequate preparation and conditioning.

Behind the bland abstractions it is evident that the authorities take it for granted that the Earth's population will need to be 'conditioned'. There is, to say the least, a loss of not only civil liberty, but also of freedom of thought and imagination entailed in the intense secrecy. Much later we discover that the authorities have decided not to let any information permeate outside the security cordon. The Earth's nations have been kept in ignorance of the monolith's existence.

---

[19] The fact that the US authorities have circulated a cover-story alleging that a serious epidemic has broken out at the site of the secret excavation speaks volumes, symbolically, about their anxiety.

In the second and third acts, technology is represented with delibe-rate ambivalence. The film played to many in the audience of the late 1960s (including the present writer) to whom its wide-screen vision of passenger-carrying space craft and the great wheels of orbiting space stations was a source of wonder. We have mentioned ways in which the aesthetics of the screen were deployed both to excite and gratify a sense of wonder and awe. However, on screen the twenty-first-century characters themselves make the electronics and advanced equipment the object of rational but unemotional attention. For them the wonderful has become the merely routine. What is more, the clichéd scientific jargon of the fictional astronauts' speech renders, with only slight exaggeration, the wooden communications lingo of NASA's men in the 1960s – so there was a direct connection with the present for the audience of the day. The banality of this impoverished human discourse contrasts with the majesty of the music. The latter carries both the power and the subtlety of the emotions generated by the awesome circumstances in which the characters find themselves, but which their limping words, sanctioned corporate-speak, are incapable of touching.[20] The contrast between the two ways of perceiving – the one dominated by the uses and control of a complex technology, the other by the musicality and poetry of the experience – develops into an unstated, but real, conflict of values. The film's scientists and astronauts focus on *the means* of space travel. The film itself – and eventually one of the astronauts – encourages its audience to contemplate *the purposes* of such a voyage.

The focal point of Dr Floyd's visit to the Moon is an on-site examina-tion of the excavated monolith. Here the high significance of what we are witnessing is signalled to the audience by the fact that no radio communi-cations between the team can be heard. Instead we listen to a ceremonial incantation composed by Ligeti, which is like the chorale sounding when the first monolith was discovered by the scientists' distant forbears. For a moment or two the incredible presence of the sheer-sided block imposes itself on the men. Floyd moves forward and touches it, just as the lead ape-man had done. However, the awe communicated through the music and the slow movements of the group of scientists toward the monolith quickly dissipates. The team then trivialises the occasion by posing for a group photograph in front of it. At this moment it emits a radio signal that pierces their ears and (we later discover) succeeds in focusing their minds on the proper issues at hand. This is the only signal it transmits. Thereafter it remains as inert as it had done for the 4 million years it was buried under the surface of the moon. But the exact timing of its emission

---

[20] I owe this thought to Jane Ryan and Miriam Sheer.

also suggests not only that it has a message to deliver, but also that the visitors may be close to a hubristic undervaluation of its significance – a mistake which the monolith itself corrects.

The amount of data on the monolith available to the audience is not large, but it does license two parallel readings. It has been on the Moon 4 million years and produces a strong magnetic field which first led lunar explorers to it. The latter believe that it must have been deliberately buried. It emits just the one radio signal, and does so at the precise moment that its vertical plane is aligned with Jupiter and the Sun. This transmission is the trigger that causes the US government to dispatch a mission to Jupiter.

Among the many uncertainties which this scant information leaves open, one question in particular tantalises. Is there a chain of monoliths (four in all by the end of the journey) which signal to each other? Or is there just the one, the manifestations and movements of which are beyond the capacity of reason to comprehend? The first proposition stimulates the thought that there must exist an older, more advanced species capable of rigging such a signalling system across our galaxy. The second idea fits sweetly with the recognition that the monolith stands for and leads humanity ever deeper into the unknown – and that it has therefore a connection with the transpersonal or collective unconscious.

I intend to produce a reading of *2001* which respects both these possibilities, arguing that the monolith is a visible metaphor for the evolving self of western humanity. In this context we should note that on its second appearance the monolith is once again vertical. Again during this phase in human development consciousness must dominate the endeavours of the species which require focusing on technology to enable travel to the more distant planet.

The third act is set 18 months later on board the Discovery. The mission to Jupiter on which it is bound has been prepared under conditions of secrecy so stringent that the crew have not been briefed on their ultimate goal before departure. None of them even know that there is a secret purpose to their mission. Dave Bowman (Keir Dullea) is in command, with Frank Poole (Gary Lockwood) his deputy. Three further crew members who comprise a survey team are in a state of hibernation and will be awakened when they reach their destination.

Once again we see the potential for boredom inherent in a routinely perfect environment. The crew members have little to do other than keep themselves fit by running the inner rim of the great wheel of their living quarters. Once again blandness governs verbal discourse and shuts off the emotions, whether in conversations between Dave and Frank, a birthday greetings message from Earth to Frank, or in a news item about the voyage. Nonetheless there is conflict latent here – and it centres on the use of the rational and conscious intellect and the extension of its powers through the on-board computer.

The HAL 9000 series computer (voiced by Douglas Rain) has a perfect operational record, a fact of which it is well aware, being apt to remind humans of its superiority whenever it can. Since it has an intelligence comparable to that of its human makers (but functions with greater speed and reliability) and is programmed to converse with people on equal terms, it is assumed for all intents and purposes to be conscious too. Of course what it actually has to a high degree is the capacity to undertake logical processing – a capacity which it demonstrates by trouncing Frank at chess. This very same skill appears to provide it with the framework for another game in which the stakes are altogether higher. We may deduce from what later happens that HAL, knowing its superior powers of reasoning, has worked out a totalising logical argument. It calculates that anything less than a total belief in its accuracy on the part of the crew would mean that they were less than wholly in thrall to its authority. In that case they would be less than perfectly committed to the mission. The machine decides to test the men for their loyalty. It does so by fabricating a bulletin anticipating the supposed breakdown of a piece of communications equipment.

When the crew test it they can find no fault. Nor can the identical HAL 9000 at mission base. Mission control reports that they suspect HAL is in error in predicting the fault. Frank and Dave lock themselves into one of the Pods – the small space vehicles that Discovery carries. They cut audio communications with HAL and confer in secret. Reaching the obvious (but wrong) conclusion that HAL has malfunctioned, they agree that if further problems occur they will have no alternative but to switch off its functions of higher consciousness and transfer control of the mission to the machine at base.

Although HAL cannot overhear Dave and Frank, it can see them and knows how to lip-read. The syllogism that it has worked out is brutal in its totalitarian simplicity. It has concluded that what it says must by definition always be correct, because it has powers of perfect logical reasoning. And this will remain the case even when, as in the present instance, it has itself falsified the data on which its first premise is based. HAL requires unquestioning faith from the human crew members. When it encounters anything less, it deals with that as if it were mutiny.

Is HAL a tool or a weapon? Perfected for its capacity as the former, it evolves into a weapon which turns its life-controlling powers against the crew of the Discovery. This occurs as a logical consequence of it applying to the maximum its most advanced function – ruthless logic. Earth's smartest tool turns on its makers and becomes a deadly weapon directed against them because its 'mind' has no capability for any other mode of functioning. Though a machine, HAL becomes in dramatic terms an epic villain, no less single-minded and dangerous than Milton's Satan, its formidable strengths combined with great weaknesses. Appropriately enough HAL's demise will have some of the absurdity that surfaced in Satan's defeat.

HAL having made its decision, the action moves fast. When Frank goes outside the Discovery to replace the unit that has been tested, HAL sends his Pod after him to cut his oxygen line and hurl him into space. Dave boards his own Pod to recover the body, and while he is out of the ship, HAL kills the three hibernating crew members. Dave returns to the parent ship, but the computer refuses to open the bay doors and admit him. HAL tells Dave that it knows of the plan to disconnect it. It concludes: 'This mission is too important for me to allow you to jeopardise it.' Dave's response to the crisis facing him, since he cannot match HAL in logic, has to be arrived at through the application of his other, human strengths. His emotions (fear for his own life, grief for his dead friend, cold rage against the computer) combine with knowledge, courage and determination and make him an opponent formidable in ways with which HAL cannot compete.

Having left his helmet behind in his rush to get to Frank, Dave has no safe means of regaining entry to the Discovery. He has no choice but to put his life at risk by blasting his way in through the emergency hatch. While doing so he must survive in an environment without air until he can manually close the hatch behind him. This is an option which HAL could not anticipate, because the practice of self-sacrifice runs counter to the priorities with which it has been programmed. Then, donning his helmet as precaution against the risk that HAL will try to starve him of oxygen, as it has done the sleeping crewmen, Dave enters the computer room and disconnects its higher functions. As he does so HAL is reduced to idiocy, eventually singing a little ditty before its voice grinds towards silence. As its conscious functions die, a security lock fails and the mission-briefing tape plays. Only now does Dave discover his true goal.

The fourth act, 'Jupiter And Beyond The Infinite', opens as Discovery approaches Jupiter, where the black monolith now orbits. An ancient mystical symbol is evoked by a shot of Jupiter's meniscus encompassing the crescents of two of its smaller moons. Reminiscent of the impossible image of Earth's old Moon cradling the new Moon in its arms, Kubrick's picture includes an important variant in that the spaceship can also be seen against the dark sphere of the planet. Since in profile the shape of the Discovery plainly recalls a spermatozoon, the visual conjunction of male and female principles could hardly be more explicitly stated. What is more, to continue the theme of fertility, the Pod in which Dave now embarks from the parent ship for the last time also carries with it the metaphor of the delivery of seed. The imagery of fertility anticipates what is still to come.

As Dave approaches the monolith (on this occasion oriented in the horizontal plane relative to both him and the audience), the Pod moves into alignment with it, Jupiter and the Sun, and his journey beyond the great outer planet to the infinite commences. The astronaut first witnesses streams of light, radiant, saturated in colour, hurling him through dimensions of time and space beyond the known. But not beyond the imaginable. The lights from the Pod's instruments reflect on to his face like war paint. Every hero fights, and Dave's battle is to hold on to consciousness. Even when his face is splayed in a silent scream against the glass of his porthole, and through every extremity of peril, he watches. While supernovae explode, galaxies wheel and plasma streams from stars in pinpoint formation, his eyes remain alert. As the journey continues he observes, foretelling what is to come, the development of a star that contains the smudged outline of a foetal shape. And then, while his eye still blinks as he watches intently, the speed of travel seems to slow while he is hurled across weird solarized un-landscapes. The celebratory choral voices that have accompanied him give way to steely scratching and deep electrical clangour, and suddenly everything 'naturalises' again. Except that the natural is also totally strange.

Dave's Pod has 'landed' in an approximate simulacrum of a Regency style hotel suite. The resemblance is approximate because, unlike most hotel suites, this is a chamber of light. Even the floor, which is white, radiates luminance. This materially impossible room is best understood as a metaphor, an expression adapted to the requirements of our times for what John Milton referred to three and a half centuries ago as the 'doctrine of accommodation'. By this he meant that numinous mysteries can only be expressed to humanity in a language that is comprehensible within the limitations of the human mind. In the final minutes of *2001*, image, music and sound replace speech, but the intention to express deep mysteries is comparable to Milton's endeavour – as the bewilderment of many commentators has made plain.

From this point time jumps forward in a succession of carefully marked elisions. Still in his Pod, Dave looks into the room and sees himself still in his space suit. But now he is a considerably older man of perhaps sixty years of age. This figure space-walks nervously into the bathroom, and looks at himself in the mirror, observing with the frank gaze that has characterised his whole solitary journey. Hearing a slight noise from the principal room, he looks round. The Pod has vanished, but a man about eighty years old is dining there. This too is Dave, and he too has heard a sound and checks the bathroom; but his younger self has disappeared. Resuming his meal, the old man knocks his wine glass on to the floor where it breaks. As he ponders this mishap he detects the faintest breathing and looks at the bed where, as an ancient man, he lies quietly waiting for the end of his life. In his final gesture, Dave slowly raises his arm and points at the black monolith, which has now reappeared at the foot of his bed. The viewpoint reverses, and we look back down at the bed from where the monolith stands. The venerable man has vanished into an effulgence of light in the womb of which coalesces the image of the foetal Star Child. We now track into and through the monolith and find ourselves once again among the planetary and stellar bodies where, to the triumphal heraldry of Richard Strauss's 'Thus Spake Zarathustra' the Star-Child Dave hangs softly luminous in the firmament.

By the end of *2001: A Space Odyssey*, an extended chain of symbols has been presented to the spectator. Their meaning bewilders every audience, but amplification and the active imagination help to bring sense out of the puzzle. Our cue that it is appropriate to work in this fashion comes from the 'room' itself, which exists like a metaphoric frame upon the action that occurs within it. In effect it puts quote marks on the sentence of time within which the existence of the hero Dave is framed, as also (because he too is de-realised) is the existence of the species. It lets us perceive that human life has two dimensions – the personal, represented by the ageing and death of Dave; and the collective, indicated in the absence of distinctive marks of character and the celebration of the new birth – a moment of growth for the species.

Dave Bowman's journey through rainbow light can be compared with the revelations of the wonders of the numinous higher world that Jung found typical of visitations by UFOs. Where the descent of the UFO/god can be taken as a metaphor for an involuntary coming to consciousness, Dave's odyssey, which he carries out for all humanity, is a voyage of discovery – an exploration of the unknown which deliberately extends the realm of consciousness by penetrating the mysteries. Dave's final voyage is a hero's journey – but this time into an over-world rather than the underworld that so many heroes have to endure. But like his chthonic counterpart, he encounters terror and emerges in a remade form. The further it progresses, the more Dave's journey becomes a dynamic image of the self as evolving, progressing, recurring through the generations. It is that great journey, characteristic of the human experience, to the very edge of the known, looking into the unknown, which is here couched in terms exactly right for our age. The symbolism of flight has long associations (through birds and insects before ever humanity grew wings) with the entry into the realm of the spiritual. Here it is updated to encompass space flight.

If we have any doubt about this, the journey beyond Jupiter to the infinite is punctuated by extreme close-ups of Dave's eye blinking as it takes in the many wonders that the journey presents him with. As Hellen and Tucker remark in relation to this episode, the eye used for intelligent observation makes an obvious symbol for increasing consciousness. Dave's eye, which changes colour every time he blinks, can be interpreted as symbolising the essential observing self that, enhanced by his experiences, will endure after the death of his body. The same authors are, however, surely mistaken in implying that the eyes of HAL have a similar meaning to Dave's (1987: 38–9). On the contrary, HAL's eyes, which keep under surveillance every inch of the Discovery, seem to be anything but windows to the soul. We never see more than one at a time, so they bring to mind the Cyclopes of Homer's *Odyssey*, who, as Grimal reminds us, were a race of gigantic savage beings with one eye, tremendous strength and murderous disposition (1986: 113). Each of HAL's eyes is cold because, despite the best attempts of voice-programmers to simulate a personality, it has none. The longer we know HAL, the more his red eye seems to signal danger – in contrast to the life-sustaining warmth associated with the astronauts' cockpits. Always alert, never blinking, each of his eyes is an instrument of espionage and control.

The basis for Hellen's and Tucker's generally helpful observations lies in a number of connections between *2001* and typical images in the writings of alchemists. In order to take the point, we need to clarify the significance of the work of these precursors of modern science for our present undertaking. Their goal was to accomplish a process of chemical transformation by refining common matter into gold. However, their complex experiments implicated more than physical matter alone and in this respect their objectives differed from today's scientists. In attempting to refine dross into gold, they did so in the confident belief that they were also trying to bring about a spiritual purification of themselves.

Jung spent years investigating the writings and emblematic imagery in the alchemists' publications. He observed the intensity of their labours which could last for years as they pursued investigative procedures that (as is obvious in the light of today's science) must have faced them with more reversals and blind alleys than successes. He deduced that the very difficulty of those procedures enhanced the force of the alchemists' projections and imaginings, so that the attempt to bring about chemical transformation became also a process of striving for individuation. In seeking appropriate images to act as vehicles for their thoughts and projections, they brought into play imagery from diverse sources, resuscitating among them certain figures familiar in the classical literature of ancient Greece and Rome. Under the pressure of the alchemists' less than fully conscious needs, these icons became imbued with a strongly archetypal cast, as Jung's immensely detailed account of their work repeatedly demonstrates. And this is the relevance that alchemy has for us.

Of the iconic figures reclaimed by the alchemists none was more prominent than that of Hermes (also known by his Roman name Mercury or Mercurius). There are strong resonances between the personal traits of Hermes/Mercurius and the figure of Dave. To take the most obvious starting-point, there is a suggestive link with his surname 'Bowman', since Hermes was the Archer of the gods (Hellen and Tucker 1987: 37). He was the god of flight, and according to some authorities, the messenger and servant of Jupiter. Universally known as the messenger of the gods at large, one of his tasks was to bear the souls of the dead to Hades (we can recall Dave's ceremonious releasing of Frank to the void). Because of this he was given the name Psychopompus, 'accompanier of souls' (Grimal 1986: 198–9). In *2001*, however, there is one development of the classical mythology which has high significance: Dave is a messenger *to* the gods rather than *from* them. This too fits his connection to Mercurius, since the latter was the traveller's guide; and Dave, if our reading of him proves correct, will be the pathfinder for the rest of humanity.

Dave Bowman shares with his divine winged forefather not only the characteristics of the psychopomp but also those of the god of revelation. Like the latter, Bowman unites the opposites (see Jung 1953: 293–5). One instance of this occurs with the conjunction masculine/feminine which Jung had identified in early pictures of UFOs: it is clearly present in the film, as we have noted on a number of occasions. As we have also seen before, the conjunction in opposition of the sexes characterises many images of the monotheistic, unified self, of which the syzygy is a case in point. In *2001* the fertile union of masculine and feminine principles is symbolic. It does not involve Dave and a woman but the conjunction of conscious with the unconscious. And it produces the new third thing, the Star Child born mysteriously through Dave's death.

A further reinforcement of the same symbolic theme is found in the configuration of the monolith. Its rectilinear form stands in opposition to the spherical shape of the planets. In its own right too, the monolith conveys the idea of opposition. We have seen it sometimes appear upright, sometimes horizontal, seeming to pull in the first instance towards deepening consciousness, in the second towards venturing into the unconscious. Mapping the two orientations on to each other produces the imaginary outline of a cross. And as we know from Christian use of that image, the cross readily signifies both the marriage of conscious and unconscious and the necessity of sacrificing the old life in order to be reborn into a new one. Both meanings fit with our reading of Dave's ultimate journey. The final manifestation of the monolith at the deathbed is vertical. Dave had previously opened himself to the unconscious as directed by the stone's horizontal stationing in Jupiter's orbit. Now his successors (in story terms the new generations, but in terms of the address from the screen, ourselves) are offered the chance to recognise the need to deepen consciousness once again, in order to bring into the frame of human knowledge an understanding of what has been witnessed but only partially comprehended. So once again the conjunction of opposites in the collective conscious and unconscious is implicated in this symbol as in the other figures.

Yet another way of expressing the same conjunction was first spotted by Hellen and Tucker in that the monolith has the qualities of the *lapis philosophorum*. The *lapis* is the Philosophers' Stone, familiar in the alchemists' treatises where it frequently has a central place in the process when used to symbolise both the beginning and the goal of the alchemical labour (Hellen and Tucker 1987: 33–6). The ancient physics, as Evola said, was also a transcendental psychology in which each physical perception had simultaneously a psychic component which animated it (cited in Jung 1953: 242n). Thus the alchemists often thought of their endeavours as falling into a pattern that conformed with the path followed by the mystic. That is, the pattern was a circular progress in which the end is contained in the beginning and the beginning in the end. Read in a manner which respects the alchemical process, the monolith takes on a double presence, first as the *prima materia*, the unrefined source-material, and secondly as the philosophical gold (the *aurum philosophicum*) which is produced from it at the end of a long and arduous process of refinement.

The narrative structure of *2001* thus incorporates both a linear voyage of exploration and a circle. It is a circle in respect of the cycle of one man's life, both in his own being and for the countless generations which he represents. This paradox is hard to think in terms of a simply human figure, but it is a familiar mental step in the case of the human who (like Christ) is also a god. So whilst we have been developing (and will continue with) the argument that *2001* conveys religious experience through imagery that reflects human knowledge and understanding in the later twentieth century, it is also well to recognise that it embodies oblique, intuitively grasped references to older types of reborn hero-gods. It is thoroughly grounded in the old mythological forms, notwithstanding it varies and develops them in a fascinating manner.

At an earlier point in the chapter, the idea was canvassed that the four sightings of the monolith might amount to the discovery of a signalling network planted in the solar system by a more advanced species. For this plot line to be fulfilled, Dave must by the end of his journey either have encountered the invisible species itself, or (more plausibly, since there is little sign of that having occurred) have come to the last symbol that it is within his power to comprehend. Either way, what he is shown in the Star Child is simultaneously himself and the choiring generations that will follow him. So, if an advanced form of life has through its network of signals enticed humanity into the 4-million-year journey, what it finally discloses is identical to what a Jungian reading of mythological and archetypal imagery reveals – namely, that the potential for the human race lies within the self, both individual and collective. This advanced life form may not yet even exist, but be coming into being as humanity itself.

All these indications that the final scenes of *2001* can legitimately be read as symbolising an encounter with the self complement the second thrust of the narrative, the powerful linear movement outwards that the entire journey depicts. If we accept that at the height of his nobility Dave Bowman undergoes an apotheosis and then can be understood as a god-like figure, it will be productive to view him in the context of Jung's concept of the god within us (previously considered in chapter 9). A key to understanding the theological dimension of the film's final act can be found in its representation of energy. God-men such as Christ and the Buddha (whether within us or outside us) have always been linked with light and energy, and even seen as sources of such power themselves – the halo ringing them is an obvious expression of it. But in *2001* there is a shift. The human image is by no means abandoned, but there is a strong visual and narrative suggestion that the god image is transmuting into energy. The balance of power personally commanded by the image of the god or goddess in his or her human form shifts away from the older model with which the western world is thoroughly familiar through Christianity. Now impersonal power surrounds Dave. His final home, the site of his rebirth, hums with energy that radiates from its walls and floor, and is expressed by the abundant light in the apartment.[21]

In the past the gods within (and outside) us have been figured as all-powerful, often as variants of the wise (or foolish) old man or woman. By contrast, Dave is an ordinary person. He possesses no extraordinary

---

[21] Perhaps the room itself suggests the form that our species, in struggling to shape that energy through culture, has given to life. The uneasy mock-Regency design nicely embodies that mix of the banal with the elegantly attained which Kubrick shows as typical of the works of humanity in its current stage of development.

powers other than unflinching determination; he shows no sign of devotion to an organised faith. He enters the cycle of rebirth simply because he gives himself fully to what Kubrick and Clarke show to be the most profoundly religious of human impulses – the passion to know both the universe and the self more deeply. This is Dave's choice, both voluntary and moral. But having committed to that ultimate journey, he then has no further alternative but to submit to the overwhelming power which moulds his fate. This force does not dress itself in quasi-human form, but is the raw energy that forms the stars.

Energy can express itself both through physical matter and through psyche. As Jung put it, 'There are indications that psychic processes stand in some sort of energy relation to the physiological substrate ... In spite of the nonmeasurability of psychic processes, the perceptible changes effected by the psyche cannot possibly be understood except as a phenomenon of energy' (1954c: 233). He went on to speculate that there might be not only a connection between the psyche and physiological and biological phenomena but some form of continuum linking psyche with physical events (ibid.: 234). Such interconnection is a distinctive characteristic of the universe represented in *2001*, and when Dave enters outer space on his final journey, his experience bears out these speculations. Hard-edged divisions familiar to us from our usual habits of classification dissolve. Matter and mind appear no longer to occupy wholly separate categories, and Kubrick makes the self a fluidly integrated part of the vast scene where the boundaries between physis and psyche bend and dissolve. A star forms and takes the shape of a foetus; the Regency room is alive with sound; and, conversely, space in its entirety is lodged within the head of the pioneering visitor. Apotheosis, the elevation of a mortal to the rank of a god, is not a new phenomenon either in religion or mythology. But the normal pattern with such a mythologem is that the hero is lifted away from the world, leaving humanity behind. Another factor that makes Dave Bowman's journey different is that the audience witnesses his story unfolding.

The nature of Kubrick's universe actually inflects the archetypal image of the self. This odyssey differs from Homer's in that this Ulysses does not return home. On the contrary, the god within us is travelling out, and in imaginary form entering the wider universe in order to take up a new position in the fluid pantheon of energy. Dave Bowman, like both Ulysses and Mercurius in their times, guides us on a new journey, heralding new adventures of the psyche.

In his late years, Jung wrote a speculative treatise, his *Answer to Job*, addressing a topic which had gripped his attention since boyhood. The question was how a good god can visit appalling evil on the world he himself created. A mark of its importance to Jung is that in this thesis he did something unique in the canon of his writings, discussing God as an *actuality*, a universal entity, rather than exclusively as the god within us that we have been dealing with hitherto. In this important respect I want to part company from him, since I do not believe that the notion of a 'god out there' is essential to recognising energy as the source of both universal and human life. On the other hand, I do want to make use of Jung's treatise as a means of describing what seem to me to be changes with immense potential for the future found in the image of the god within us that are projected through *2001: A Space Odyssey*.

On Jung's reading, the Book of Job focuses sharply the abundant evidence revealing the Old Testament God, Yahweh, as not only a loving god but also a tyrant capable of acts of great harm. His deliberate persecution of Job is the result of a wager with Satan to test whether the devotion of the most loyal of Yahweh's servants can be corrupted by tormenting him beyond measure. In Jung's opinion, the endless punishments visited on Job have no purpose other than for Yahweh to prove his own power to himself. God appears to have been bamboozled by Satan into forgetting his omniscience and proving his might at the expense of love for his creature (1952b: 378–9). But in doing so he reveals his dual nature to Job, and the latter perceives the unconscious split in his God's nature. The very fact that Job can see this is immensely significant, because it entails that Yahweh has also to learn to know himself. It is inconceivable that one of his creatures could have knowledge of Yahweh that the latter does not have of himself. 'Whoever knows God has an effect on him. The failure of the attempt to corrupt Job has changed Yahweh's nature' (ibid.: 391). Thus began the long process that was to culminate in God becoming man with the advent of Christ. These events brought about, Jung argues, nothing less than a world-shaking transformation of the divinity: 'The encounter with the creature changes the creator' (ibid.: 428).

In this, Jung advanced a radical thesis about the interdependence of god and man, arguing that this interdependence was vital to both parties, not just to poor weak humankind. The utterly new element was the hypothesis that the godhead needed to become human in order to activate his omniscience, for although Yahweh had possessed this power, he did not seem to use it. His consciousness seems not to have been more than a primitive awareness, his actions and perceptions paralleling the blindness of one who acts from the instinctive unconscious (ibid.: 404–5). But the entry into the Christian era was designed to express changes in the old regime.

The father wants to become the son, God wants to become man, the amoral wants to become exclusively good, the unconscious wants to become consciously responsible (ibid.: 424)

Considering this thought strictly in the context of the god within us, Yahweh's urgent need to become human corresponds to the need of the archetypal image of the self to bring itself ever more fully into consciousness in order the more fully to know itself.

However, this was by no means the end of the story. Jung had no difficulty in showing that although the Christian God became more loving than Yahweh in letting himself become man, he did not lose the capacity for harm. The signs are numerous. For example, to choose a minor tribulation, there is the disquieting hint in the Lord's Prayer in Christ's petition to his father, 'Lead us not into temptation', which leaves open the possibility that God might be a devilish tempter (ibid.: 410–11). This is to say nothing of the altogether more savage fact that the Christian God of love and goodness is so unforgiving of his own creatures that he can only be appeased by a human sacrifice – and the killing of his own son at that (ibid.: 430). All in all, Jung concludes,

God is not only to be loved, but also to be feared. He fills us with evil as well as with good, otherwise he would not need to be feared; and because he wants to become man, the uniting of his antinomy must take place in man. This involves man in a new responsibility. He can no longer wriggle out of it on the plea of his littleness and nothingness, for the dark God has slipped the atom bomb and chemical weapons into his hands and given him the power to empty out the apocalyptic vials of wrath on his fellow creatures. Since he has been granted an almost godlike power, he can no longer remain blind and unconscious (ibid.: 461)

The fundamental problem encountered in attempting to discuss the godhead is, as Jung recognises, that whenever we speak of religious matters we are operating in a world of images which point to something ineffable. It is particularly interesting from our point of view to note his concession that 'we can imagine God as an eternally flowing current of vital energy that endlessly changes shape just as easily as we can imagine him as an eternally unmoved, unchangeable essence' (ibid.: 361). However, despite this recognition, Jung does not test the merits of conceiving the godhead as a current of energy, but – understandably, given both his Christian background and the nature of his argument as to the burden on humanity – he preserves the image of god in the image of a powerful father-figure, as we have seen. Nonetheless, there are distinct benefits to be gained from reducing the personal component of the imagery that touches on the numinous.

Depersonalising the numinous in the way that *2001* does shows humanity as the servant of overmastering energy. That energy is perceived as rushing through both physical matter and the psyche, and as bringing life to both the conscious and the unconscious mind. We have already said that revising the image of deity does what all religions have striven to achieve in the time of their greatest conviction. It both revitalises the image and brings it as close as possible to the knowledge and experience people have of the world – both physical and cultural – that they inhabit. But locating the source of the numinous in energy does more than that. It allows a rapprochement of religious experience with the forms of knowledge uncovered by the natural sciences. Also, it makes it easier, since energy is wholly amoral, to understand how we are profoundly capable of acts of both the finest good and the greatest evil.

A film with the impact that *2001* had can bring to consciousness, and then leave latent in the cultural unconscious for years afterwards, a trace which modifies the culture by seeding a new image of great potential. In *2001* it is not just what *arises from* the unconscious that is so exciting, but also what consciousness gives back to and animates in the unconscious. What is at stake, in the stage of development to which Clarke and Kubrick show humanity to have arrived, is nothing less than enhancing knowledge and consciousness of the unconscious and the unknown, both personal and universal. Theirs is a revised version, updated for the late twentieth century, of the religious responsibility with which Jung believes humanity is charged.

It would be false to claim that the image of the numinous recognised in the western world has changed radically in the thirty years since 1968. But change in the collective unconscious can be a slow process that may be measured in hundreds rather than tens of years as the psyche reaches out and finds symbols that better express its needs. We began by speaking of the phenomenon that dreams and visions of extraordinary power sometimes predict future constellations of meaningful symbols. The imagery of inner and outer space that Kubrick, Clarke and (after them) many other artists have offered the twentieth century is emotive and powerful, and could yet become a popular and enduring symbolic cluster to convey our sense of what is magical about human experience of the universe and the self.

Conclusion

The publication of Krin and Glen O. Gabbard's *Psychiatry and the Cinema* (1987) started a debate between screen analysts and clinicians about the therapeutic potential of movies. As we saw in chapter 1, the Gabbards believe films give spectators the opportunity through role- and symbol-play (buttressed by their sense of an emotional connection with other fans) to gain mastery over their terrors and repressions. My own book supports this case and goes further in suggesting that screen fictions can stimulate and support individuation as part of the positive processes of maturation. As clinicians, however, Christoph Hering and David Hewison take up more sceptical positions, justified by their work with patients who have had extreme difficulty in accommodating what Hering terms their internal scenario of terror (Hering 1994: 403). And Hewison refers to patients who, governed by their internal scenarios, force-read films to match their own psychological circumstances or to firm up an insecure sense of identity (Hewison 2000: 292–3).

Hering focuses on the *Alien* films, applying object-relations theory to the presumed response of spectators to the monster. Describing the Alien as absolute evil devoid of any mitigating features, he agrees with the Gabbards that in Kleinian terms, given the immense horror it generates, it gathers around itself certain split-off facets of the spectator's personality. These embody aggressive tendencies and anxieties imperfectly repressed from infancy about nurturing figures who turn hostile. In the plot, the crew endeavour to exterminate the Alien using all the ingenuity they can muster and do not try to reach an accommodation with it. It troubles Hering that the dramatic intensity of their attempts to destroy the Alien tends to reinforce viewers' primitive defences against terror, arousing them to mirror the action in their own attitude. Like the crew, their passionate desire to annihilate the monster endures through the entire film (Hering 1994: 391–5). As a consequence spectators do not find the peace of mind in which to humanise and integrate their own bad impulses by recognising them as something that they have in common with the Alien. Instead, their response is likely

204

to reinforce the very defence mechanisms that caused a state of terror in the first place – an infantile splitting and projection of the bad
from the good mother in the attempt to force absolute evil outside while
keeping absolute good inside. For Hering, the films thereby elevate a
paranoid view of the world to the level of truth, and feed the kind of
delusions about moral supremacy that legitimise cruelty and ultimately
fascism (ibid.: 395–7). He accuses the film industry of exploiting the
audience's psychotic anxieties in the interests of its own profitability
(ibid.: 406).

The problem with Hering's Kleinian analysis from the film and media
studies perspective is that it attempts to determine the spectator's sub-
jection to the text, much as, in the 1980s, Freudian film theory had done
with the concept of subject positioning. Spectators are assumed to be
identical victims of the text.

I believe that...the spectator is plunged into utter despair and helplessness,
because he is denied any access to the possibility of empathic identification with
the alien monster, and particularly the one in himself. (ibid.: 405)

In contrast to this approach, a Jungian might start from the popularity of the *Alien* films, noting the way they grabbed the attention of so
many people. Whether or not Hering is right to accuse the industry of
feeding paranoia for profit, it has to be said that audiences worldwide
turned out in large numbers. The Jungian reading (while not ruling out
investigating mass paranoid anxiety if that seemed justified by the historical conditions of the day) would certainly consider whether the films
might have presented an unconscious compensation for a distinctive bias
of consciousness. Such a reading would probably not follow Hering in
dwelling on the supposed moral nature of the Alien any more than it
would argue that a disease, say a cancer, has a moral quality. It would
take this attitude because in action the Alien has a single dominant and
amoral characteristic: it slaughters every human it can. This narrative
fact makes it an icon linked to death rather than evil. Therefore a Jungian
reading might find its explanation for the collective appeal of the film in
its compensating for the cultural repression of the taboo topic of the late
twentieth century – death. Where Hering's interpretation looks back to
seek unresolved infantile anxieties aroused by the absence of caring parents (ibid.: 402), a Jungian would be more likely to analyse the monster
as a manifestation of terrors still to be faced.

Active imagining and amplification seem to me to offer spectators the
virtual space, the safe haven, in which to work through the scenario
of terror to which the overwhelming emotional intensity of films such
as the Alien series can give rise. Those procedures have the potential

to provide the individual with the interior equivalent to the relational space that the clinical analyst keeps secure for the analysand (see Hering 1994: 403).

It has, however, to be conceded, as Hewison argues (referring to cases where patients have brought movies to his consulting room), thinking into and about feeling so that one both experiences something intensely and has sufficient distance from it to know what it is requires a degree of maturity and stability (Hewison 2000: 290–3)

[It] requires the ability to stay in states of emotional arousal without seeking to resolve the considerable tension which may arise by either rationalization or abreaction . . . (ibid.: 291)

That kind of balanced, emotional tension is indeed the state of mind that the Jungian textual analyst should aim at exploiting, and the one advantage he or she brings should be extensive knowledge of films, television and the wider cultural field. Beyond that, each spectator can only interpret films from within the sphere of his or her own subjectivity, bounded by the limits of knowledge, memories and personality.

The less stable the individual's subjective sphere, the more likely that external influences might shake it. Hewison makes the point that not everyone is able to master symbols in the way that I have advocated. He instances some of his patients whose ego is splintered or only partially developed, and who experience symbols playing with them, rather than vice versa. When such clients bring recollected films into the consulting room, active imagining would be dangerous and other techniques must be brought into service (Hewison 2000: 291–3).

Hewison argues incontrovertibly that, since there is no escaping the profound impact of the clinician's intervention on their lives, he or she is engaged with patients in a procedure which is profoundly moral (ibid.: 289). It seems to me that, although the work of the screen analyst does not raise matters of life or death with the same immediate impact, it should nonetheless engage with issues of the highest moral significance. We can argue this by focusing on one of the commonest devices of fiction – coincidence.

From their earliest lessons in scripting, novice writers learn that fictional characters are not people. They are goal-driven. Their function is to try to fulfil the overriding purpose that (whether they know it or not) is their object. The business of writers includes ensuring, in order to heighten their drama, that characters want things that are hard to get. Screen events are usually so organised that protagonists can only attain their dreams (or alternatively discover that they can never be won) near the end of the final act.[22] To bring this about requires that, in plotting their characters' fates, writers arrange meaningful coincidence.

No question, then, but writers and directors manipulate their characters. In the process (notwithstanding that, as argued in chapter 1, spectators make their own input when interpreting what appears on screen) filmmakers offer audiences vicarious involvement in the meaningful coincidences that characters undergo. When done well, such experience usually hits spectators with powerful emotions. This is not surprising when we recall that meaningful coincidence is a prime characteristic of synchronicity.

We saw earlier that Jung used the term synchronicity to express his perception that certain events which appear to be related are connected without necessarily obeying the rules of space, time and causality (Jung 1952a). At first sight, therefore, the practice of screenwriters in moving their characters along a chain of events linked by cause and effect seems to run counter to the idea of synchronicity: Event A causes the protagonist to respond with Action B which in turn triggers the antagonist to Reaction C. To this extent causality rules fiction. However, the unexpected almost always intrudes. It can, for example, infiltrate where plot lines meet. We described such a moment in chapter 6 with the raid on Buffalo Bill's lair. The unexpected may also result from an unforeseeable deepening of (or twist in) a character's psychology. Or the writer may, in time-honoured fashion, introduce an unexpected intervention, a *deus ex machina*, to bring matters to a head. Synchronicity can also occur on screen when two forms of reality – inner and outer – intersect, visiting not only characters but also the spectator with the emotionally overwhelming sense of being presented with 'absolute knowledge', the feeling that both Dana Scully and Daniel Feeld had.

Most spectators take pleasure from meaningful coincidences in fiction whether or not they have experienced synchronicity in their own lives. Such coincidences fit the psyche's need to explore beyond the rational. But because that need can be the subject of scepticism in a culture that focuses on rationality, some spectators will find that the chance to empathise with characters undergoing meaningful coincidences reinforces a private knowledge of synchronicity which they may be reticent to discuss in public.

Some movies go so far as to simulate the actual occurrence of synchronicity for spectators. For example, *Don't Look Now* (1973) and almost every other film directed by Nicolas Roeg, and more recently

---

[22] I owe these observations to Chris Dolan. (*Opening Shots*, May 2000, a Scottish Screen short course for screenwriters.)

The Sixth Sense (M. Night Shyamalan, 1999) all successfully draw spectators into feeling they have that extra sense without their being exposed to
ridicule. Far from feeling isolated, they are part of an audience buffeted
collectively by the same perceptions.

Through emotionally charged meaningful coincidence, synchronicity
on screen offers to bring into consciousness matters from the depths
that either an individual spectator or the collective audience may need
to become aware of, and can do so in a gripping way. If it has this effect
(and that is contingent on spectators' responses), then, from our point of
view, screen-based synchronicity has the qualities of an enhanced, highly
charged form of the symbolic and, like the Jungian symbol, it has potential to assist the process of individuation. At the personal level, it
can open a route to discovery of more about the self; for the collective audience it can open the possibility of enhancing awareness of deep
currents in the social psyche. So whether in life an individual gives credence to synchronistic experiences or not (though once lived they are
hard to deny), in their virtual worlds screen fictions have the capacity
through meaningful coincidence not merely to give access to the archetypal but actually to encourage both individuals and groups to engage
with it.

In showing how a Jungian methodology might shape the analysis of
certain kinds of film – in particular those which are charged with a high
level of imaginative energy – this book has dealt with a variety of representations that have about them the kind of 'dangerous' energy charge
which is usually associated with the numinous. Screen fictions can assist
many viewers to find truths for themselves and even help them to face the
basic question upon which all morality is founded, the necessity, if they
are to mature as individuals, of knowing the potential for evil and good
in themselves. I hope to have shown that at the deepest level it is possible
for spectators to exploit the transient symbols which the screen throws
up in ways that approximate the uses of the modes of self-knowledge that
in former epochs might have been passed from generation to generation
through organised religion. Nowadays for many people these mysteries
find their most effective mode of transmission via the stories and myths
that play on our screens.

Filmography

COLD LAZARUS (Renny Rye, GB, 1996)

Television networks: BBC and Channel 4
Executive producers: Michael Wearing (BBC), Peter Ansorge (Channel 4)
Producers: Kenith Trodd, Rosemarie Whitman
Screenplay: Dennis Potter
Director: Renny Rye
Director of photography: Remi Adefarasin
Supervising art director: Andrew Munro
Production designer: Christopher Hobbs
Stunt coordinator: Rod Woodruff
Special effects supervisor: Tom Harris
Film editor: Clare Douglas
Sound recordist: Clive Derbyshire; editor: Andy Glen
Music – Composer: Christopher Gunning; Performed by: London Symphony Orchestra
Leading players: Frances de la Tour (Emma Porlock), Carmen Ejogo (Blinda), Albert Finney (Daniel Feeld), Henry Goodman (Dave Siltz), Ciaran Hinds (Fyodor), Ganlat Kasumu (Luanda), Diane Ladd (Martina Masdon), Claudia Malkovitch (Kaya), Grant Master (Tony Watson)
Running time: 4 parts, 60 minutes each

DIVA (Jean-Jacques Beineix, France, 1981)

Distributor: Palace Pictures
Production company: Les Film Galaxie/ Greenwich Film Production. In association with Antenne 2
Producer: Irène Silberman
Screenplay: Jean-Jacques Beineix, Jean Van Hamme. Based on the novel by Delacorta
Director: Jean-Jacques Beineix

Director of photography: Philippe Rousselot
Production designer: Hilton McConnico
Editor: Marie-Josephe Yoyotte, Monique Prim
Sound recordist: Jean-Pierre Ruh; editor: Claude Villand
Music extracts: Aria from *La Wally* by Alfredo Catalina, 'Ave Maria' by Charles Gounod, performed by Wilhelmenia Wiggins Fernandez
Leading players: Frédéric Andrei (Jules), Richard Bohringer (Gorodish), Jacques Fabbri (Inspector Jean Saporta), Thuy An Luu (Alba), Dominique Pinon (Le Curé), Wilhelmenia Wiggins Fernandez (Cynthia Hawkins, the Diva)
Running time: 117 minutes

GHOST (Jerry Zucker, 1990, USA)

Distributor: UIP
Production company: Paramount, Howard W Koch
Executive producer: Steven-Charles Jaffe
Screenplay: Bruce Joel Rubin
Director of photography: Adam Greenberg
Video effects: Steve Price
Special video effects: Industrial Light and Magic
Editor: Walter Murch
Production designer: Jane Musky
Music: Maurice Jarre
Supervising sound editor: Leslie Shatz
Leading players: Patrick Swayze (Sam Wheat), Demi Moore (Molly Jensen), Tony Goldwyn (Carl Bruner), Whoopi Goldberg (Oda Mae Brown)
Running time: 127 minutes

INTERVIEW WITH DENNIS POTTER (GB, 1994)

Television network: Channel 4
Presenter: Melvyn Bragg
Running time: 80 minutes

KARAOKE (Renny Rye, GB, 1996)

Television networks: BBC and Channel 4
Executive producers: Michael Wearing (BBC), Peter Ansorge (Channel 4)
Producers: Kenith Trodd, Rosemarie Whitman

Screenplay: Dennis Potter
Director: Renny Rye
Director of photography: Ashley Rowe
Production designer: Gary Williamson
Film editor: Clare Douglas
Sound recordist: John Midgley; editor: Mark Auguste
Music: Christopher Gunning
Leading players: Hywel Bennett (Arthur 'Pig' Mailion), Saffron
   Burrows (Sandra Sollars), Julie Christie (Lady Ruth Balmer),
   Albert Finney (Daniel Feeld), Richard E. Grant (Nick
   Balmer), Keeley Hawes (Linda Langer), Roy Hudd (Ben
   Baglin), Ian McDiarmid (Oliver Morse), Alison Steadman
   (Mrs Haynes)
Running time: 4 parts, 60 minutes each

THE PASSION OF DARKLY NOON
(Philip Ridley, UK/ Germany/ Belgium, 1996)

Distribution: Entertainment
Executive producers: Jim Beach, Ray Burdis, Shelly Bancroft
Producers: Dominic Anciano, Frank Henschle, Alain Keytsman
Screenplay: Philip Ridley
Director of Photography: John de Borman
Production designer: Hubert Pouillé
Editor: Leslie Healey
Sound recordists: Jan van Beuer, Benoît Bruwier; design: Nigel
   Galt
Music: Nick Bicât
Leading players: Brendan Fraser, (Darkly Noon), Ashley Judd
   (Callie), Viggo Mortensen (Clay), Loren Dean (Jude), Grace
   Zabriskie (Roxy), Lou Myers (Quincy)
Running time: 101 minutes

THE PIANO (Jane Campion, Australia, 1993)

Distribution: Entertainment
Production company: Jan Chapman productions in association
   with CIBY 2000
Producers: Alain Depardieu, Jan Chapman, Mark Turnbull
Screenplay: Jane Campion
Director of photography: Stuart Dryburgh
Production design: Andrew McAlpine
Editor: Veronika Jenet

Music: Michael Nyman; solo piano: Holly Hunter
Sound design: Lee Smith; sound editors: Gary O'Grady, Jeanine Chialvo
Leading players: Holly Hunter (Ada), Harvey Keitel (Baines), Sam Neill (Stewart), Anna Paquin (Flora).
Running time: 120 minutes

THE SILENCE OF THE LAMBS
(Jonathan Demme, USA, 1990)

Distribution: Orion Pictures/Rank (theatrical), Columbia-Tristar (video)
Producers: Kenneth Utt, Edward Saxon and Ron Bozman
Screenplay: Ted Tally, based on the novel by Thomas Harris
Director of photography: Tak Fujimoto
Production designer: Kristi Zea
Editor: Craig McKay
Music: Howard Shore; editor: Susana Peric
Sound designer: Skip Lievsay; associate editor: Lisa Bromwell; recordist: John Fundus
Leading players: Jodie Foster (Clarice Starling), Anthony Hopkins (Dr. Hannibal Lecter), Scott Glenn (Jack Crawford), Ted Levine (Buffalo Bill/ Jame Gumb)
Running time: 118 minutes

TRULY, MADLY, DEEPLY
(Anthony Minghella, UK, 1990)

Distribution: Samuel Goldwyn Co
Production company: BBC Films
Executive producer: Mark Shivas
Producer: Robert Cooper
Screenplay: Anthony Minghella
Director of photography: Remi Adefarasin
Visual effects: Ian Legg
Editor: John Stothart
Production design: Barbara Gasnold
Music: Barrington Pheloung
Sound recordists: Jim Greenhorn, Aad Wirtz; editor: Helen Whitehead
Leading players: Juliet Stevenson (Nina), Alan Rickman (Jamie), Bill Paterson (Sandy), Michael Maloney (Mark)
Running time: 106 minutes

2001: A SPACE ODYSSEY (Stanley Kubrick, GB, 1968)

Production and Distribution: Metro-Goldwyn-Mayer
Producer: Stanley Kubrick
Screenplay: Stanley Kubrick and Arthur C. Clarke
Director of photography: Geoffrey Unsworth
Production designers: Tony Masters, Harry Lange, Ernest Archer
Special effects supervisors: Wally Veevers, Douglas Trumbull, Con Pederson, Tom Howard
Editor: Ray Lovejoy
Music: Richard Strauss, 'Thus Spake Zarathustra'; Johann Strauss, 'The Blue Danube'; György Ligeti, 'Atmospheres,' 'Lux Aeterna,' 'Requiem'; Aram Khatchaturian, 'Gayaneh Ballet Suite'
Sound: Winston Ryder
Leading players: Keir Dullea (David Bowman), Gary Lockwood (Frank Poole), William Sylvester (Dr Heyward Floyd), Douglas Rain (Voice of HAL)
Running time: 141 minutes

THE X-FILES: PARANORMAL ACTIVITY

An episode in the series "The Truth Is Out There" (USA 1997)

Production company: Twentieth Century Fox Film Corporation
Executive producers: Chris Carter, Howard Gordon, R. W. Goodwin
Producers: Joseph Patrick Finn, Kim Manners
Director: James Charleston
Script: John Shiban
Director of photography: Joel Ransom
Production design: Graeme Murray
Editor: Jim Gross
Supervising sound editor: Thierry J. Couturier
Music: Mark Snow
Leading players: David Duchovny (Fox Mulder), Gillian Anderson (Dana Scully), Steven M. Porter (Mr Angie Pintero), Alex Bruhanski (Harold Speuler)
Running time: 43 minutes

Glossary of Jungian and related terms

Active imagination   A technique of concentrating on dream or fantasy images by lowering the level of conscious activity. This allows the images to develop according to their own logic and provides a means of exposing unconscious contents.

Affect   Emotion. A primary force exercised by the unconscious leading to an intense excitation of nervous energy over which the individual has little control.

Amplification   A process of interpretation, important in the analysis of dreams, it depends upon finding the appropriate context for images by searching for parallels in other dreams or myths. Images in films can be amplified by cross-reference to other images whether in the same film or in comparable sources.

Androcentrism   Belief system centred on men's views of the world. Male sexism.

Androgyne   (Also hermaphrodite.) An imago having the sexual characteristics of both male and female in equal measure. In its perfected form it represents the linkage of anima and animus in a syzygy that reflects the balancing of opposite elements in the differentiated self.

Anima and animus   The contrasexual archetypes. According to Jung's formulation, the first, experienced by men, represents the hidden feminine aspects of their personalities; and the second (present in the dreams of women) symbolises the concealed masculine in them. They mediate between the ego and the unconscious, and thus are opposites to the persona. Some post Jungians argue that both anima and animus are present in all individuals to varying degrees (see Hopcke 1991). See also syzygy.

Apperception   A process whereby a new psychic content is recognised so that it becomes clear. Directed apperceptive processes, like thinking, depend on rational, conscious activity; undirected apperception, such as dreaming and fantasising, is irrational (Samuels, Shorter and Plaut 1986: 25–6).

Archetypal images   The images which clothe the archetypes and enable the conscious mind to know unconscious contents. Often recognisable by their numinosity or magical charge. See also symbol.

Archetypes   The contents of the collective unconscious. They are not inherited ideas, but inherited modes of psychic functioning. Until activated, they are forms without content; when activated they control patterns of behaviour. The centres of energy around which ideas, images, affects and myths cohere.

Association   'The spontaneous linkage of ideas, perceptions, images, fantasies according to certain personal and psychological themes, motifs, similarities, oppositions or causalities' (Samuels, Shorter and Plaut 1986: 28).

Child   Archetypal image usually signalling a beneficial change of personality before it occurs, it represents to the adult instincts experienced in childhood and subsequently split off.

Collective or transpersonal unconscious   The deeper, impersonal layer of the unconscious whose contents are more or less the same in all individuals. It is the functioning of the inherited brain structure which in its broad outlines is the same in all human beings. Since Jung also held that the thinking function could have a shared quality when it referred to agreed ideas or observations, he also referred to the –

Collective conscious   The social values to which the individual's persona must adopt.

Complex   An emotionally charged cluster of ideas or images arising from the personal unconscious.

Consciousness   Described by Jung as the relation of psychic contents to the ego, in so far as this relation is perceived by the ego. For our purposes it generally suffices to think of consciousness as awareness.

Constellation   Whenever someone experiences a strong emotional reaction, a complex has been constellated or activated (Henderson 1984: 113).

Constructive method   As opposed to the reductive method which Jung alleged Freud used, the constructive method tries to get consciousness and the unconscious to work in tandem to re-balance the psyche. It deploys active imagination in alternation with amplification as the means to gain this end.

Cultural unconscious   A concept that explicitly opens Jungian models of the psyche to the recognition that social and cultural pressures join with both personal and archetypal factors in forming all but the deepest psychic images. It is the site of a collision of psychic energies from two separate origins – first, archetypal images having their source in the collective unconscious, and second, repressed contradictions from oppressive social formations (Rushing and Frentz 1991: 391).

Demon   An extreme form of the shadow.

Differentiation   The separation of parts from a whole, the process of untangling what was formerly joined unconsciously (Jung 1921: 424; Samuels, Shorter and Plaut 1986: 45).

Duality   See enantiodromia.

Ego-complex   The centre of consciousness, in so far as psychic contents which the ego perceives are conscious. It is the feeling-toned complex that consists of representations of oneself – the way one sees oneself (Hopcke 1992: 77). Although we have knowledge of it, the ego is inferior to the *self* which is the ordering principle of the human personality.

Emblems   Called allegories or signs by Jung, they are distinct from symbols in being paraphrases of contents that are already conscious. Unlike symbols they do not signify meanings for which no other expression yet exists.

Emotion   See affect.

Enantiodromia   The tendency of every psychological extreme to contain its own opposite and to run towards it. This principle is the key to the essential duality of Jungian analyses of myth, since the more extreme a position is, the more readily it can be expected to convert into its opposite.

Feeling   Has a specific meaning for Jungians as a distinct psychic, rational function which evaluates the worth of relationships and situations. As Henderson says, feeling must be distinguished from emotion, which is due to an activated complex (Henderson 1984: 113).

God-image (Imago Dei)   See self.

Great mother   (Also Earth Mother.) The collective maternal imago, both a figure of benign fertility and nurture, and the devourer who pulls her children down to the abyss. For Jung the profound ambivalence of the imago signified the need for the young to break away from their mother's embraces in order to enter adulthood. Thus the hero's return to the world from the cave of the Earth Mother marks an early step on the way to individuation.

Group unconscious   (See cultural unconscious).

Hermaphrodite   (See androgyne).

Hero/ine   A human or quasi-human figure, symbol of the libido and 'the ideas, forms, and forces which grip and mould the soul' (Jung 1956a: 178). He or she 'represents the will and capacity to undergo repeated transformations in pursuit of wholeness or meaning', and at times appears to be ego, at times the self (Samuels, Shorter and Plaut 1986: 66).

Hieros gamos   Sacred copulation, consummation of the sacred marriage. Often a seasonal ritual ensuring the fertility of a people or their land. In analytical psychology, the union of hero and anima (often the mother) represents a preliminary stage of transformation towards individuation.

Imago   Refers to an image generated subjectively and therefore often having archetypal qualities because it is shaped by the internal state of the subject (ibid.: 73–4).

Incest   See hieros gamos. Union of the hero(ine) with the parent of the opposite sex represents the regressive entry into the unconscious, a step which must be followed by rejection of the parent imago if he or she is to progress towards discovery of the self.

Individuation   The process of discovery by which the individual approaches knowledge of the self. It entails not only an enhancement of consciousness but also the more complete fulfilment of the collective qualities of the human being.

Inflation   Described by Henderson as a state of mind in which one has an unrealistically high or (in the case of negative inflation) low sense of identity. 'It indicates a regression of consciousness into unconsciousness, which typically happens when the ego takes too many unconscious contents upon itself and loses the faculty of discrimination' (Henderson 1984: 113).

Integration   Either the recognition, or the process of bringing about the interaction of conscious and unconscious.

Introjection   The opposite of projection. A process of assimilation in which objective experience is internalised (Samuels, Shorter and Plaut 1986: 85; Jung 1921: 452).

Intuition   'The irrational function which tells us the possibilities inherent in the present. In contrast to sensation (the function which perceives immediate reality through the physical senses) intuition perceives via the unconscious, for example, flashes of insight of unknown origin' (Henderson 1984: 113).

Lapis philosophorum   The philosophers' stone, believed by alchemists to have the power to convert matter to gold, and interpreted by Jung as an image of the self.

Libido   Psychic energy. Desire and appetite in their natural state, unchecked by any kind of authority.

Mana personalities   (See also hero/ine.) Imagoes of personalities such as priests or magicians, radiating extraordinary energy and having divine or magical powers, which appear when the ego is consciously confronted with the self (Samuels, Shorter and Plaut 1986: 89–90).

Mandala   An image having numinous powers, and often combining rectilinear (representing conscious) and circular (unconscious) components. Jung interpreted his patients' mandalas as intuitively produced and detailed maps of their psyches.

Mythologem   A figure in myth.

Myths   Revelatory narratives which Jung argued were not so much invented as experienced. He thought they resembled a projection of the collective unconscious of each nation and thus provided a means to study it.

Numinosum   Transcendent energy (mediated by the archetypes) wholly outside the control of the individual's will. It can transport the subject into a state of rapture and transform consciousness. Jung thought that experience of the numinous was an important factor in the religious life of the individual, and produced a personal faith in what is beyond the power of the psyche to know.

Numinous   Having the qualities of the numinosum.

Persona   The public face or mask of the individual. It is the means by which the ego confronts the world. Its countertype is the anima or animus.

Personal unconscious   That layer of the unconscious that owes its existence to personal experience and stores forgotten and repressed contents.

Pneuma   Literally air, wind, breath or spirit. Pneuma and spirit refer to the immaterial aspect of humanity, 'in their archetypal character [they] are dynamic and half-substantial agencies; you are moved by them as by a wind . . . ' (Jung 1935b: 155–6). Psychic manifestations of the spirit are autonomous complexes (like the wise old man) which may lead to enhanced intuitive self-knowledge.

Projection   Occurs when individuals find either good or problematic aspects of their own personality transferred on to other people or objects. It gives subjects who are aware of this function the opportunity to identify some of the contents of the unconscious. Opposite of introjection.

Psyche   The total activity and contents of the mind, both conscious and unconscious. Also used to mean soul.

Psychopomp   In myth, a figure that leads souls down to the underworld; in analytical psychology a symbol of interchange between consciousness and unconsciousness.

Psychosis   'A personality state in which an unknown 'something' takes possession of the psyche to a greater or lesser degree and asserts its existence undeterred by logic, persuasion or will' (Samuels, Shorter and Plaut 1986: 123).

Quaternity   Division into four parts, frequently seen in mandalas. Represents the wholeness of psychic life through the conjunction of opposites in the self.

Reductive method   Freud's analytical method as described by Jung. The latter believed it was limited because it insisted on the reduction of all psychological phenomena to infantile processes.

Regression   The turning back of the libido to the depths of the unconscious (often symbolised by the Great Mother). It may be caused either when an individual recoils before a daunting task, or by neurosis.

Self   An archetype whose nature is contested within Jungian Studies. Classical Jungians, like the founder of the movement himself, reckon it to be analogous to the monistic imago Dei, the central archetype in the human psyche; the image of totality achieved through the balancing out of opposites; and both the source and goal of our psychic life. Archetypal analysts like Hillman think it preferable to attend to all the voices and images that emerge from the psyche, integrating each in its own right. The resultant picture favours a multi-centred (or, where the archetypes are represented by types of god, polytheistic) image where the self is de-emphasised and the analyst seeks better insights into emotions and relationships between the parts of the psyche (Samuels 1990: 107–8).

Shadow   The archetype that represents the 'dark side' of human nature, that is those elements of the personality which the individual does not recognise in him or herself. Sometimes appears as a dark figure.

Sign   See emblems.

Soul   Sometimes used by Jung interchangeably with psyche; sometimes employed to refer to deep level activity in the psyche (Samuels, Shorter and Plaut, p. 140).

Spirit   See pneuma.

Symbol   Expression of an intuitive idea that cannot yet be formulated in any other way. It performs a compensatory function in mediating between and rebalancing conscious and unconscious. See archetypal images and emblems.

Synchronicity   An 'acausal connecting principle' by which events that may have no causal relationship in space or time are nonetheless experienced by an observer as meaningfully linked. Covers such parapsychological phenomena as telepathy and clairvoyance.

Syzygy   The linking of opposites in a pair. Sometimes found as interlinked symbols such the Yin and Yang but usually as male – female couples representing the anima and animus. This syzygy expresses the impossibility of men and women talking without their contrasexual projections encountering each other. See also androgyne.

Transitional objects   Something tangible which an infant holds onto as a defence against separation anxiety and to stand in for the absent mother. Winnicott calls such things as teddy bears 'the first not-me possession'. Thus transitional objects are the child's first experience of symbols.

Transpersonal unconscious   See collective unconscious.

Trickster   A specialised variant of the shadow typified by changeability. Can partake (like Mercurius) of the nature of both devil and saviour, yet *prima facie* is an anti-type to the hero. His fondness for jokes, and his ability to transform himself make him a symbol of enantiodromia.

Unconscious   See collective unconscious, cultural unconscious and personal unconscious.

Uroboros   The circular snake that eats its own tail: symbolic of the perfect beginning state in which opposites are united, having not yet flown apart, and differentiation has yet to commence. (The androgynous Great Mother can have the same value.) Also an emblem of eternity.

Will   Thought of by Jung as 'the amount of psychic energy at the disposal of consciousness' (1921: 486). Refers to a drive focused by consciousness.

Wise old person   Represents knowledge, reflection, insight, wisdom, cleverness and intuition, as well as positive moral qualities. May constellate spontaneously when all the subject's spiritual and physical forces are challenged and there is no going back. Sometimes exhibits an ambiguous elfin personality such as Merlin's (Jung 1948b: 219–30).

References

Anthony, Maggy (1990), *The Valkyries: The Women Around Jung*. Shaftesbury: Element Books.

Auty, Martin (1982), 'Breathless: *Diva*', *Sight and Sound* 51, 4, 302.

Bale, John (1991), 'Playing at Home: British Football and a Sense of Place', in John Williams and Stephen Wagg (eds.), *British Football and Social Change: Getting into Europe*. Leicester University Press.

Beebe, John (1992), 'The Anima in Film', on Don Williams's web site 'C.G. Jung, Analytical Psychology, & Culture', http://www.cgjung.com/films.

(1996), 'Jungian Illumination of Film', *Psychoanalytic Review* 83, 4, 579–87.

Bolen, Jean Shinoda (1985), *Goddesses in Everywoman: A New Psychology of Women*. San Francisco: Harper and Row.

Bordo, Susan (1993), '"Material Girl": The Effacements of Postmodern Culture', in Schwichtenberg.

Bowie, Malcolm (1991), *Lacan*. London: Fontana.

Branigan, Edward (1992), *Narrative Comprehension and Film*. London: Routledge.

Branson, Clark (1987), *Howard Hawks: a Jungian Study*. Santa Barbara: Capra Press.

Browne, Pat (ed.) (1987), *Heroines of Popular Culture*. Bowling Green, Ohio: Bowling Green State University Popular Press.

Campbell, Joseph (1973), *The Hero with a Thousand Faces*. Princeton University Press.

Carrette, Jeremy R. (1994), 'The Language of Archetypes: A Conspiracy in Psychological Theory', *Harvest: Journal for Jungian Studies* 40, 168–92.

Chetwynd, Tom (1982), *Dictionary of Symbols*. London: Aquarian, 1993.

Christ, Carol P. (1975), 'Spiritual Quest and Women's Experience', *Anima* 1, 2.

(1976), 'Margaret Atwood: The Surfacing of Women's Spiritual Quest and Vision', *Signs* 2, 2.

Clarke, Alan and Clarke, John (1982), 'Highlights and Action Replays – Ideology, Sport and the Media', in Hargreaves, Jennifer.

Clarke, Arthur C. (1968), *The Promise of Space*. Harmondsworth: Penguin, 1970.

Cook, John R. (1995), *Dennis Potter: A Life on Screen*. Manchester University Press.

Dervin, Daniel (1985), *Through A Freudian Lens Deeply: A Psychoanalysis of Cinema*. Hillsdale, NJ: The Analytic Press.

Dixson, Miriam (1976), *The Real Matilda: Women and Identity in Australia 1788 to the Present.* New York: Penguin.

Donaldson, Mara E. (1987), 'Woman as Hero in Margaret Atwood's *Surfacing* and Maxine Hong Kingston's *The Woman Warrior*', in Browne.

Dunning, Eric (1971), *The Sociology of Sport: A Selection of Readings.* London: Frank Cass.

Dyer, Richard (1998), *Stars.* 2nd edn. London: British Film Institute.

Eberwein, Robert T. (1984), *Film & the Dream Screen: A Sleep and a Forgetting.* Princeton University Press.

Ehrenreich, Barbara, Elizabeth Hess, and Gloria Jacobs (1992), 'Beatlemania: Girls Just Want to Have Fun', in Lisa A. Lewis (ed.), *Adoring Audience: Fan Culture and Popular Media.* London: Routledge.

Elias, Norbert (1971), 'The Genesis of Sport as a Sociological Problem', in Dunning.

and Dunning, Eric (1971), 'Folk Football in Medieval and Early Modern Britain', in Dunning.

Fiedler, Leslie A. (1967), *Love and Death in the American Novel.* London: Paladin.

Firth, Raymond (1973), *Symbols: Public and Private.* London: George Allen and Unwin.

Francke, Lizzie (1993), '*The Piano*', *Sight and Sound* 3, 11, 50–1.

Fredericksen, Don (1979), 'Jung / Sign / Symbol / Film', Part 1, *Quarterly Review of Film Studies* 4, 2, 167–91.

(2000), 'Why Should We Take Jungian Screen Studies Seriously?' Paper presented to Society for Cinema Studies Conference, Chicago (10 March).

Gabbard, Krin and Gabbard, Glen O. (1987), *Psychiatry and the Cinema.* London: University of Chicago Press.

Gimbutas, Marija (1989), *The Language of the Goddess.* San Francisco: Harper & Row.

Goldenberg, Naomi R. (1990a), 'Looking at Jung Looking at Himself: a Psychoanalytic Re-reading of *Memories, Dreams, Reflections*', *Soundings* 73, 2–3, 383–406.

(1990b), *Returning Words to Flesh: Feminism, Psychoanalysis, and the Resurrection of the Body.* Boston: Beacon Press.

Goldie, Terry (1988), 'Signifier Resignified: Aborigines in Australian Literature', in Anna Rutherford (ed.), *Aboriginal Culture Today.* Sydney: Dangaroo.

(1989), *Fear and Temptation: The Image of the Indigene in Canadian, Australian and New Zealand Literatures.* Kingston: McGill-Queen's University Press.

Gray, Richard M. (1996), *Archetypal Explorations: An Integrative Approach to Human Behavior.* London: Routledge.

Greenberg, Harvey (1994), '*The Piano*', *Film Quarterly* 47, 3, 46–50.

Greenfield, Barbara (1985), 'The Archetypal Masculine: Its Manifestation in Myth, and Its Significance for Women', in Andrew Samuels (ed.), *The Father: Contemporary Jungian Perspectives.* London: Free Association Books.

Grimal, Pierre (1986), *Dictionary of Classical Mythology.* London: Penguin.

Guttmann, Allen (1978), *From Ritual to Record: the Nature of Modern Sports.* New York: Columbia University Press.

Hargreaves, Jennifer (ed.) (1982), *Sport, Culture and Ideology*. London: Routledge & Kegan Paul.

Hargreaves, John (1986), *Sport, Power and Culture: A Social and Historical Analysis of Popular Sports in Britain*. Cambridge: Polity Press.

Hellen, Richard A.J. and Philip M. Tucker (1987), 'The Alchemical Art of Arthur C. Clarke', *Foundation: the Review of Science Fiction* 41, 30–41.

Henderson, Joseph L. (1984), *Cultural Attitudes in Psychological Perspective*. Toronto: Inner City.

Henderson, Lisa (1993), 'Justify Our Love: Madonna & the Politics of Queer Sex', in Schwichtenberg.

Hering, Christoph, (1994), 'The Problem of the Alien: Emotional Mastery or Emotional Fascism in Contemporary Film Production', *Free Associations* 4, 3, 391–407.

Hewison, David, (2000), ' "Loving the Alien?" A Response to John Izod's "Active imagination and the analysis of film",' *Journal of Analytical Psychology* 45, 2, 287–93.

Hillman, James (1975), *Re-Visioning Psychology*. New York: Harper Collins.

(1988), *Suicide and the Soul*. Dallas, Texas: Spring Publications.

(1990), *The Essential James Hillman: a Blue Fire*. (ed.) Thomas Moore. London: Routledge.

and Michael Ventura (1992), *We've Had a Hundred Years of Psychotherapy – And the World's Getting Worse*. San Francisco: Harper.

Hopcke, Robert H. (1991), *Jung, Jungians, and Homosexuality*. London: Shambhala.

(1992), *A Guided Tour of the Collected Works of C.G. Jung*. London: Shambhala.

Iaccino, James F. (1994), *Psychological Reflections on Cinematic Terror: Jungian Archetypes in Horror Films*. London: Praeger.

(1998), *Jungian Reflections Within The Cinema: A Psychological Analysis of Sci-Fi and Fantasy Archetypes*. London: Praeger.

Izod, John (1992), *The Films of Nicolas Roeg: Myth and Mind*. London: Macmillan.

Jacoby, Mario (1992), 'The Witch in Dreams, Complexes, and Fairy Tales: The Dark Feminine in Psychotherapy', in Mario Jacoby, Verena Kast and Ingrid Riedel, *Witches, Ogres, and the Devil's Daughter: Encounters with Evil in Fairy Tales*. London: Shambhala.

Jhally, Sut (1989), 'Cultural Studies and the Sports/Media Complex', in Wenner.

Jung, Carl Gustav (1921), *Psychological Types, The Collected Works*, vol. 6, rev. edn. Princeton University Press, 1976.

(1929), 'The Aims of Psychotherapy', *The Practice of Psychotherapy, The Collected Works*, vol. 16, 2nd edn. Princeton University Press, 1985.

(1931a), 'On the Relation of Analytical Psychology to Poetry', *The Spirit in Man, Art and Literature, The Collected Works*, vol. 15. London: Routledge & Kegan Paul, 1966.

(1931b), 'The Stages of Life', *The Structure and Dynamics of the Psyche, The Collected Works*, vol. 8, 2nd edn. London: Routledge & Kegan Paul, 1981.

(1934), 'A Review of the Complex Theory', *The Structure and Dynamics of the Psyche, The Collected Works*, vol. 8, 2nd edn. London: Routledge & Kegan Paul, 1981.

(1935a), 'The Relations between the Ego and the Unconscious', *Two Essays on Analytical Psychology, The Collected Works*, vol. 7, 2nd edn. London: Routledge & Kegan Paul, 1966.

(1935b), The Tavistock Lectures, *The Symbolic Life, The Collected Works*, vol. 18. London: Routledge & Kegan Paul, 1977.

(1936), 'The Concept of the Collective Unconscious', *The Archetypes and the Collective Unconscious, The Collected Works*, vol. 9, 1, 2nd edn. London: Routledge & Kegan Paul, 1968.

(1938), *Dream Analysis*, Part I. London: Routledge, 1995.

(1939), 'Conscious, Unconscious, and Individuation', *The Archetypes and the Collective Unconscious, The Collected Works*, vol. 9, 1, 2nd edn. London: Routledge & Kegan Paul, 1968.

(1942), 'Paracelsus as a Spiritual Phenomenon', *Alchemical Studies, The Collected Works*, vol. 13, London: Routledge & Kegan Paul, 1983.

(1943), 'On the Psychology of the Unconscious', *Two Essays on Analytical Psychology, The Collected Works*, vol. 7, 2nd edn. London: Routledge & Kegan Paul, 1966.

(1946a), 'The Psychology of the Transference', *The Practice of Psychotherapy, The Collected Works*, vol. 16, 2nd edn. Princeton University Press, 1985.

(1946b), 'Psychotherapy Today', *The Practice of Psychotherapy, The Collected Works*, vol. 16, 2nd edn. Princeton University Press, 1985.

(1948a), 'The Spirit Mercurius', *Alchemical Studies, The Collected Works*, vol. 13. London: Routledge & Kegan Paul, 1983.

(1948b), 'The Phenomenology of the Spirit in Fairytales', *The Archetypes and the Collective Unconscious, The Collected Works*, vol. 9, 1, 2nd edn. London: Routledge & Kegan Paul, 1968.

(1948c), 'General Aspects of Dream Psychology', *The Structure and Dynamics of the Psyche, The Collected Works*, vol. 8, 2nd edn. London: Routledge & Kegan Paul, 1981.

(1950), 'Psychology and Literature', *The Spirit in Man, Art and Literature, The Collected Works*, vol. 15. London: Routledge & Kegan Paul, 1966.

(1951), 'The Psychology of the Child Archetype', *The Archetypes and the Collective Unconscious, The Collected Works*, vol. 9, 1, 2nd edn. London: Routledge & Kegan Paul, 1968.

(1952a), 'Synchronicity: An Acausal Connecting Principle', *The Structure and Dynamics of the Psyche, The Collected Works*, vol. 8, 2nd edn. London: Routledge & Kegan Paul, 1981.

(1952b), 'Answer to Job', *Psychology and Religion: West and East, The Collected Works*, vol. 11. London: Routledge and Kegan Paul, 1958.

(1953), *Psychology and Alchemy, The Collected Works*, vol. 12, 2nd edn. London: Routledge & Kegan Paul, 1981.

(1954a), 'Archetypes of the Collective Unconscious', *The Archetypes and the Collective Unconscious, The Collected Works*, vol. 9, 1, 2nd edn. London: Routledge & Kegan Paul, 1968.

(1954b), 'Psychological Aspects of the Mother Archetype', *The Archetypes and the Collective Unconscious, The Collected Works*, vol. 9, 1, 2nd edn. London: Routledge & Kegan Paul, 1968.

(1954c), 'On the Nature of the Psyche', *The Structure and Dynamics of the Psyche, The Collected Works*, vol. 8, 2nd edn. London: Routledge & Kegan Paul, 1981.

(1955/1956), *Mysterium Coniunctionis, The Collected Works*, vol. 14, 2nd edn. Princeton University Press, 1977.

(1956a), *Symbols of Transformation, The Collected Works*, vol. 5, 2nd edn. London: Routledge & Kegan Paul.

(1956b), 'On the Psychology of the Trickster-Figure', in *The Archetypes and the Collective Unconscious, The Collected Works*, vol. 9, 1, 2nd edn. London: Routledge & Kegan Paul, 1968.

(1957), 'Commentary on "The Secret of the Golden Flower"', *Alchemical Studies, The Collected Works*, vol. 13. London: Routledge & Kegan Paul, 1983.

(1958), 'The Transcendent Function', *The Structure and Dynamics of the Psyche, The Collected Works*, vol. 8, 2nd edn. London: Routledge & Kegan Paul, 1981.

(1959a), *Aion, The Collected Works*, vol. 9, 2, 2nd edn. London: Routledge & Kegan Paul, 1968.

(1959b), 'Good and Evil in Analytical Psychology', *Civilization in Transition, The Collected Works*, vol. 10. London: Routledge & Kegan Paul, 1964.

(1959c), 'Flying Saucers: A Modern Myth of Things Seen in the Skies', *Civilization in Transition, The Collected Works*, vol. 10. London: Routledge & Kegan Paul, 1964.

(1961), *Memories, Dreams, Reflections*. Glasgow: Collins, 1973.

Jung, Emma (1957), *Anima and Animus: Two Essays*. Zurich: Spring Books.

Kaplan, E. Ann (1993), 'Madonna Politics: Perversion, Repression, or Subversion? Or Masks and/as Master-y', in Schwichtenberg.

Kemp, Sandra (1996) (citing Andrew Benjamin) 'Reading Difficulties', in Patrick Campbell (ed.), *Analysing Performance: a Critical Reader*. Manchester University Press.

Kilborn, Richard and John Izod (1997), *An Introduction to Television Documentary: Confronting Reality*. Manchester University Press.

Konigsberg, Ira (1996), 'Transitional Phenomena, Transitional Space: Creativity and Spectatorship in Film', *Psychoanalytic Review* 83, 6, 865–89.

Larson, James F. and Nancy Rivenburgh (1991), 'A Comparative Analysis of Australian, US, and British Telecasts of the Seoul Olympic Opening Ceremony', *Journal of Broadcasting and Electronic Media* 35, 1, 75–94.

Lear, Jonathan (1998), *Open Minded: Working Out the Logic of the Soul*. Cambridge, Massachusetts: Harvard University Press.

Lipsky, R. (1975), *Sports World: An American Dreamland*. New York: Quadrangle.

MacAloon, John J. (1984), *Rite, Drama, Festival, Spectacle: Rehearsals Towards a Theory of Cultural Performance*. Philadelphia: Institute for the Study of Human Issues.

Macnab, Geoffrey (1996), '*The Passion of Darkly Noon*', *Sight and Sound* 6, 6, 49–50.

Mannoni, O. (1964), *Prospero and Caliban: The Psychology of Colonization*. New York: Frederick A. Praeger.

McLeish, Jamie (1996), 'Darkness Visible: Philip Ridley on *The Passion of Darkly Noon*', *Sight and Sound* 6, 6, 16–17.

Mercer, Kobena (1991), 'Monster Metaphors: Notes on Michael Jackson's *Thriller*', in Christine Gledhill (ed.), *Stardom: Industry of Desire*. London: Routledge.

Milne, Tom (1982), '*Diva*', *Monthly Film Bulletin* 49, 190–1.

Moore, Thomas (ed.) (1990), *The Essential James Hillman: a Blue Fire*. London: Routledge.

Moss, Stephen (1998), 'Movie Shots', *The Guardian* (7 October) G2, 4.

Mulvey, Laura (1975), 'Visual Pleasure and Narrative Cinema', in *Visual and Other Pleasures*. London: Macmillan (1989), 14–26.

    (1981), 'Afterthoughts on 'Visual Pleasure and Narrative Cinema' Inspired by King Vidor's *Duel in the Sun* (1946)', in *Visual and Other Pleasures*. London: Macmillan (1989), 29–38.

    (1985). 'Changes: Myth, Narrative and Historical Experience', in *Visual and Other Pleasures*. London: Macmillan (1989), 159–76.

Munsterberg, Hugo (1916), *The Photoplay: a Psychological Study*. London: Constable, 1970.

Neumann, Erich (1954), *The Origins and History of Consciousness*. Princeton University Press, 1973.

O'Donnell, Hugh and Raymond Boyle (1997), 'Playing the Game: The Lillehammer Winter Olympics on British Television and in the UK National Press', in Roel Puijk (ed.) *Global Spotlights on Lillehammer*. University of Luton Press.

Palmer, James and Michael Riley (1995), 'Seeing, Believing and "Knowing" in Narrative Film: *Don't Look Now* Revisited', *Literature/Film Quarterly* 23, 1, 14–25.

Potter, Dennis (1953), 'The Artist', cited in Cook (1995).

Preston, John (1970), *The Created Self: The Reader's Role in Eighteenth-Century Fiction*. London: Heinemann.

Pribram, E. Deirdre (1993), 'Seduction, Control, & the Search for Authenticity: Madonna's *Truth or Dare*', in Schwichtenberg.

Rodowick, D. N. (1991), *The Difficulty of Difference: Psychoanalysis, Sexual Difference and Film Theory*. London: Routledge.

Ross, Kristin (1996), *Fast Cars, Clean Bodies: Decolonization and the Reordering of French Culture*. Cambridge, Massachusetts: MIT Press.

Rushing, Janice Hocker and Thomas S. Frentz (1991), 'Integrating Ideology and Archetype in Rhetorical Criticism', *Quarterly Journal of Speech* 77, 3, 385–406.

    (1993), 'Integrating Ideology and Archetype in Rhetorical Criticism, Part II: A Case Study of Jaws', *Quarterly Journal of Speech* 79, 61–81.

Samuels, Andrew (1990), *Jung and the Post-Jungians*. London: Routledge.

    (1993), *The Political Psyche*. London: Routledge.

    Bani Shorter, and Fred Plaut (1986), *A Critical Dictionary of Jungian Analysis*. London: Routledge & Kegan Paul.

Schwichtenberg, Cathy (ed.) (1993), *The Madonna Connection: Representational Politics, Subcultural Identities, and Cultural Theory*. Oxford: Westview Press.

Slotkin, Richard (1973), *Regeneration Through Violence: The Mythology of the American Frontier 1600–1860*. Middletown, Connecticut: Wesleyan University Press.

Smith, Henry Nash (1970), *Virgin Land: The American West as Symbol and Myth*. London: Harvard University Press.

Smith, Murray (1995), *Engaging Characters: Fiction, Emotion and the Cinema*. Oxford University Press.

Stevens, Anthony (1991), *On Jung*. London: Penguin.

Sundelson, David (1993), 'The Demon Therapist and Other Dangers: Jonathan Demme's *The Silence of the Lambs*', *Journal of Film and Popular Television* 21, 12–17.

Taubin, Amy (1991), 'Killing Men', *Sight and Sound* 1, 1, 14–19.

Tetzlaff, David (1993), 'Metatextual Girl', in Schwichtenberg.

Trujillo, Nick and Bob Krizek (1994), 'Emotionality in the Stands and in the Field: Expressing Self Through Baseball', *Journal of Sport and Social Issues* 18, 4, 303–25.

Ulanov, Ann Belford (1971), *The Feminine in Jungian Psychology and in Christian Theology*. Evanston: Northwestern University Press.

and Barry Ulanov (1994), *Transforming Sexuality: The Archetypal World of Anima and Animus*. London: Shambhala.

von Franz, Marie-Louise (1993), *The Feminine in Fairy Tales*. 2nd edn. London: Shambhala.

Wehr, Demaris S. (1987), *Jung and Feminism: Liberating Archetypes*. Boston: Beacon Press.

(1990), 'Religious and Social Dimensions of Jung's Concept of the Archetype: A Feminist Perspective', in Robert L. Moore, and Daniel J. Meckel (eds.), *Jung and Christianity in Dialogue: Faith, Feminism and Hermeneutics*. New York: Paulist.

Wenner, Lawrence A. (ed.) (1989), *Media, Sports, & Society*. London: Sage.

and Walter Gantz (1989), 'The Audience Experience with Sports on Television'.

Winnicott, D. W. (1971), *Playing and Reality*. London: Routledge, 1996.

Wood, Robin (1986), *Hollywood from Vietnam to Reagan*. New York: Columbia University Press.

Wright, Elizabeth (1987), *Psychoanalytic Criticism: Theory in Practice*. London: Methuen.

Index